"Arguing that equities have been no more volatile than bonds in the long run—and therefore need not bear a higher risk premium—they say the Dow could be 36,000 now . . . the authors present their case clearly, tempering their audacious claims with sensible cautions."

—John T. Landry, *Harvard Business Review*

"Glassman and Hassett offer a vision of the future that breaks sharply with the contours of the past . . . but we would be foolish not to consider that they might be right."

—Zachary Karabell, *Los Angeles Times*

"Hassett and Glassman offer a compelling case that market skeptics are wrong."   —Ira Carnahan, *Investors Business Daily*

"I debated Jim Glassman . . . I got slaughtered. The crowd embraced Glassman and his theory and carried him off in a sedan chair."

—Barton Biggs, Morgan Stanley Dean Witter

"James K. Glassman and Kevin A. Hassett's . . . work may influence investing in the first half of the 21st century as much as Benjamin Graham's did in the last half of the 20th century."

—*Kansas City Star*

"Their explanation of the current bull market is certainly more compelling than the arguments of those whose predictions have been consistently wrong and whose current market analysis amounts to little more than repetition of the word 'bubble.' "

—Brit Hume, *The Weekly Standard*

DOW
36,000

THE NEW STRATEGY FOR PROFITING FROM
THE COMING RISE IN THE STOCK MARKET

James K. Glassman
and
Kevin A. Hassett

THREE RIVERS PRESS

NEW YORK

Published by Three Rivers Press, New York, New York.
Member of the Crown Publishing Group.

Random House, Inc. New York, Toronto, London, Sydney, Auckland
www.randomhouse.com

Three Rivers Press is a registered trademark and the Three Rivers Press colophon is a trademark of Random House, Inc.

Originally published in hardcover by Times Books in 1999

Printed in the United States of America

Design by Robert Olsson

Library of Congress Cataloging-in-Publication Data
Glassman, James K.
Dow 36,000 : the new strategy for profiting from the coming rise in
the stock market /
James K. Glassman and Kevin Hassett — 1st ed
p. cm.
Includes bibliographical references and index.
1. Dow Jones industrial average.   2. Stocks—Prices—United States.
3. Investments—United States.   4. Stock exchanges—United States.
I. Title: Dow thirty-six thousand.   II. Hassett, Kevin A.   III. Title.
HG4915.G55   2000
332.63´22—dc21   00-064841

ISBN 0-609-80699-8

10   9   8   7   6   5   4   3   2   1

First Paperback Edition

For Zoë Glassman and Kate Glassman Maddox

and

For John Walter Stokes Hassett

'Tis sweet to know that stocks will stand
When we with Daisies lie—

—Emily Dickinson

Contents

Preface   xi

PART I: THE IDEA

CHAPTER 1 Introduction: Why Stocks Are Such a Good Buy   3

CHAPTER 2 The History of Stocks: A New Interpretation   20

CHAPTER 3 Dividend and Conquer   38

CHAPTER 4 A Conservative Look at How High
the Stock Market Can Go   56

CHAPTER 5 A More Reasonable Look at How
High the Market Can Go   74

CHAPTER 6 Unrisky Business   91

CHAPTER 7 The Jungle Stocks Live In   108

CHAPTER 8 Today, When Stocks Were Still Cheap   126

PART II: IN PRACTICE

CHAPTER 9 How to Profit from the Dow 36,000 Theory   143

CHAPTER 10 How to Build a Winning Relationship
with Your Stocks   151

CHAPTER 11 Making Sense of Mutual Funds   162

CHAPTER 12 Getting Started in Stocks   196

Contents

CHAPTER 13 Which Stocks Should You Buy? 215

CHAPTER 14 Stocks, Bonds, or Cash?
How to Allocate Your Assets 239

CHAPTER 15 The Wealth Explosion 257

Glossary 269

Notes 275

Index 287

Preface

One theme that occurs time and again in the history of mathematics is the gradual evolution of a new concept—from its initial rejection as being too abstract, through grudging acceptance of its usefulness, despite the fact that it appears "unnatural" and counterintuitive, to its eventual elevation to the status of a basic and indispensable tool in applications.
                                    —Robert Osserman, *Poetry of the Universe*

WHEN THE hardcover version of this book was published in the fall of 1999, it sparked a much-needed debate. For decades, the opinion leaders of the financial establishment had been in thrall to an outdated theory on how to value stocks. As the Dow Jones Industrial Average rose from under 800 in the early 1980s to over 11,000 by the end of the 1990s, their model could not explain what was happening. It kept signaling, "Crash ahead!" But no crash came—and, remarkably, the old model continued to be the darling of many observers. That model contends that there are limits, set by history, on how high the market can go. The limits are ratios, or relationships, between a stock's price and a company's profits, or its assets or its dividends. These limits had been exceeded for about ten years, but the high priests of the stock-market religion would not change their beliefs.

Then came *Dow 36,000*. We have been gratified at how, in a very short time, our book changed the way that Wall Street, the media, the scholarly community, and investors look at the stock market.

The two of us wrote the book because we, too, were baffled by the behavior of stocks. No apples plonked our heads. No light bulbs flashed. We began, instead, with simple curiosity. Stocks had been rising for more than a decade, and the experts were saying that they had breached the stratosphere. They were heading for a fall, we were told. But no fall came; in fact, the opposite kept happening.

Were the laws of financial gravity, hypothesized by scholars and financial pundits, simply wrong? One thing was for sure: Their model wasn't working. So we set to work on our own. We had offices next to each other on the eleventh floor of the downtown Washington office building that houses the American Enterprise Institute, a think tank where the research normally runs to matters of public policy considered much deeper than the stock market: telecommunications, regulation, taxes, foreign affairs. But the truth was, the market was starting to affect politics and policy as more Americans gained wealth through owning a piece of corporate America.

One of us was a journalist writing columns for *The Washington Post* and the other, an economist writing papers for scholarly journals. We got to talking about the market. Our talks turned to research, and our research became an op-ed piece in *The Wall Street Journal,* on March 30, 1998. The reaction—hot anger from academics, head nodding from investors—convinced us we were on to something, and the result is the book you hold in your hands.

When the hardcover was published, the reaction was even more intense. While the conventional wisdom of Wall Street and academia held that stocks were vastly overvalued, *Dow 36,000* states unequivocally that they are cheap. Between August 1982 and January 1999, when we made the calculations that brought us to our conclusion, the Dow had soared from 777 to about 9,000—a nearly twelve-fold increase. That rise, we argued, was far from over. The Dow would quadruple in a fairly short time, about five years. This result came, step by step, from financial theory and analysis, as well as from assumptions about the U.S. economy that should not be controversial to any serious economist.

But controversial it was. The book was attacked from every direction. Some critics (who neglected to notice that one of us taught Ph.D students Econometrics at Columbia University) falsely accused us of making mathematical errors; others said that we had naively fallen for claims about a "New Economy"; and others simply contended that, whatever the logic of our conclusions, the market would "revert to the mean," or go back to its old ways. In fact, in the early months of 2000, *Irrational Exuberance,* a new book by a Yale professor named Robert Shiller (who makes several appearances in our own book), was published, making the case for mean-reversion. Shiller had been saying since 1996 that stocks had to fall sharply to put their valuation ratios back in line and warning that investors had become overenthusiastic and unreasonable.

As we traveled the country, none of the criticisms we heard in the year since our book was published changed our views. We still believe stocks are a great buy. We still believe that individual investors are revising their views of how risky stocks are and are becoming more willing to own stocks. This increases the demand for stocks and drives up prices. As we show in the pages that follow, the evidence supporting this position is almost irrefutable, and the likelihood is very high that the process will take us to its logical resting place: a Dow of 36,000.

In 1995, the Standard & Poor's 500-Stock Index, which even more than the Dow has become the benchmark by which market performance is measured, returned, including dividends, more than 37 percent. In 1996, the S&P returned 23 percent; in 1997, another 23 percent; and in 1998, more than 28 percent. Then in 1999, the year of our book's initial appearance, the S&P returned 21 percent and the Dow 25 percent.

However, in 2000, to the delight of the bears, stock prices began to level off. For the first half of the year, the Dow dropped 9 percent, the S&P fell 1 percent, and the Nasdaq—an index dominated by technology stocks—was off 2.5 percent. Such declines are not ruled out in the Dow 36,000 theory. To the contrary, we tell readers that corrections and even bear markets are inevitable, but in the longer term stocks will rise sharply. The key to making money in the market is to ignore day-to-day and even month-to-month fluctuations and to hold onto great stocks and mutual funds, waiting for the bad times to pass.

Many of the stocks we write about admiringly in *Dow 36,000* have performed exceptionally well since the book appeared. The giant Internet infrastructure firm Cisco Systems, for example, returned 84 percent for investors between September 1, 1999, and June 30, 2000. We pointed out in the hardcover version of this book that Cisco was trading at a price-to-earnings ratio of 85. "Pretty expensive stock?" we wrote. "Not really." We stated that it was reasonable to postulate that Cisco should rise by a factor of four to five. Automatic Data Processing, which we called "a magnificent company that the market has consistently underpriced," returned 34 percent over the same nine-month period. General Electric, which we said was "trading two-thirds below its perfectly reasonable price," returned 44 percent. Of course, not every stock we mentioned was so successful. Biogen, a volatile drug company, fell 20 percent, and Tootsie Roll Industries, one of our favorites, rose just 4 percent.

But for the market as a whole, what was remarkable about the first half of 2000 was not that stocks fell at all but that they fell so little. From late 1999 through May 2000, the Federal Reserve Board raised interest rates six times by a total of 1.75 percentage points. The ten-year Treasury bond rose from 4.9 percent to 6.5 percent, and as a result borrowing costs for consumers, investors, and businesses rose by about one third. In the face of rising rates, the S&P and the Dow barely budged. Over the course of twelve months, the Dow moved between a low of 9,700 and a high of 11,700 while the S&P bounced between 1250 and 1520—the equivalent of a stock fluctuating between $25.00 and $30.40 a share.

The Nasdaq was another matter. It proved extremely volatile. The index nearly doubled in 1999, then dropped by 40 percent in the spring of 2000, before recovering about half its lost ground by June. As the Nasdaq rushed from 2,300 to above 5,000, some pundits were saying that we should have called our book "Nasdaq 36,000" instead of *Dow 36,000*. At any rate, the critics said, the Nasdaq advance disproved our theory since we place such a high priority on investing in blue-chip firms that have reliable earnings while prominent Nasdaq companies, such as Amazon.com, have never made a profit.

In fact, the rise of Nasdaq stocks during the late 1990s (they sextupled in five years) can be *explained* by our theory. Smaller companies, such as those in the Nasdaq, carry higher risk premiums than large companies do. In other words, investors are more afraid of their volatility, so they demand higher returns as compensation. Therefore, in a period when risk premiums are falling back to reality, the journey is longer (and the price rises greater) for Nasdaq than for blue-chip stocks.

Still, the data on Nasdaq companies are hazier than for the more established companies of the Dow and S&P, and it could be that higher risk premiums are indeed *warranted* for Nasdaq firms. Our decision in writing *Dow 36,000* was to emphasize firms with well-established patterns of profit-making. They are very cheap by our analysis. Nasdaq stocks might be cheaper, but in a market as undervalued as this one, there is no need to mess with stocks whose earnings you can't depend on, or can't even count. The Nasdaq, in fact, has become a "sector fund"—in effect, a technology index. Nearly every sector—including "old-economy" industries such as oil and consumer products—is riskier than the market as a whole, so it is no surprise that the Nasdaq itself has endured severe ups and downs. For that reason, we advise our readers to diversify—own profitable Nasdaq stocks like Cisco but also traditional blue chips like General Electric.

The troubles of the Nasdaq—and the apparent stagnation of the broader market—cheered critics of *Dow 36,000*. A common thread was that the book's publication itself was "a symptom of a bubble market" (as Jeremy Grantham wrote in *Forbes Magazine*) or that the Dow would sooner hit thirty-six *hundred* than thirty-six thousand. Farther from New York, however, the welcome was warm. Typical was Jerry Heaster of the *Kansas City Star,* who wrote that our "work may influence investing in the first half of the twenty-first century as much as Benjamin Graham's did during the last half of the twentieth century." Bill Barnhart of the *Chicago Tribune,* who is probably the best financial columnist working in newspapers today, wrote, "The authors have asserted a method of regarding the stock market that is both comforting and rigorous."

When we first began to develop our theory, we ourselves were puzzled that a series of simple and logical steps, using modest assumptions, led inexorably to the conclusion that the Dow should be at about 36,000 today. Only after months of working through the nuances of the theory, and confronting the suggestions and criticisms of people we trust, did we become convinced that it was correct. In the year since the hardcover version of our book was published, we have not changed our conviction. Indeed, nothing we heard in opposition has caused us to alter one word of our theory. This is not because we ourselves have adopted a new religion. As you will see in the pages below, we take arguments against our view very seriously, and even devote a chapter to them. Rather, we spent years testing out our theory on some of the best economists and financiers in the country. Their thoughts and suggestions anticipated almost perfectly the response of the harsher critics, and our reactions were already contained in the pages of the hardcover.

We hardly expected that economists, after decades of studying and teaching the old model, would read our book and suddenly exclaim, "Oh, yes! Now I see the light. I was wrong." Still, nearly all the scholars who commented on the book said that our argument was worth close consideration—and that was a more accommodating reception than we had anticipated. For example, Gregory Mankiw, professor of economics at Harvard and author of the college textbook that is replacing the standard by Paul Samuelson, wrote in *Fortune* magazine, "In explaining the market's amazing performance in the 1990s, therefore, Glassman and Hassett may have a point. Perhaps investors, gradually learning that stocks are a terrific investment, are shrinking the risk premium toward where it should be and bidding stocks higher. It is hard to think of any other good explanation." Burton G. Malkiel, author of *A Random Walk Down Wall Street* and professor of economics at Princeton, wrote, "In sum, *Dow 36,000* is a provocative and well-written treatise that cannot be dismissed." Jeremy J. Siegel, author of *Stocks for the Long Run* and professor of finance at the Wharton School, wrote that our "thesis demands serious discussion."

The most gratifying response to *Dow 36,000* is not that the ideas have been swallowed hook, line, and sinker but that the focus of debate on the stock market has shifted away from a facile discussion of whether investors have lost their heads to a more sophisticated colloquium on how stocks should be valued, by the old model or the new. That new model, which you will find laid out in the first half of this book, stresses the importance of risk in valuing stocks. For reasons we have never understood, many analysts believe risk is a constant, a given, something that can't change. For instance, in a pessimistic and widely quoted article that appeared in the November 22, 1999, issue of *Fortune* magazine, Warren Buffett—the highly successful investor whom we quote frequently in this book—wrote that for investors "to achieve juicy profits in the market over ten years or 17 or 20," either interest rates must fall or "corporate profitability in relation to GDP must rise."

But there is a third factor that Buffett neglects, like so many adherents of the old model. It is that the "risk premium"—the extra return over benchmark Treasury-bond rates that investors demand—can fall. Indeed, it is the decline of the risk premium, not lower interest rates or higher profits, that explains the stock market's boom since 1982 and that forecasts a climb by the Dow to 36,000 in the next few years.

In November, shortly after our book appeared, few analysts were talking about the risk premium. That has now changed. Even Alan Greenspan, who as recently as 1996 was an acolyte of the old religion warning of the "irrational exuberance" of investors, has been rethinking his position. He has now endorsed one of our main conclusions: "Because knowledge once gained is irreversible," he said, "so too are the lowered risk premiums." But the battle over how to value stocks continues, and we are pleased that it has moved into our playing field.

Professor Shiller of Yale has become our main antagonist, and he is the best kind of foe to have: intelligent, gracious, and candid. "We're at an unusual point in history," wrote Shiller in 1999. "Historically, after a period of success in the stock market, the price goes back down. Currently, it's a little uncomfortable because it has never gotten this out of whack." Back in 1996, with the Dow around 6,000, it was Shiller who told the governors of the Federal Reserve Board that stocks were dangerously high and headed for a fall. But over the next three years, share prices continued to rise at a record pace. Shiller explained the increase this way in a debate with us that was published in May in *Time* magazine: "People believe stocks are safe. . . . It suggests this is what we call a speculative bubble. When stock prices go up—and they have been consistently for a while—people get the feeling that they must go up."

We disagree. Rather than believing stocks are safe, investors have adopted the more sophisticated (and correct!) view that stocks are highly risky over the short term, but no riskier than bonds, and far more profitable over the long term. The problem is not the insanity of investors but the inadequacy of the old models. That is what we wrote in early 1999 as we drafted the hardcover version of this book, and that is what we still believe today.

This book is the product of more than the two of us. Our editor, John Mahaney, and his colleague, Luke Mitchell, gave us important advice, as did our agent, Raphael Sagalyn, who had the smarts to keep nagging Jim to write a book for, oh, the past fifteen years or so. We also thank those economists who helped us explore the nuances of our method of valuing companies, especially Alan Auerbach, Ricardo Caballero, Charles Calomiris, Jason Cummins, Peter Diamond, John Donaldson, Bruce Chelimsky Fallick, Paolo Fulghieri, Glenn Hubbard, Larry Lindsey, John Makin, Allan Meltzer, Steve Oliner, Steve Sharpe, and Sandy Struckmeyer.

We had vital research help, primarily from Alex Brill, Matthew Clement, and Rebecca Lane of the American Enterprise Institute, and from Sharon Utz, also of AEI. Christopher DeMuth, president of AEI, and David Gerson, the executive vice president, backed the project to the hilt. We also thank James Taranto and Max Boot of *The Wall Street Journal,* who published that first op-ed piece, when our ideas were just forming, and another one a year later.

Jim acknowledges the support of his two editors at *The Washington Post,* Jill Dutt and especially David Ignatius, and of all his mentors in finance and economics, including Arthur Levitt, Larry Kudlow, Ian Arnof, Virginia Postrel, Neal Freeman, Chip Block, Joe Rosenberg, Tom Tisch, Larry Tisch (who will undoubtedly be appalled by the conclusions we reach here), Mary Glassman, and Stanley Glassman, who taught him, among other things, to adore math. For general inspiration, Jim also thanks his mother Elaine Garfield, Jon Newlin, his guide in all things literary, and Nancy Hechinger, who offered acute and affectionate suggestions.

Kevin is grateful for the tireless support of his wife, Kristie. He thanks his parents, John and Sylvia Hassett, who taught him just about everything important; his sister, Julie, who filled in the gaps; and the many people who provided encouragement, insight, and assistance, including Fred deGroot, Tom Gee, Drew Hutchison, Bruce Kovner, Al Lee, Alex Lapidus, Rick Lord, and Fred Smith. Finally, having heads to pat made writing the book much easier, so Kevin also thanks Rusty and Penny, the dogs of the Dow.

DOW 36,000

PART I: THE IDEA

CHAPTER 1

Introduction:
Why Stocks Are
Such a Good Buy

*I have steadily endeavored to keep my mind free so as to give up
any hypothesis, however much beloved (and I cannot resist forming one on every subject), as soon as facts are shown to be opposed to it.*

—Charles Darwin (1809–1882)

NEVER BEFORE have so many people owned so much stock. They
depend on their shares not just to enjoy a comfortable retirement, but
also to pay tuition, to buy a house or a car, to help their children, to
take a long vacation, or simply to lead a good life.

Today, half of America's adults are shareholders—up from one-fifth
in 1990 and just one-tenth in 1965. Stocks are the largest single asset
that families own, topping even the net value of their homes.

But investors—many of them novices—are as frightened as they are
enthusiastic. The market has been a great boon, but it remains a great
and ominous mystery.

It should not be. This book will give you a completely different perspective on stocks. It will tell you what they are really worth—and give
you the confidence to buy, hold, and profit from your investments. It
will convince you of the single most important fact about stocks at the
dawn of the twenty-first century: They are cheap.

A ONE-TIME-ONLY RISE

Throughout the 1980s and 1990s, as the Dow Jones industrial average rose from below 800 to above 11,000, Wall Street analysts and financial journalists warned that stocks were dangerously overvalued and that investors had been caught up in an insane euphoria.

They were wrong.

Stocks were *undervalued* then, and they are *undervalued* now. Tomorrow, stock prices could immediately double, triple, or even quadruple and still not be too expensive.

Market analysts, and media pundits have also persistently warned that stocks are extremely risky. About this, they were wrong too. Over the long term, stocks, in the aggregate, are actually less risky than Treasury bonds or even certificates of deposits at a bank.

While the experts may not be very good at predicting what the market will do, they are brilliant at scaring people—not out of malice but out of a profound misunderstanding about stock prices. Whatever their intentions, they have performed a disservice to millions of investors by frightening them away from the market.

If you own stocks or mutual funds, this book will remove the fear.

If you are worried about missing the market's big move upward, you will discover that it is not too late.

Stocks are now in the midst of a one-time-only rise to much higher ground—to the neighborhood of 36,000 on the Dow Jones industrial average. After stocks complete this historic ascent, they will still be profitable, but their returns will decline. You won't be able to make as much money from them each year. In the meantime, however, astounding profits will be made. This book will show you how easy it is to participate.

Many small investors are already catching on. They have ignored the dire warnings from professionals that have accompanied nearly every step of the Dow's rise from 777 on August 12, 1982. They are rejecting the outdated model that Wall Street has been using to assess whether stocks are overvalued—a model based largely on historical price-to-earnings, or P/E, ratios. That rejection reflects not their nuttiness but their sanity. After all, the stock market itself long ago repudiated the model. Contrary to the famous warning of Federal Reserve

Board Chairman Alan Greenspan—made on December 5, 1996, with the Dow at 6437—investors are not irrationally exuberant, but *rationally* exuberant. They have bid up the prices of stocks because stocks are a great deal.

Still, even the most enthusiastic investors have doubts. They know vaguely that stocks are wonderful, but they have no real framework for analysis. They don't have an explanation for *why* prices are going up and up.

We do.

How did we come to hold our views? We began nearly three years ago by wondering what on earth was going on in the market. Stocks had quintupled in price in the dozen years up to 1994. Then, in 1995, 1996, and 1997, the Standard & Poor's 500-stock index, generally considered a good proxy for all U.S. stocks, scored returns of more than 20 percent. ("Returns" means dividends plus "capital appreciation," which is a fancy name for the increase in a stock's price.) Never before in modern history had the market had three years this good in a row.

Why were prices rising so quickly and consistently? We weren't satisfied with the explanations we heard in the press and on Wall Street: that investors were acting irrationally—reflecting what Charles MacKay called, in the title of his 1841 book, *Extraordinary Popular Delusions and the Madness of Crowds*—or that baby boomers all of a sudden remembered they should invest for retirement and decided to dump huge sums into stocks as protection against a penurious future.

No. There had to be better answers.

THE RIGHT PRICE

We decided to begin with the core question. If the issue was whether the market was overvalued, we wanted to know this: What is the *right* price for a stock?

The experts did not have an answer. Their model—or view of the financial world—typically focused on what are called "valuation indicators," such as the P/E ratio. Wall Street analysts figure that, if P/Es are too high, stocks are overpriced.

But the term "too high" relates only to history—not to substance. We decided, first of all, to look at substance. At dollars. At how many dollars a stock puts in your pocket over time.

As John Burr Williams, a brilliant young economist with the ability to cut through the muck, wrote in 1938, "In short, a stock is worth *only what you can get out of it* [his italics]."

So, first, we developed a method for estimating the flow of cash an investor can get from a stock. Next, we determined what that cash flow was worth.

A house that throws off $1,000 in rental income a month might be worth, say, $150,000. A restaurant that generates $100,000 in profits a year might be worth $1 million. What, then, is a share of IBM worth? What is the "perfectly reasonable price"—or, as we put it, the PRP—for *any* share of stock?

In our research, we were shocked at how high PRPs turned out to be. Could it be possible? After refining our analysis for a year, listening to the criticisms and suggestions of people we trust, we became convinced that our theory explains—as no other theory does—the rise in stock prices over the past two decades. More important, we concluded that the rise will continue, at least until Dow 36,000.

You will find, after reading this book, that you can determine the right price for any stock. But if analyzing individual companies is too time-consuming or unappealing, we will show you how to construct a portfolio of mutual funds that will accomplish much the same purpose.

But picking the right stocks and funds does not guarantee success. More important than your selections is what you do after you make them. We will show you how to build a *personal* relationship with your investments so that you are less likely to act rashly—and unprofitably—in a volatile market.

The reason to invest in stocks immediately is that changes are afoot that will cause shares to rise powerfully toward their true value, their PRP. Stocks, of course, will not go straight up. They never do. There will be dips, possibly even brief bear markets, along the way. Those declines will provide great buying opportunities—but only for investors who know what stocks are really worth.

THE POWER OF DIVIDENDS

For too long, the value of stocks has been seriously underrated.

Consider dividends, which are the part of a company's earnings that it gives out in cash, usually in the form of quarterly checks, to its share-holders. Most stocks today pay what the experts say are paltry dividends. But the truth about dividends is that they increase as earnings increase—and over time, these increases compound so that even tiny dividends today will provide shareholders with loads of cash in the long term.

Take General Electric Co., a giant diversified corporation with interests ranging from lightbulbs to broadcasting to jet engines to plastics to consumer finance. GE is superbly managed but hardly the sort of fresh, go-go business associated with parabolic growth. After all, it is more than a century old. In Chapter 13, we will closely examine GE, but here are the highlights on the company's dividends.

First, we took the price of GE in 1989 and adjusted it for splits that occurred later. (When a company splits its stock, it issues new shares to current owners, but the value of their total holdings does not change. For instance, if you own 100 shares with a market price of $100 each, and the stock splits two-for-one, you will own 200 shares with a market price of about $50 each.)

In 1989, you could have bought a share of GE for $11, after accounting for splits. At the time, the stock was paying an annual dividend of 41 cents, or 3.7 percent of the share price. The dividend rose each year, so that, by the start of 1999, it was $1.40—or more than three times the annual dividend ten years earlier.

In other words, in 1999, your GE stock was paying you a dividend return—in that year alone—of 12.7 percent on your original investment, or well over twice the rate of a ten-year Treasury bond, and rising. At this pace, in another twenty years, GE will be paying an annual dividend that represents a 50 percent return on your initial investment!

GE is a profitable company that passes on its gains to shareholders, but it is not exceptional. In the year 1999 alone, dividends on a share of Philip Morris exceed the stock's 1980 purchase price.

This is the difference between what bonds and stocks put into your pockets: Bonds may make higher interest payments to start, but over time stocks outstrip them because the profits of healthy firms increase, and so do their dividends.

For example, over the twenty years starting in 1977, a $1,000 investment in American Brands, a modest consumer products company that later sold some divisions and changed its name to Fortune Brands, put five times as much money (in dividends alone) into the pockets of its shareholders as a $1,000 investment at the same time in a long-term Treasury bond.

Our research found that, since 1946, dividends have risen, on average, more than 6 percent a year. The after-tax earnings that companies report to shareholders have risen more than 7 percent. Something growing that fast doubles about every ten years through the miracle of compounding.

Those growth rates are at the heart of our theory about rising stock prices. They have largely been ignored by analysts, who prefer to judge stocks by backward-looking valuation techniques that, much of the time, have argued against investing in stocks at all.

The measures you see in the stock tables and hear mentioned on television have been so wrong for so long that it is hard to see why anyone continues to pay attention to them. But old ideas die hard.

THE EMPIRE STRIKES BACK

New ideas, on the other hand, disturb.

On March 30, 1998, we unveiled our theory in *The Wall Street Journal* under the headline, "Are Stocks Overvalued? Not a Chance." At the time, the Dow stood at 8782, and we said we were comfortable then, as now, with the index rising to 36,000 or even higher.

The article provoked criticism because it challenged the cherished assumptions of the financial establishment—for example, that dividend yields of 2 percent are too low and that P/E ratios of 25 are too high. But the truth is that clinging to the conventional wisdom can be very costly to investors.

(Don't worry. We'll explain all the jargon. For example, a "price-to-earnings ratio" indicates how many dollars an investor has to pay today for one dollar's worth of a company's profits. The average P/E since 1872 has been 14. A high P/E indicates that a stock is popular—some would say *too* popular—with investors.)

At the same time, our views have led some professionals to begin reconsidering the old rules of the stock market. After our *Wall Street Jour-*

nal piece, Byron Wien, the respected Morgan Stanley strategist, wrote a letter to his clients laying out our arguments—for example, that "the fair-market P/E multiple of the market could reach 100." The article, he said, "did start me thinking."

It's smart to be skeptical when someone (like us) claims that "this time it's different"—that something new is happening in the stock market. But, as Wien points out, there have been times "when recognizing that something was, in fact, different paid off significantly."

Still, a more common response to our ideas by the financial establishment was anger and resentment. Following our second piece in *The Wall Street Journal*—on March 17, 1999, just after the Dow passed 10,000—Bob Brusca, then chief economist at Nikko Securities, was quoted in the *New York Post* as saying "This stupid article does not make any sense."

THE USES OF HISTORY

You can learn a lot from the past. For instance, research shows that stocks have been incredibly generous to the people who have bought them, returning an average of 11 percent a year—including both dividends and price increases—since 1926. If those averages hold and you keep reinvesting your dividends, you will double your original stake in six and a half years. And, in less than twenty years, $10,000 will grow to $80,000.

But history can also become tyranny. Just because something has happened in the past doesn't mean it will keep happening in the future. Maybe it has rained three days in the row. That doesn't mean you need to build an ark. To move from observations of history to faith in the future requires knowledge. You need to know whether you are looking at the *right* facts from the past.

When it comes to stocks, the financial establishment chose to look at a particular slice of history and conclude that valuations have a low ceiling. (A "valuation" is a number that measures what a stock is worth since the raw price of a stock alone doesn't tell you much.) According to this view, if the ratio of a stock's price to its earnings—the P/E ratio—gets too high, the price will inevitably collapse or, as economists say, revert to the mean.

But why? It is not enough simply to answer, "Well, that's the way it has always been."

What if something has changed to raise the historic "ceiling" on the P/E ratio? What if the low ceiling was the result of irrationality or ignorance? And what if investors have become more rational and intelligent?

But on Wall Street, the iron-clad rules of history seem to permit no change. On January 18, 1999, *Barron's*, the financial weekly, published a transcript from a discussion among nine strategists and money managers invited to give their forecasts. The participants concluded, as they had in the previous three years, that the market was overpriced but that individual bargains could be found. (Without such discrete bargains, of course, the money managers might as well close up shop.) The main message, though, was "overpriced." The headline on the article was "Tulipmania," a sly reference to the seventeenth-century pandemonium—discussed in more detail in the next chapter—that pushed the prices of Dutch tulip bulbs into the stratosphere before they crashed back to earth.

Typical was the remark of panelist Oscar S. Schaefer of Cumberland Associates in New York: "If you look at stock valuations on a historical basis—especially big companies'—there is nobody who will now not say that they are overpriced."

Schaefer actually had it right. Looking at valuations through the telescope of history—or, more precisely, from a specific historical vantage point—you would have to conclude stocks were overpriced. And all nine of the roundtable participants agreed—as does practically every other observer of the financial scene.

While they were right in their observation of history, they were wrong in their conclusion. It doesn't matter what the price, or the valuation, was ten years ago. The only thing that matters is what the right price is *today*.

History is continually repudiated. For instance, through 1996, the stock market had never posted gains above 20 percent for more than two years in a row. But, through 1998, it posted such gains for *four* years in a row. Until recently, the average dividend yield for a stock in the Standard & Poor's 500-stock index, a proxy for the market, had never been as low as 1.5 percent. Now, it's lower. Wall Street traditionalists will tell you that the market's sharp rise is an anomaly and that P/Es of 25 and more can't be sustained. But, so far, they have been.

Sometimes, historical trends change for good, even in finance. Mainly through the research and proselytizing of investment banker Michael Milken, investors learned in the early 1980s that "junk bonds"—debt issued by corporations that lacked top credit ratings—were nowhere near as risky as they had previously thought. The spread—that is, the difference in interest rates—between junk and Treasury bonds narrowed significantly and, except for brief periods, stayed there. Even more striking was the change that occurred in the late 1950s, when, suddenly, the dividend yields on stocks dipped below the interest rates on long-term Treasury bonds.

For decades, investors had demanded high dividends to compensate them for the risk of buying stocks. Why? One argument was that if a company goes bankrupt, stockholders by law stand in line behind bondholders when the failed company's assets are distributed. That sounds absurd when you consider that the companies involved are the thirty behemoths that make up the Dow Jones industrial average.

Still, in the 1950s, it was the conventional wisdom on Wall Street that investors should sell stocks when dividends dipped below Treasury bond rates—since shares were obviously too expensive and risky. But in 1959, stock yields fell below bond yields and stayed there. Recounting this episode forty years later in discussing our *Wall Street Journal* article, Wien wrote:

> This time the models didn't seem to be working. Stocks kept going higher, and the gap between the current returns for stocks widened. Equities rose 60% in real terms in the ten years after 1958. During that period, some of [the] strategists turned even more bearish. . . . What these forecasters failed to recognize was that investors had begun to appreciate the growth characteristics of equities, compared with the fixed returns on bonds.

Investors came to realize, almost in a blinding flash, that stocks weren't as risky as they had thought and that a dividend that grew as profits grew was far better than a static yearly payout from a bond. As a result, investors didn't need the enticement of high dividends to get them to buy stocks. This new realization caused investors to bid up stock prices sharply in the late 1950s—to a permanent new level. For example, from 1940 to 1957, the average P/E ratio never exceeded 15 in a single year. Since then, it has exceeded 15 in a majority of years.

In the 1980s and 1990s, a similar process of rethinking began again as investors started to look at stocks through a different lens. The process will continue, and as it does, the old view of valuations, based on a specific historical vantage point, will come to be rejected.

When observers say that "history" dictates certain results, they really mean a particular perspective on history. Karl Marx, for example, viewed history as class struggle, picking and choosing events and nations to make his case. The same with stocks. By focusing on such indicators as P/Es, dividend yields, and price-to-book ratios (the relationship between what investors pay for a share of a company and its net worth on the balance sheet), the current generation of observers sees only part of the picture—and it is badly distorted, as the soaring market of the past several years has confirmed.

HOW WE VALUE STOCKS

Turn from history to the here and now. Say that you own shares of IBM trading at $150 each. You want to know, simply, whether $150 is high or low. Should you buy, sell, or hold?

The financial expert today looks at historical valuation measures. For example, how does IBM's price-to-earnings ratio compare with the past P/Es of IBM, or with those of similar companies and the market as a whole?

But this crude instrument is meaningless if stocks have perennially been undervalued, as we believe they have. Instead, we look at what investors really want out of a stock or any other investment: a flow of cash into their pockets.

Whether IBM's price was $100 or $200 last week is irrelevant. The real question is this: *Going forward,* how much money will you earn by owning IBM? And how does that amount compare with what you could earn from an equivalent investment?

Some estimating is required, but not so much as you might think. And the math is fairly easy. After you have determined what IBM will pay you today and how that amount should grow over time, you can come up with a price that a perfectly reasonable person would pay right now for the stock.

What our research shows is that such prices—the PRPs—are far, far higher than prices that currently prevail. Stocks, in other words, are cheap.

Will they stay that way? Not forever. In recent years, investors have come to understand that stocks are a better deal—more profitable and less risky—than they had previously thought. In this judgment, they are far ahead of the Wall Street experts. As a result, we believe, stock prices will rise sharply as demand from more knowledgeable investors increases. Then, at some point, the returns of stocks will trail off.

When that happens (and we will tell you how to identify the point it does), the returns of stocks and similar investments will be roughly interchangeable. It won't much matter whether you buy a stock or a bond. The determining factor will be your personal needs, just as today, top-rated municipal bonds and Treasury bonds return about the same after taxes; whether you buy one or the other depends mainly on your own tax situation.

Stocks *should* be priced two to four times higher—today. But it is impossible to predict how long it will take for the market to recognize that Dow 36,000 is perfectly reasonable. It could take ten years or ten weeks. Our own guess is somewhere between three and five years, which means that returns will continue to average about 25 percent per year.

But the amount of time it takes for the Dow to hit 36,000 is not crucial. What's important is to understand that stocks are significantly undervalued today and that the run-up since 1982 is part of a process of moving toward more rational prices. That process is far from complete—and you can benefit handsomely as it unfolds. In the meantime, you can hold a diversified portfolio of stocks in comfort, knowing that for a solid company with good earnings growth, a P/E below 100 is not a cause for concern.

PARADIGM SHIFT

In 1962, Thomas Kuhn, a professor of linguistics and philosophy at the Massachusetts Institute of Technology, published an influential book called *The Structure of Scientific Revolutions.* Kuhn argued that in sectors of science a paradigm—a way of looking at the world, based on historical information—comes to dominate and then is replaced, swiftly and completely, by a new paradigm.

When does this shift occur? "Sometimes," he wrote, "a normal problem, one that ought to be solvable by known rules and procedures, resists the reiterated onslaught of the ablest members of the group within whose competence it falls. . . . Normal science repeatedly goes astray." Eventually, "the profession can no longer evade anomalies that subvert the existing tradition."

One example Kuhn uses is astronomy. The Ptolemaic paradigm, which had the earth at the center of the universe, gave way to the Copernican, with the earth revolving around the sun, when it became clear that because of the accumulation of new observations, Ptolemy's model could not provide accurate predictions of the movements of stars and planets.

The new paradigm was founded on the same initial set of facts as the old—the same basic information about the positions of the planets, for example—but it was able to incorporate new facts that the old paradigm could not.

No area of inquiry is more ripe for a paradigm shift than modern finance. The old model, which focuses on historical valuations, does not seem to work any longer. Everyday investors, spurred on by the efforts of creative thinkers like Tom and David Gardner, the brothers who launched the Motley Fool website and books, are learning to ignore the experts. Ridiculed for acting like tulip-maniacs, these small investors have acted more intelligently than the professionals and, by doing so, have profited. For example, when the Dow fell 554 points on October 27, 1997, the pros saw the decline as confirmation of their warnings about an imminent bear market and rushed to sell. But not small investors. Many bought stocks at what turned out to be bargain prices.

"I'm kind of floored," said David Castellani, senior vice president for 401(k) retirement plans at Cigna in Hartford, on the day after the big drop. Fully 40 percent of the callers were asking to move money from fixed-income funds into stock funds. "In the past," he said, "90 percent of the calls would have been, 'Get me out of stocks!' I'd like to think that a lot of the education—both written and in seminars—is taking hold."

That education teaches that stocks are the place for long-term investments, through thick and thin, since stocks not only return more than bonds but, over long periods, are no more risky. But the new financial paradigm continues to be resisted by the establishment—and no wonder. As Kuhn wrote, "[The] emergence of new theories is generally preceded by a period of pronounced professional insecurity. As one might expect, that insecurity is generated by the persistent failure of the puzzles of normal science to come out as they should. Failure of existing rules is the prelude to a search for new ones."

Failure? Yes. Not only have financial pundits warned inaccurately of apocalypse in recent years but, worse, money managers devoted to the old model have been unable to beat simple, unmanaged index mutual funds. A majority of human-managed funds failed to beat the S&P 500 in every year from 1994 to 1998. In that last year, the portfolios of 86 percent of managers produced returns lower than the popular averages.

In the years ahead, a new paradigm will at last be accepted by financial professionals—after the public has already stumbled on it. Historian Herbert Butterfield calls this reorientation "picking up the other end of the stick," a process that involves "handling the same bundle of data as before, but placing them in a new system of relations with one another by giving them a different framework."

Is such a reorientation—really, a revolution—a certainty? No, but we believe the weight of the evidence, which we will present in the chapters that follow, is overwhelming. We ourselves have acted on it, reorienting our own investment strategies, with pleasing results, both in profits and in peace of mind.

As investors digest the evidence about stocks, they will start to understand the new paradigm intuitively—again, more quickly than the professionals. For example, the economists who discovered that stocks were no more risky than bonds did not take the next logical step: If stocks and bonds are equally risky, then they should provide roughly the same cash flow to investors, so let's figure out what a stock should return today to be the equivalent of a bond returning, say, 5.5 percent.

In Chapter 4, we work out the answer, but here's a hint: Because a stock's earnings and dividends grow, it doesn't need to return very much at the time you buy it in order to match a bond over the long run. Or to put it another way, our calculations show that the stock dividend yield that is equivalent to a 5.5 percent interest rate may be as little as one-half of one percent.

Could it be that investors are finally recognizing that stocks and bonds are equally risky and are—quite rationally—bidding up the prices of stocks to levels which make much more sense? Are everyday Americans connecting the dots and creating a new map of the financial world ahead of the experts who have so much invested in the old way of looking at things? We think so and believe that you will too after reading this book.

THE NEW INVESTOR

One reason that stock ownership is soaring—from 10 percent of adults in 1965 to 21 percent in 1990 to 43 percent in 1997 to an estimated 50 percent today—is that Americans have begun to understand that equities offer both high returns and, over the long term, low risk.

Another reason is that with low-cost mutual funds and tax-advantaged retirement accounts, it has never been easier to invest. In 1980, just 6 million families owned mutual funds; by 1998, that figure had jumped to 44 million, or two out of five households. From 1980 to 1998, assets held in stock mutual funds have increased from $44 million to $3 trillion. The average fund-holding family has $98,000 socked away in stocks, bonds, and money market funds. Meanwhile, 401(k) retirement plans are also booming. More than 25 million Americans participate, and total assets top $1.4 trillion.

But, with all this money sunk into mysterious equities—which, to many investors, are simply names and numbers on the stock pages—no wonder Americans are worried. This book should allay the fears. Armed with the knowledge of what your stocks are really worth, you can resist the daily drumbeat of news reporting that previously would shake your faith in what you own.

The press and the financial analysts are continually saying that stocks are overvalued, and they have continually been wrong. By contrast, Warren Buffett, chairman of Berkshire Hathaway, Inc., and the most successful investor of the past century, told investors at his company's 1998 annual meeting in Omaha: "The market is not overvalued, in our view, if two conditions are met: namely, number one, that interest rates stay at or near present levels or go lower and, number two, that corporate profitability stays close to current levels."

We concur, but take a slightly more optimistic view. Profit growth can revert to historical levels and interest rates can actually rise—as long as real (or after-inflation) rates stay roughly where they are. In that case, stocks are not overvalued. In fact, they are significantly *undervalued*. In the pages ahead, you will hear our argument, which goes like this:

1. Over the long term, a diversified portfolio of stocks is no more risky, in real terms, than an investment in bonds issued by the United States Treasury.

2. Stocks have historically paid shareholders a large premium—about seven percentage points more than bonds. (In other countries, the premium has been only slightly smaller. In Britain, for example, writes Martin Wolf of the *Financial Times,* it has been about six percentage points since 1918.)

3. This equity premium, based on the erroneous assumption that the market is so risky that anyone who invests in it should get higher returns as compensation, gives investors a delightful unearned dividend.

4. Evidence abounds that investors are catching on, realizing that the equity premium is unnecessary. So they are bidding up the price of stocks to take advantage of this terrific deal.

5. If there is no risk premium, then, over time, stocks and bonds should put about the same amount of money into the pockets of the people who buy them.

6. Therefore, the correct valuation for stocks—the perfectly reasonable price—is one that equalizes the total flow of cash from stocks and bonds in the long run.

7. Several complementary approaches show that the P/E that would equalize cash flows is about 100.

8. The Dow Jones industrial average was at 9000 when we began writing this book, and its P/E was about 25. So, in order for stocks to be correctly priced, the Dow should rise by a factor of four—to 36,000.

9. The Dow should rise to 36,000 immediately, but to be realistic, we believe the rise will take some time, perhaps three to five years.

10. In the meantime, as we show in the second part of the book, you can profit by taking our approach to your investment planning and your stock portfolio.

In other words, stocks are an exceptional investment. They are just as risky as bonds over long periods of time, and their returns—at least for now—are much higher.

THE CHAPTERS AHEAD

Our book is divided into two parts.

The first brings the reader through the theory—why stocks are significantly undervalued. Simple, real-world examples lead to the conclusion that a fourfold market increase—Dow 36,000—is not a pipe dream, but rather the logical consequence of careful analysis. We also provide the arguments on the other side, so that readers can judge for themselves and be armed to ask the right questions.

We begin by looking at the history of stocks and why they have risen so much lately. Then in Chapter 3, we show how to value shares in a company. In Chapter 4, we look in a cautious way at how high the market can go. In Chapter 5, we take a more reasonable—and aggressive—approach to growth. Chapter 6 presents our views on risk: why stocks are not as dangerous as they seem. The next two chapters examine the real-life market and confront challenges to our theory.

The second part of the book lays out, in detail, the investing strategies you need to adopt now in order to profit from the new financial paradigm. It also serves as a primer for both novice and seasoned investors. We tell you how to find the best stocks and mutual funds; how to allocate your assets among stocks, bonds, and cash; and how to develop the kind of personal relationship with your holdings that will produce success.

A colleague of ours, a seasoned economist, laughed when he heard the title of this book. "As long as you don't say *when,* I suppose it is all right," he added. But we aren't laughing. The case is compelling that 36,000 is a fair value for the Dow *today*. And stocks should rise to such heights very quickly. As you read on, you will realize why—and learn to invest in ways that take advantage of a remarkable time in financial history.

CHAPTER 2

The History of Stocks: A New Interpretation

If the Past has been an obstacle and a burden, knowledge of the past is the safest and surest emancipation.

—Lord Acton (1834–1902)

O N THE EVENING of October 28, 1929, the day before the most famous stock market crash in history, Charlie Chaplin, the film star, and Irving Berlin, the songwriter, were having dinner together. Berlin had $5 million invested in the market, which had soared 37 percent in 1927, had gone up another 44 percent in 1928, and had risen 28 percent in the summer months of 1929 alone.

"Berlin was ebullient about the market's prospects," writes Martin Fridson in his book, *A Very Good Year: Extraordinary Moments in Stock Market History.* Chaplin was not. Once again, he was trying to persuade Berlin to sell all his stocks and take his profits, as Chaplin himself had done the previous year. Chaplin told his friend that "owning stocks was unwise . . . while unemployment stood at 14 million." But Berlin wouldn't listen—and, the next day, took the consequences.

If Chaplin looks like a market-timing genius, he was not. He was wildly inaccurate about how many Americans were unemployed. The figure was not 14 million, but 2 million. In fact, the unemployment rate in 1929 was just 3.2 percent—far lower even than during the economic boom of the late 1990s. Never in U.S. history have 14 million people been out of work—not even when the population was far higher than in 1929. It was only in 1933, in the depths of the Great Depression, that unemployment, at 13 million, approached the number that Chaplin used in pleading with Berlin to sell. (By the way, in 1933, the market *rose* a record 54 percent.)

This deliciously ironic story illustrates the existential nature of investing: It doesn't matter whether you are wrong about the reason, as long as you are right about the action.

But more important, while Chaplin *seemed* to be right, Berlin may have turned out the true winner. Since no solid record of Berlin's stock activity is available, we cannot say with certainty what happened to the songwriter's investments. But we can make some educated guesses. Assume that Berlin began investing with $2 million at the start of 1926. In that case, if he held a diversified portfolio of stocks, then, by the eve of the crash, he would have had about $5 million, as Fridson suggests in his book. Also assume that he used his dividends to buy new shares of stocks (ignore any taxes). Using statistics from the Standard & Poor's 500-stock index and its predecessor, along with analysis by Ibbotson Associates, we calculated that, if Berlin had a broad-based portfolio of well-known large-cap stocks, his $5 million would have dwindled to $1.3 million by the end of 1932. That's a loss of 74 percent from the pre-crash peak.

But, by February 1937, he had recouped all his losses. By 1945, his portfolio would have grown to $8 million; ten years later, to $37 million. And, by the time of his death in 1989, at the age of 101, Berlin's original $2 million would have become $1.1 billion.

As for Chaplin, it would be interesting to know when—if ever—he got back into the market. If he waited until World War II ended, then Berlin would have outperformed him by tens of millions of dollars.

THE MONEY MACHINE

Pick any day in the past century, and you will find someone—usually lots of people—warning that the stock market is heading for disaster. Either the market is too high, so it has to fall; or the market has been falling and the downhill momentum will continue. What is remarkable about these predictions is how often they have been wrong.

On December 5, 1996, we both attended the annual dinner of the American Enterprise Institute, the Washington public-policy think tank where we work. The speaker was Alan Greenspan. In the tradition of the dinner, he delivered his formal lecture in the ballroom of the

Washington Hilton Hotel while the guests, more than a thousand of us, sat patiently at our tables, stomachs growling, heads spinning from the cocktail hour, waiting for the soup course. The talk was erudite (mainly a history of the Fed)—and long. Toward the end, Greenspan mentioned the terrible Japanese experience and then warned of "irrational exuberance" in our own stock market. At the time, the Dow stood at 6437, having risen from 3686 just two years earlier. The day after the speech, the chairman's admonition jolted U.S. shares. But they quickly recovered and, two and a half years later, the Dow had returned another 77 percent.

Greenspan is a smart economist and a brilliant Fed chairman, yet a generation earlier he had warned, in a March 1959 article in *Fortune* magazine, of similar "over-exuberance." After all, in the year just ended, 1958, the S&P returned 43 percent. But the bull market continued, with shares returning another 43 percent over the next three years.

It is important to remember that naysayers have always been around.

Sometimes, they even get the timing right, but that hardly matters. The history of the market is clear: In the short term, stocks have extreme ups and downs (none of them predictable), but in the long term, stocks go in only one direction. Up. They have risen at an average rate of 11 percent a year, including dividends—or, when inflation is factored out, of more than 7 percent.

The stock market is a money machine: Put dollars in at one end, get those dollars back and more at the other end. The history of these remarkable returns is vivid and undeniable, yet few investors seem to be able to make it out in the fog of hourly jabber and the haze of daily fear, and many experts seem always to draw the lesson from the past that stocks are headed for a fall.

Here, instead, are the lessons that we draw from history—the foundation of our theory that the Dow will rise to 36,000

LESSON 1: STOCKS HAVE BEEN STEADY WINNERS THROUGH THICK AND THIN

Forget Irving Berlin. Imagine buying $10,000 worth of stock yourself on the very eve of the great crash, at the beginning of October 1929. Over the next two months, if you held a portfolio similar to the modern S&P 500, you would have lost $3,000. It gets worse: After big losses in 1930, 1931, and 1932, your $10,000 stake is reduced to $2,800.

Naturally, you are tempted to sell as troubles brew in Europe. But you decide to hang on and are rewarded, as stocks enjoy their four best years in modern history, tripling from 1933 through 1936. Remember that these are some of the darkest times on the planet, with fascism infecting Europe and Asia, Stalin ruling Russia, bread lines everywhere and Franklin Roosevelt forced to remind Americans that they had nothing to fear "but fear itself." Yet stocks rose 200 percent.

As the decade wears on, Hitler marches into Czechoslovakia, Poland, and Austria, and Japan invades China. By the end of 1939, your account is back up to $7,200. And since the decade of the 1930s is characterized by deflation, or falling prices, the buying power of your $10,000 has dropped by only $1,000.

As the 1940s begin, the war broadens, and the United States is soon fighting both Japan and Germany. The market falls and rebounds, and by the end of 1944—fourteen years and three months since you bought your portfolio of stocks for $10,000—you are ahead, by $400. Despite the the worst-timed investment imaginable, the worst depression of the century, and the worst war in history, your initial investment has actually grown 4 percent.

Over the next sixteen years, through the hot war in Korea and the Cold War elsewhere, through nuclear threats and labor turmoil, the market continues to rise powerfully. By the time of John F. Kennedy's election as president in 1960, your $10,000 has become $93,000.

The Vietnam War begins and seems never to end. Protests disrupt U.S. campuses, and riots burn Detroit, Washington, Los Angeles, and other cities. Inflation worsens. Then come the Arab oil embargo, wage and price controls, the closing of the gold window, and the impeachment of President Richard Nixon. The years from 1961 through 1975 are nasty and often depressing and include the two worst back-to-back years (by far) for the market since 1931 and 1932. Nevertheless, stocks more than double, and your $10,000 rises to $262,000.

Inflation accelerates to 9 percent in 1977 and to 13 percent in 1978. The rate on long-term Treasury bonds takes off as well, hitting 15 percent in 1981. It is hardly an attractive climate for stocks. Who would want to own equities when Treasury bonds are paying four percentage points more interest than stocks have returned historically? Yet the market continues to climb, and by 1985 the original $10,000 stake has become $999,000.

Over the next fourteen years, inflation declines, taxes are cut, the Berlin Wall falls, and U.S. businesses renovate themselves. The stock market soars, and by the end of 1998 your investment is worth $8,414,000. It has grown by a factor of 841—or by a factor of 124, after accounting for inflation.

The calculations for this little history come from a series developed by Ibbotson Associates, a Chicago research firm. We tried to pick the worst possible scenario and then chose subsequent dates at random, but long-term stock market returns are so steady that you can pick any lengthy period you want and the results will be roughly the same.

The consistency of returns in the stock market over long periods is an important lesson. In his book, *Stocks for the Long Run,* Jeremy J. Siegel, professor of finance at the Wharton School of the University of Pennsylvania, divided U.S. market history into three eras: 1802–1870, when stocks returned 7 percent in real (inflation-adjusted) terms; 1871–1925, when they returned 6.6 percent; and 1926–1997, when they returned 7.2 percent.

That last figure is especially convenient because it works well with the rule of 72: Divide the rate of growth, in percentage terms, into 72, and you find the number of years it takes an initial investment to double. So, at 7.2 percent, it takes ten years. This means that if stocks behave as they have over the past eight decades, a woman who invests $20,000 when she is 25 years old will have $320,000 in today's buying power when she reaches sixty-five. She could use that money to buy an annuity that would pay her a decent income she could live on until she dies.

LESSON 2: IN THE LONG RUN, STOCKS ARE NOT VERY RISKY

So why doesn't everyone invest lots of money in stocks?

Good question.

The main reason is that people are naturally cautious, especially with their own money, and the return on stocks is highly volatile from day to day. This inclination toward caution is perfectly reasonable, reflecting an intuitive understanding of an important financial truth: the average return is not the only thing that matters when evaluating an investment. You must also consider the likelihood of profits and the chances of losses. In other words, remember risk.

As an example, would you be willing to bet $100,000 on a coin flip? Unless you are very rich, it would be an absurd wager. Although your average chance of winning is 50 percent, the returns are highly volatile—you win or lose $100,000 per flip rather than, for example, winning $5 on some flips and losing $5 on others. A loss would mean you might have to mortgage your house or tell your son to get a job instead of going to college. While the average rate of return on the bet is zero (you'll win half and lose half if you flip enough times), the risk to you personally is extremely high.

Another game of chance you are probably unwilling to play is Russian roulette. A six-shot revolver is loaded with a single bullet. You point the gun at your temple, spin the chamber, and pull the trigger. Say that if you survive, you win $1,000. That would seem a good bet: five chances out of six of winning. But consider the effects of losing. (The Russian stock market recently has also provided a kind of Russian roulette, soaring until the financial crises of 1997, then dropping 77 percent in less than a year, when losses are measured in U.S. dollars.)

Like flipping a coin or playing Russian roulette, buying stocks offers an uncertain return. You could invest in a company today and lose everything. Boston Chicken, for example, went from 38 dollars in November 1996 to 38 *cents* in November 1998. You can even lose massive amounts with a diversified portfolio of companies. Over twenty-four months from the start of 1973 to the end of 1974, the five hundred stocks of the Standard & Poor's index lost 37 percent of their value. And, over a thirteen-month stretch from October 1989 through October 1990, the 2,000 stocks in the Russell small-cap index fell 34 percent.

While the stock market is very risky, it is risky in a special way. When you understand that risk, you learn there is little to fear from it.

What is risk, anyway? It's a question we explore in detail in Chapter 6. But, for now, in simple terms, think of financial risk as the volatility of returns—the severity of the ups and downs of a stock's performance.

Consider two made-up stocks: Over the past decade, Acme Utility

Corp. has been incredibly consistent, paying a 3 percent dividend and growing 7 percent in price—thus, returning 10 percent per year. Over the same period, Tiger Technology, Inc., has also returned an average of 10 percent, but it pays no dividends. In some years, its price triples, and in other years its price falls by half or more. Tiger, in financial parlance, is extremely risky, or volatile; Acme is not. Both, however, provide the same average annual return over time.

The most common way to quantify risk is through an analysis of "standard deviation," which tells how much a stock's return has varied from its own average. Another risk indicator, beta, compares the stock's volatility to that of the market as a whole. Volatility is important. Most people feel more comfortable with an investment that pays $10 every year rather than $20 in some years and nothing at all in others.

But all risk indicators have two drawbacks: First, they can only describe what has happened in the past, not what will happen in the future. The past is a good predictor, but it is far from perfect. Second, the risk indicators don't account for cataclysmic events, like a bankruptcy, where the price of the stock might drop to zero. After all, one characteristic of a stock that is actively traded is that the company behind it has never gone bust. As a result, the Russian roulette factor doesn't show up in the standard-deviation numbers.

But, despite its inadequacies, history is the best source of information we have when analyzing risk, and the history of stocks is clear and consistent: In the short run, stocks are very risky; in the long run, they are no more risky than Treasury bonds.

Turn again to Jeremy Siegel, who examined U.S. stock prices going all the way back to 1802, using his own original research, supplemented by that of G. William Schwert, Robert Shiller, the Center for the Research in Stock Prices, and others. Siegel found that in the worst year of the past 196, the inflation-adjusted return on stocks was *minus*-38.6 percent. In other words, an investment of $100 became $61.40 in real terms, when both declines in price and income from dividends were taken into account. He found that in the best year, the return was 66.6 percent. A $100 stake became $166.60 in real terms.

That is an enormous range. No wonder stocks scare so many people. Over the past seventy-three years, the Ibbotson Associates data show, stocks have produced positive returns fifty-three times. So the chances, based on history, that you will lose money in a single year are more than one in four—not a very cheerful prospect. And worse, the chances that your losses will be in double digits are one in eight.

But the research shows something else about risk, and it is striking: The longer you hold on to stocks, the less volatile your returns and the more likely you will make money. Stocks have appeared to obey a kind of reversion to the mean—whatever goes down, must go up.

Assume you hold a diversified portfolio of stocks—such as the S&P 500—for ten years instead of one year. Risk shrinks significantly. For the sixty-four overlapping ten-year periods between 1926 and 1998 (that is, 1926–35, 1927–36, etc.), the S&P stocks scored positive returns sixty-one times. For the fifty-eight periods of fifteen years, they were positive *every* time. In fact, over the worst twenty-year period, from 1929 to 1948, the total gain was 84 percent.

Siegel's research also shows risk declining over time in another way. While the worst single year since 1802 showed a loss of 38.6 percent after inflation, the worst five-year period in the last two centuries produced an average annual loss of only 11 percent; the worst ten-year period, an average annual loss of 4.1 percent; the best, an average annual gain of 16.9 percent.

Now, go out thirty years. The worst average annual return for stocks was *positive* 2.6 percent. In other words, an investment of $10,000 grew to $21,598. Never in American history has the basket of large-caps that comprises the S&P 500 (or its predecessors) failed to double in buying power over a generation. Never.

Here's another way to express the amazing decline in risk as time passes. Over a one-year period, the standard deviation for stocks is 19 percent. This means that, in two-thirds of the years, the return on a stock will vary by no more than nineteen percentage points from the average—in either direction. Since the average real return is about 7 percent, returns should vary two-thirds of the time between plus 26 percent and minus-12 percent. That's very risky. But, over ten-year holding periods, standard deviation drops to 5 percent; over thirty-year periods, to 2 percent. So the range, two-thirds of the time, is from 5 percent to 9 percent. That's not risky at all.

What is truly incredible about these long-term risk figures is that they are *lower* than those for Treasury bonds and even Treasury bills, which mature in a year or less. If you keep your money at work for twenty years or more, then stocks are actually less risky than short-term T-bills rolled over annually.

Over twenty-year periods, the worst inflation-adjusted return for stocks was an annual average of plus-1 percent. For bonds, however, the worst was minus-3.1 percent; for T-bills, minus-1.8 percent. Over one-year periods, stocks have outperformed bonds only 61 percent of the time, but over twenty-year periods, stocks beat bonds 92 percent of the time; over thirty-year periods, 99 percent of the time.

In the television program *Early Edition,* Gary Hobson receives a copy of the newspaper a day ahead of time. He then attempts to use the information to change history and prevent disasters and personal tragedies. Of course, the newspaper also contains information that could be used for personal profit, as one of Hobson's friends continually reminds him. The paper has a list, for example, of the results for every sporting event of that day. With such a list, it would be easy to make immense profits. Just scrape together as much money you can and bet on racehorses or football teams most unlikely to win. You would quickly double or triple your money, and do so with no risk.

Stocks have historically presented shareholders with a similar opportunity, but without the need for an advance edition of the newspaper. At any point in the past century, you could have put everything in stocks and made a profit—in many cases, a fortune—as long as you stuck with your shares for the long run. In the market, risk vanishes with time.

LESSON 3: TRADITIONAL VALUATION METHODS HAVE PREDICTED CATASTROPHE THROUGHOUT THE BULL MARKET OF THE 1990s

But the fact that stocks weren't risky in the past doesn't mean you can buy them now and be certain you will make lots of money.

When you buy a stock, you are buying an asset, just like a house. If you buy in a particularly hot neighborhood, you might not find it reassuring that prices there had doubled in the past three years. On the contrary, you might feel you are running a big risk of buying at the top, just as a real estate bubble is about to burst.

Is there any way to figure out what an asset—specifically, now, a stock—is worth? Traditionally, market analysts have used several differ-ent measures of what is called "valuation," each based on hard data about a company. The most popular are the dividend yield, the ratio of a stock's price to its earnings per share, or P/E, and Tobin's Q. In our view, these measures are limited, shortsighted and anachronistic. Let's look at each.

DIVIDEND YIELDS

When you are thinking about whether to put your money in the bank or spend it on, say, a new television, one of the things you look at—besides the reception of your old television—is the interest rate the bank will give you after you deposit your money there.

If the bank pays you 20 percent interest, you might be more in-clined to postpone buying the TV.

If you put your money in a stock, you will get whatever dividends the company pays you, plus the increase in the price of the stock. Divi-dends are fairly predictable, while the change in the price is not, so one quick-and-dirty indicator of value focuses simply on the current divi-dend that the firm pays. If a stock pays a $5 annual dividend and the price of the stock is $100, then analysts compute the ratio and say that the stock yields 5 percent ($5 ÷ $100 = .05), just as a bank account that paid you $5 for a $100 deposit would be said to yield 5 percent.

Drawing on a long series of data on stocks put together by Robert Shiller of Yale, we tracked the history of dividends back to the 1870s. In the late 1800s, dividend yields were typically around 6 percent. Buy $100 worth of stock, and each year you received about $6 in dividends. Interest rates on long-term Treasury bonds were about the same at the time. Between 1900 and 1930, dividend yields stayed fairly close to the interest rate, wandering as high as about 10 percent and as low as about 4 percent, the level just before the crash of 1929.

After stock prices plummeted, dividend yields rose—at least for the companies that survived. That stands to reason. For example, if a stock that cost $100 before the crash paid a $4 dividend, it was yielding 4 per-cent. If, after the crash the firm traded at only $50 and had reduced its dividend to $3 because of lower profits, the yield rose to 6 percent ($3 ÷ $50 =.06). For the market as a whole, the yield stayed in that 6 percent range until the 1950s. At that point, a long and fairly steady decline brought yields by mid-1999 to 1.5 percent for the thirty stocks of the Dow Jones industrial average and 1.2 percent for the five hundred stocks of the S&P. Those yields are the lowest in history.

Another reason that many people use dividend yields as an indicator of value is that actual dividend payouts—in dollars—are fairly steady for a corporation. They tend to rise as earnings rise. Remember that a dividend *yield* is the payout divided by the price. So, if the price rises at the same rate as the payout, the yield will stay the same.

Take Cleco Corp., a utility company that serves central Louisiana. In 1986, the company paid a dividend of $1.04 per share. Since the price of the stock was $16.75, the yield was 6.2 percent ($1.04 ÷ $16.75 = 0 .062). By 1999, Cleco's dividend had grown by more than half—to $1.62 per share—as earnings grew at nearly the same rate, from $1.61 to $2.37. The stock price had risen to $28, so the yield was 5.8 percent ($1.62 ÷ $28 = 0.058), very close to what it had been thirteen years before.

But Cleco is unusual. Utility stocks have been out of favor in the 1990s, so its price has risen far slower than the average stock on the S&P. The examples the Wall Street pessimists find alarming are companies like IBM. In 1994, IBM paid a dividend of 50 cents a year, and the stock traded at $26 a share—for a dividend yield of 1.9 percent. In early 1999, IBM paid a dividend of 88 cents and was trading at $180, a yield of 0.5 percent. While the company's dividend payment barely doubled, its earnings tripled and its price rose by a factor of seven. Management decided it could use much of the cash it was generating better than its shareholders could—not a bad policy when one judges by IBM's spectacular performance over five years.

But many analysts look at low yields like IBM's and conclude that stock prices are far too high. They're too far out of whack with dividends and earnings, the measures to which they should always be tied.

The only problem is that dividend yields have been falling for a half a century, so if you believe that the dividend yield is the true measure of the value of a stock, you would have to conclude that stocks have almost always been too expensive. Around 1950, a $100 investment bought annual dividends of $6, just as it did in the 1870s. But, except for a blip in the inflation-racked 1970s, when bond rates soared, that $100 has bought less and less. In the early 1990s, it bought only $3 in dividends. By the end of the decade, it bought less than $1.50.

Consider the Boeing Co., which in 1999 paid a dividend of 56 cents while trading at $37 a share—a yield of 1.5 percent. If you believe that the appropriate yield for a stock is the historic 6 percent and if Boeing's dividend remains at 56 cents, then its price would have to drop to $9.25 a share. To achieve a yield of 3 percent, the price would have to drop to $18.75. Since Boeing's yield is roughly the same as the S&P's, the entire market would have to fall by one-half to three-quarters to return to its old dividend-yield levels.

Isn't it time for the crowd that keeps pointing to alarmingly low dividend yields to reassess the usefulness of that indicator? Certainly, a high yield may be a signal that a particular stock is attractively underpriced. But a low yield tells us very little about whether the market is dangerously overpriced. If investors have realized stocks are not so risky, they don't have to be "bribed" with high quarterly dividends to buy them.

P/E RATIOS

The second popular measure is the P/E, or price-to-earnings, ratio. Many firms including wildly profitable ones like Microsoft, have loads of earnings, but choose not to pay dividends. Think of a wispy corporate veil hanging over the company whose stock you own. When the firm pays you a dividend, its managers pass the money through an opening in the veil. When they keep profits inside the firm, then the money stays behind this veil. Since you own the firm, it shouldn't matter much to you whether the managers decide to pay dividends or not, just as your watch is still yours if you wear it or leave it at home on the night table next to your bed. Academic research has shown that this logic is supported by the data: shareholders "peer through the corporate veil" and are indifferent to whether their companies pay dividends or retain earnings. If the firm you own earns $5, it is your $5 whether the firm formally hands you the money through the veil or not.

One reason dividend yields are no longer a useful tool for valuing stocks is that companies now recognize their shareholders' indifference to receiving quarterly payouts. In fact, owners may *prefer* to keeping profits inside the company because taxes are lower.

So earnings may be even more important than dividends when it comes to valuing a company—which is why the P/E ratio has become such a closely followed indicator. We think it's easier to look at the P/E ratio upside down.

Just as you can calculate a dividend yield comparable to a bond interest rate, so also can you calculate an *earnings* yield that takes into account all the profits a company makes after taxes—whether those profits are distributed to shareholders or kept in the company.

A stock that earns $5 per share and costs $100 has an earnings yield of 5 percent—the earnings per share ($5) divided by the current price of the share ($100). That's the earnings-to-price, or E/P, ratio. Most analysts, however, like to talk about the *inverse* of the earnings yield, the P/E ratio.

The P/E has a much more interesting history than the dividend yield. Firms tend to set their dividend yields at a level which they are comfortable they can maintain or increase. Cutting dividends is nasty business, so payouts tend to be fairly smooth from year to year. Earnings, on the other hand, swing down sharply in recessions and up sharply in boom years. For example, from 1890 to 1900, the average dividend yield for the market was around 4 percent just about every year; but the P/E ranged from a low of 13 to a high of 27. Such exaggerated P/E swings have been common. From 1917 to 1922, the average annual market P/E rose from 5 to 25, then fell back below 10 the next year. During the Bush administration in the late 1980s, the P/E swung between 15 and 27.

Since the P/E is so volatile, it is harder to get a handle on a "reasonable" historical ratio. The average since the 1870s is about 14 (which is the same as an E/P, or earnings yield, of 7 percent). In the late 1970s, the P/E dipped below that, perhaps flashing a "buy" signal to market strategists. (Buying in the 1970s was a smart thing to do—but also very brave. The decade was the worst in modern times for the stock market, with the S&P 500 index falling 6 percent after factoring out inflation. Even in the 1930s, the S&P more than doubled in real terms.) From the time Ronald Reagan took office to the end of the 1990s, the market's P/E has climbed from below 10 to between 25 and 30.

If you were adamant that the level of the late 1970s was the "correct" value for the P/E, as many analysts were, then you would have stayed away from stocks through the greatest bull market in our history. Even if you took the longer-term view and didn't bail out of stocks until the

P/E climbed above its long-run average of 14, you would have sold out in the late 1980s and missed an octupling of your money.

Again, like the dividend yield, the P/E is a good sign to investors that an individual stock may be a bargain. But yields and P/Es (or E/Ps) do not create a kind of *ceiling* on stocks. Consider Merck & Co., the pharmaceutical house. From 1983 to 1998, its P/E averaged 19. But if investors had accepted that figure as a limit, they would have dumped shares in early 1995. Over the next four years, Merck quadrupled in price. By May 1999, it was trading at a P/E of 32 and was still, according to our analysis, significantly undervalued. The stock had a dividend yield of 1.5 percent, and dividend growth between 1993 and 1998 averaged 13 percent.

A profound change has occurred in the attractiveness of stocks since the early 1980s as investors have become more rational. The old "limits" of yields and P/Es do not apply any more—if they ever did.

TOBIN'S Q

The third measure of market valuation, developed by Nobel Prize–winning Yale economist James Tobin, is called, appropriately, "Tobin's Q." It measures the ratio between a company's market value and the value of machines that it owns to produce its profits. Tobin's Q is followed mainly by professionals, but like P/E, it has risen sharply—and, some believe, dangerously.

Here is how it works: Suppose you decide to start a vending machine business. You purchase, as your only asset, a candy-selling machine for $10,000 from a company that promises to take it back and refund your $10,000 if you ever become dissatisfied. Suppose you put the vending machine at a good location and start making money. In fact, things are going so well that you decide to incorporate and try to sell stock in your company. What should your stock be worth? Tobin's answer is $10,000.

Why just $10,000?

What if you were making tons of money from that $10,000 machine—$2,000 in profits a month? Wouldn't the company be worth far more than $10,000? At first, it might, but some other entrepreneur will probably notice how much money you are making and see that his own $10,000 investment can turn to riches if *he* buys a vending machine.

He does so and, quite likely, starts eating into your profits. In theory, new entrants should keep buying vending machines until profit margins dwindle down to a little more than the cost of financing the machine if you had bought it on credit.

Tobin's Q is simply the ratio of the market value of a company's stock to the replacement cost of the company's machines. So, if your vending-machine company had 1,000 shares of stock outstanding and the stock were trading at $20 per share, then its market value would be $20,000 (1,000 $\times$ $20 = $20,000), and its Q ratio would be 2 ($20,000 $\div$ $10,000 = 2).

But measuring a company's machines—or, really, all of its assets—can be a very tricky business, especially for firms that have established a powerful product identity over the years. The Coca-Cola Co., for example, has a high Q ratio since the machines that produce Coke are not that expensive, but the profits of the company are nonetheless enormous thanks to the brand name.

Still, the Q for the stock market as a whole was in the neighborhood of 1 for most of the post–World War II period. It rose in the early 1990s, however, touching off dire warnings from the Q contingent. By the end of the 1990s, the Q was about 1.5, meaning that the value of a firm in the stock market was 50 percent higher than the amount of money that it would cost to "reproduce" the company from scratch. This discrepancy scared Q devotees out of the market during the bull run.

Each of the prime valuation measures that market analysts have traditionally used has been flashing an "overvalued" signal for many years—decades, in some cases. If the market were to return to historical valuation levels, by these measures, then declines of 50 to 90 percent would be necessary. Yet, instead of waiting for the market to regress to its old averages, we view the measures themselves as woefully mistaken. What are they missing?

THE $33,000 TULIP BULB

If you look only at the course of stock prices, history is clearly on your side when you invest in stocks for the long term. If you are saving to buy a house in the next three years or to retire in the next five, then the past shows that stocks may be too risky. But if you can keep your money at work for ten years or more, then the past performance of stocks indicates that putting most of your money into bonds or bills or certificates of deposit is plain foolish.

Stocks outperformed corporate and Treasury bonds, Treasury bills, and inflation in 84 percent of the ten-year periods from 1926 to 1998. Stocks produced positive returns in 97 percent of those periods.

But the fact that a particular stock—or even a diversified portfolio that tries to mimic the entire market—was a good buy yesterday does not mean that it is a good buy today or tomorrow. Things change. Horses were a fine investment before the automobile. The Japanese stock market was roaring until the end of 1989, when the Nikkei 225 index peaked at just under 40,000. Ten years later, it had fallen to 15,000. Gold rose powerfully to $800 an ounce in 1980, but in mid-1999 it was trading at $256.

Maybe the history from which we should draw our lessons is the history of bubbles, or manias.

Perhaps the greatest investment mania of all time was the tulip-bulb frenzy that gripped Holland between 1634 and 1637. Tulip bulbs are susceptible to a type of mosaic virus that can cause an effect called "breaking," which produces random variations in colors or patterns, some of which are particularly beautiful and exotic.

One of the features of these sick bulbs is that they do not reproduce very well, so exotic tulips are rare indeed. In early seventeenth century Holland, the appeal of bulbs that could hatch gorgeous tulips reached a frenzy, and their prices started to rise. By November 1636, even ordinary bulbs had become the object of buying and selling by the public, with active markets springing up in local taverns.

The prices of unusual varieties soared. A single Semper Augustus bulb traded hands at 5,500 guilders, equal to about $33,000 at today's prices, or roughly six times the annual earnings of a middle-class Dutch family of the time. But while prices were high, they reached those heights only gradually. The average rate of return on tulip bulbs prior to the final year's craze was about 12 percent annually.

In fact, judging from history alone, you can see why bulbs appeared to the Dutch in 1636 to be an excellent and logical investment. But in February 1637, the tulip bubble burst and prices collapsed. There were no rewards for bottom fishing, either. A century later, prices of many of the prized bulbs had dropped to less than one-tenth of 1 percent of their peak.

Ever since Holland's tulipmania, investors have been haunted by the fear that some kind of financial law of gravity will draw prices back to earth with a thud.

Investors are right to be worried. Manias and bubbles exist. They are usually driven by what is called the "greater fool" theory—the idea that if I buy a tulip bulb I may be foolish, but I can usually find someone who is even more foolish to whom to sell it.

The way to protect yourself against the bubble mentality is to look carefully at the asset you are buying. Can you tell what it is truly worth?

With the tulip bulbs, such an assessment was nearly impossible. A bulb whose tulip offspring did not capture the popular imagination was worthless, but no one could tell what the Dutch would like. Similarly, Japanese companies in the 1980s were notoriously difficult to evaluate, lacking the strict accounting standards of U.S. firms and traditionally paying tiny dividends. As for gold: like old paintings, it generates no income.

In all these cases, the assets could be undervalued or overvalued. The average investor just can't tell. Many stocks today have this same characteristic of mystery. How should Amazon.com the online retailer, be priced? Without a history of earnings, any valuation would be a wild guess. Could Internet stocks today be the focus of a mania or a bubble? Absolutely. But could the stocks of the Dow Jones industrial average? As you will see, it is highly unlikely. Companies like General Electric have a strong tradition of earnings and dividends that we can analyze and project. We can assign a perfectly reasonable price to each of the thirty stocks based on what it will put in your pocket over time.

It is to avoid buying into bubbles that followers of the Dow 36,000 Theory take the long view and count the cash. There are hundreds of stocks (and hundreds of mutual funds, if they are your preference) that offer high rewards at low risk. Choose them and you won't have to worry about manias.

But remember that history is not enough—either on the upside or the downside. To have the confidence to risk your money, you need to know not just how stocks performed but *why* they performed as they did. If, as in the case of tulips, a reasonable explanation is not forthcoming, then a wise strategy is abstention.

In the end, it all boils down to a single question: What measures should we use to value stocks? If the traditional ones, such as the P/E ratio, are the correct ones, then running for the exits is the correct strategy.

But so far, they have failed miserably. It is time for new measures.

CHAPTER 3

Dividend and Conquer

Do you know the only thing that gives me pleasure? It's seeing my dividends roll in.

—John D. Rockefeller, Jr. (1874–1960).

A FLUKE? A lucky seventeen years?

From August 12, 1982, to June 30, 1999, the Dow Jones industrial average rose fourteen-fold. An investment in a portfolio made up of the five-hundred stocks in the Standard & Poor's index, with all the dividends reinvested, turned $10,000 into $194,000. During the entire period, stocks suffered only two brief bear markets (defined as declines of at least 20 percent), lasting a total of 143 days. The bull-market rallies lasted 5,917 days. And, from 1995 to 1998, the S&P returned at least 23 percent for four years in a row—an unprecedented feat in modern market history.

Simply chalking up this amazing performance to mass insanity is absurd. Yes, investors can get carried away with a few stocks or a few sectors—or even the market as a whole for a short time. But the nature of the recent boom in stocks is neither concentrated nor transitory. Nearly every industry has participated, and stocks lost money in only one year (a 3 percent drop in 1990) out of the seventeen—while the average over the preceding fifty-six years was one negative year in every four.

The only adequate explanation for this stock market revolution, we believe, can be found in the Dow 36,000 Theory.

For decades, stocks were cheap because investors believed stocks were very risky. When something is risky, you don't want to pay too much for it. Would you pay a fortune for a house perched on an eroding cliff next to the sea?

But starting in the early 1980s, two profound changes occurred: First, investors began to understand—thanks to better research and education—that stocks were not as risky as they had thought. And, second, stocks actually *became* less risky because of positive changes in government policies and in the way corporations did business.

Investors responded to this reduced risk—both perceived and real—by bidding up the prices of stocks. They were willing to pay $52 for every $1 of Pfizer's earnings—instead of the $14 they paid in 1982—because they were more confident that those earnings would continue to grow well into the future.

They were willing to accept a dividend amounting to just $100 for every $10,000 they invested in Coca Cola—instead of the $650 they received in 1982—because they saw dividends growing consistently at a rate of better than 10 percent a year.

Another way of saying this is that investors demanded a *lower risk premium*. They were satisfied with Pfizer giving them an earnings yield of just 2 percent instead of 7 percent. They didn't require those extra five points to compensate them for owning a risky stock. They were happy with a 1 percent yield on their Coke stock; they didn't need 6.5 percent.

And the process won't end here. Risk premiums will keep falling and prices will keep rising until stocks reach their PRP—reflected in a Dow of about 36,000.

But to understand exactly how the process works—so that you can become comfortable with today's "high" stock prices and tomorrow's much higher ones—we need to go back to basics, to a set of six eternal truths about the market.

ETERNAL TRUTH NO. 1: VALUE A SHARE OF STOCK THE WAY YOU WOULD VALUE A PIECE OF A BUSINESS

You're at a dinner party, sitting next to a woman who owns the neighborhood dry cleaning shop. In between the soup and the chicken, she makes a proposal to you. She wants to open another store across town, and she wants you to be an investor, a part-owner.

To set up her current shop, she originally invested $100,000—in machinery, leasehold improvements, and working capital to meet the losses in the early stages. After a few years of building a loyal clientele, that store now provides an annual cash flow of $30,000 per year—the profits she takes out of the business after all expenses, including her own salary. For the next store, she asks you to invest $50,000 in exchange for half the profits.

How do you respond?

Assume you have $50,000 in the bank earning interest of 5 percent a year. Your neighbor, the dry cleaner, says her existing store earns $30,000 on a $100,000 investment—or 30 percent a year. If the new shop does as well, your return will be six times greater than that of the bank account. But unlike a bank deposit, a dry cleaning shop presents uncertainties, or risks.

How can you assess them? You might scout out the neighborhood of the new store. Is there competition across the street? Is another shop likely to move in? Are the neighbors likely to provide the requisite soiled clothes?

After some investigation, you conclude that the key characteristics of the new location are precisely the same as those of the current one and that it would be reasonable to expect the same level of profits. Thus, the cash flow for the new store would also be $30,000 a year, with your share (half) being $15,000.

Now you have a sensible choice: You can keep your money in the bank and earn a guaranteed cash flow of $2,500 annually. Or you can invest it in the dry cleaning shop, where you might earn $15,000—or more, or less. In fact, you might lose your entire $50,000 investment. (Even if the neighborhood looks accommodating, the risk is far greater than that of a federally insured bank deposit. For one thing, you have to worry about whether your partner, the woman sipping her soup, is honest.) What should you do?

The answer depends both on two things: (1) your willingness to accept risk and (2) your time horizon.

If you are going to lose sleep worrying about your money, you probably should not invest in the store. And since the investment is not particularly liquid—that is, easy to sell to someone else—you would be foolish to put up $50,000 if you think you'll need it back in a year or two to send the twins to college.

But if you are willing to accept the risk and if you can keep your money at work long enough, you should probably take the plunge. The reason is simple: You put your money in the store because it is highly likely, based on a sensible analysis, to earn a higher cash flow than alternative investments.

When you decide to purchase stock in a company, you are making precisely the same kind of decision. Exxon, for example, is a business that throws off profits each year, and you are buying a share of those profits.

Whether the investment is a good idea or not will depend on many factors: the price of oil, the skill of management, the chances of increased competition. If you can acquire a convincing answer for each of these questions, then the choice to buy Exxon stock is just like the choice to become a partner in the dry cleaning store.

ETERNAL TRUTH NO. 2: THE IRON LAW— A STOCK IS WORTH SOMETHING ONLY IF IT PUTS CASH IN YOUR POCKETS

So a stock is like an interest in a dry cleaner's. It represents nothing more, and nothing less, than a share of the current and future cash flow of a business. A stock will be a good buy for you if it puts more money in your pockets over time than other investments with similar risk attached.

This concept is very simple but often very difficult to grasp. For instance, one dangerous misconception is that there is a difference between income stocks and growth stocks. An income stock, like Exxon, is one that pays a consistent and generous dividend. But the dichotomy between income and growth gives the impression that when you buy growth stocks, you are buying something different—booming sales and profits but no discernible dividends—and that growth is somehow a valuable characteristic in and of itself. According to this view, the normal rules of asset valuation are suspended for a growth stock like Microsoft.

We're not saying that growth is a bad thing (we love it!), but it can be a distraction to concentrate on growth alone. Why?

People who study financial markets disagree about a lot, but not about one universal truth, called the Iron Law: In a well-functioning market, the value of a business is the value of the stream of current and future dividends that it generates. Dividends are the only thing that matter. Period. *Every* stock is an income stock—even, stocks that don't pay traditional dividends year after year, like Amazon or Dell Computer Corp. The reason is that the anticipation of a future payoff gets built into the price of the stock. We'll explain how when we look at Eternal Truth No. 3, but, first, a more fundamental question: How much are a stock's dividends worth?

Suppose that IBM, a big and sound company, decides to issue a special type of security (or stock) that will guarantee to pay $1 per share one year from now and then become worthless. How much would such a security be worth today?

Simply calculate the amount of money you would have to put in the bank right now in order to have $1 in a year. Simple. If the bank interest rate is 5 percent, then the price of the special shares should be about 95 cents ($1.00 ÷ 1.05 = $.952).

Since you can put 95 cents in the bank today and have $1 a year from now, you shouldn't have to pay more than 95 cents for a share of IBM that delivers the same promise. That dividend payment a year from now is what determines the value of the security.

What if IBM offered instead a special share that promised to pay you $1 *two* years from now and then become worthless? That share should, again, cost the amount of money that you have to put in the bank today in order to be sure to have $1 in two years. The amount: about 91 cents [$1.00 ÷ (1.05 × 1.05) = $.907].

The value of a $1 dividend paid ten years from now would be considerably cheaper today (about 61 cents). A $1 dividend paid thirty years from now would be cheaper still (about 23 cents), and so on. This simple reasoning would allow us to value an infinite set of possible IBM securities. IBM merely announces the year in which the company will pay the dollar dividend, and we figure out how much we would have to put in the bank today to generate a dollar at the appropriate date in the future. That value determines what we are willing to pay.

Of course, stocks don't pay you money once and for all, but rather, they give you a whole stream of payments for many, many years. Suppose that IBM offered special shares that pay a $1 dividend every year for the next thirty years. What would they be worth?

Easy. Just add up the values of the year-from-now dividend (95 cents) plus the two-years-from-now dividend (91 cents) and so on all the way up to the thirty-years-from-now dividend (23 cents). When you do this calculation, you are finding the *present value* of the cash stream generated by IBM—again, the amount of money these promises are worth today.

The present value is determined by two things: what IBM will pay in the future and what interest rate you use to "discount" that flow of cash—in other words, the bank rate (in this case, 5 percent). If the bank interest rate is higher, then IBM's future dividends aren't worth as much. At 8 percent, IBM's year-from-now dividend is worth just 93 cents today ($1.00 ÷ 1.08 = $.926), instead of 95 cents. For now, we are assuming IBM is not significantly riskier than the government. If a company were riskier, the discount rate would be higher.

Of course, the real stock of IBM doesn't *guarantee* $1 per year. Instead, it pays an uncertain dividend—determined mainly by the company's success at earning profits—every year for as long as the company exists, which could be a century or more.

By extending our example, we could calculate the value of that stream of cash as well—as long as we could take two educated guesses: First, how much will IBM's future dividends be? And second, how much will the interest rate at the bank will be?

This calculation is not as hard as it seems for a couple of reasons.

First, dividends tend to be fairly smooth from year to year, and looking at annual payouts from the past can often be very informative in predicting future ones. For example, for the past ten years, Minnesota Mining and Manufacturing Co., or 3M, maker of Scotch tape and Post-it notes, has increased its dividend by an average of 8 percent. Every year, like clockwork, the payout is boosted by between 5 percent and 10 percent. It's a good bet that pace will continue.

Second, as we saw earlier, dividends far out in the future are not particularly valuable in today's dollars (remember that a $1 dividend thirty years from now is worth only 23 cents today). As a result, the tremendous uncertainty attached to questions about where IBM, or indeed the world, will be fifty years from now, is surprisingly unimportant in this exercise.

But let's go back to the Iron Law: Growth can be wonderful, but growth without dividends is meaningless.

The dry cleaning store can make copious profits, but if all those earnings have to go toward buying new machines—rather than toward paying the shareholders—then investors are wasting their money. They could be making 5 percent at the bank rather than zero percent at the dry cleaner's.

Similarly, stocks will be worth something only if they put money in the pockets of shareholders from now until the firm stops operating.

Even sexy Internet companies like Priceline.com, an online auctioneer, or biotech firms like Entremed, a startup firm that is attempting to cure cancer by starving tumors of their blood supply, are valuable to investors only if they ultimately throw off profits. Priceline has never posted a profit and lost $112 million in 1998, but it was worth $20 billion in May 1999. This valuation implies that investors expect huge earnings to emerge in the future—enough to exceed the heavy up-front losses the firm posts in its early stages. Of course, those earnings may never show up. If not, then at some point, the stock's price will plummet.

ETERNAL TRUTH NO. 3: THE IRON LAW APPLIES EVEN TO BUSINESSES THAT DON'T PAY DIVIDENDS

The big money in the market has been made because prices of stocks have gone up and up—not because dividends, which lately have represented less than 2 percent of stock prices, have put lots of cash into investors' pockets. The most remarkable success stories have been companies like America Online, which have never paid a penny in dividends.

True. But the Iron Law on cash flow still holds. Why? Because a dividend is not just the quarterly check you get from a company.

This is not an easy concept to absorb—but it is essential to understanding the true nature of stocks and the foundation of our theory that the Dow will move quickly to 36,000.

This example should help. Suppose that Microsoft were to operate for the next one hundred years and never once pay a dividend. For ninety-nine years, Microsoft makes big annual profits, but it keeps those earnings in the firm, using the money to expand, to buy other companies or simply to accumulate as cash and securities. Shareholders live and die without ever seeing a dividend check from Microsoft.

But in the hundredth year, Microsoft closes up shop and liquidates its holdings—its cash, real estate, machines, patents, and everything else—and distributes the proceeds to shareholders. As far as the Iron Law is concerned, this payment would constitute a gigantic, one-time-only dividend. Indeed, this is the only future for *any* company: Unless it pays regular dividends, is bought out by another company (another form of one-time-only dividend), or goes bankrupt, at some point it will turn its assets into cash. Nothing, not even a great corporation, lasts forever.

But since Microsoft's hypothetical dividend is paid one hundred years from now, how does it affect the value of the company today? Simple: At any point in time, that future, anticipated dividend is the anchor that determines the value of Microsoft.

What would a prospective investor ninety-nine years from now want to pay for the firm? He would look at how much money the stock will pay him in a year (when he gets that huge dividend), look at the rate of return he could get in a different asset, such as a bank account, compare the risks of the different assets, and then buy the stock if it paid at least as much as the next-best alternative.

For example, if he could anticipate $100 per share from Microsoft's liquidation, he would want to pay around $95 per share one year before the event—the amount of money he would have to put in the bank in year 99 in order to have $100 in year 100.

Now, consider an investor ninety-eight years from now. He would take the liquidation value ($100) and, again figuring what he could earn elsewhere, decide to pay no more than $91. If, after buying for $91 in year 98, he sells to another investor a year later for $95, he will receive a capital gain of $4, passing up his dividend a year later. But the underlying reason he gets the gain at all is still the dividend in the final year—the anchor. Without that, there would be no $4 profit. (After all, in 1999, Microsoft had $20 billion in its cash hoard.)

We can draw this same exercise back to the present day. Microsoft has value now even if we expect that it will never pay regular dividends as traditionally defined because, ultimately, *someone* will take cash out of the firm—either after a liquidation or after a buyout by another company. Between now and the time that this cash-out occurs, the stock market value of Microsoft depends on investors' assessments of how much cash the business will generate in total.

Now, a company that could somehow *guarantee* that it would never,

ever pay a dividend of any sort would have no value. The company has value only so long as it is expected to deliver cash, in one way or another, to its shareholders.

ETERNAL TRUTH NO. 4: IT DOESN'T MATTER WHEN YOU GET PAID, AS LONG AS YOU ULTIMATELY DO GET PAID

General Electric is a company that has regularly paid dividends. What would happen to the price of GE's stock today if its board announced that the company will forgo all quarterly payments for twenty years because the firm wants to use the cash profits for corporate investment opportunities?

In all likelihood, nothing.

Such an announcement may change the notions of investors about when they will receive dividends, but they will recognize that what really matters is whether the firm makes profits—not whether it pays those profits out to shareholders every year.

If a company decides to keep its profits to itself, then its managers must be making the judgment that the firm can make an investment in, say, a new plant that will give shareholders a return that is at least as high as the alternative use of the money—putting it in a bank account, for instance. The fact that the dividend is not paid out is a signal to you that these nice investment opportunities are available to GE, and you should, if anything, be pleased.

This commonsense conclusion—that it doesn't really matter whether you get a regular dividend or not—helped win a Nobel Prize for the two economists who thought it up: Franco Modigliani of the Massachusetts Institute of Technology and Merton Miller of the University of Chicago. They showed that dividend policy is irrelevant to the value of a company. Along with the Iron Law, the Merton-Modigliani theorem forms the basis of the study of modern finance.

But at this point, it would seem that financial theory has led us into a paradox. The two truths about stocks are (1) dividends are the only thing that matter and (2) dividends are irrelevant. We could stop here if we were talking about the Tao instead of the Dow.

But it is not really so difficult to reconcile the two statements.

Think of it this way: The value of a business is always equal to the value of the entire stream of money that it will deliver to its owners—whenever that delivery is made.

Again, go back to the dry cleaning shop: What if the owner said that instead of trying to generate a cash flow of $30,000 a year (distributed as dividends to the shareholders), she wanted instead to liquidate the company at the end of ten years, paying out $500,000? The reward to investors would be much the same since, if they invested their annual $30,000 dividends for ten years, they would have about $500,000. However, the risk to the investors might be greater since they wouldn't get their mitts on any money for a decade.

The point is that cash flow does not need to take the form of traditional dividends.

So, those dividend checks aren't a complete measure of the potential money that a stock will put in your pockets? If not conventional dividends, what?

This is a profound question—one that can't as yet be answered to anyone's satisfaction.

But it is obvious that the dividend that gets printed in a newspaper's financial tables is the *minimum* figure for the in-your-pockets money that a stock generates.

In 1998, General Electric paid a dividend of $1.20. At the start of 1999, the company boosted its quarterly dividend to 35 cents. We can be reasonably sure that the stream of cash from GE to an investor owning one share is at least $1.40 in 1999.

But can we really rely on the figure? How do we know that the dividend is the minimum cash flow from a company? Why don't dividends bounce up and down?

Firms like GE use dividends to signal to the market how healthy they are, and they are very reluctant to reduce their annual payouts. GE has raised its dividend by about 12 percent in every year since 1989, paying out a remarkably consistent 42 percent of its earnings to shareholders.

A lowered dividend is a sign that a company is in serious trouble. Investors conclude that the management is worried that the firm will be unable to generate healthy cash flows in the future. Ford Motor Co., for instance, cut its dividend from $1.50 in 1990 to 98 cents in 1991 and

80 cents in 1992. In both 1991 and 1992, the company suffered net losses, totaling nearly $3 billion. But, while reducing its dividends, Ford management was extremely reluctant to eliminate them altogether—even though the company lacked the earnings to justify sending checks to shareholders.

One good way for a company to avoid cuts in dividends is by raising dividends very, very cautiously. Managers generally boost payouts only when they are so comfortable with their cash flow forecasts that they believe the probability of having to lower the dividend in the future is very low.

So dividends are clearly the lower boundary of cash flow. But what is the upper boundary?

Remember that many companies pay no dividends at all, and even those that do, often retain and reinvest a huge proportion of their earnings. As Warren Buffett has written: "The best business to own is one that over an extended period can employ large amounts of incremental capital at very high rates of return." That incremental capital, of course, can come from the firm's own profits.

When we turn to figuring out the true underlying value of a firm, the money that is left inside and reinvested on behalf of shareholders should count too as a potential future dividend. We can't count all of it, of course—since some of the money is used to buy new buildings and machines that replace old ones that are worn out. In other words, some earnings go simply to keep the business running in place. But other earnings help boost future profits—and dividends. We'll discuss this thorny question in depth in Chapter 5, but for now, we want to be clear: The Dow 36,000 Theory is not based on a model that uses all of a company's earnings to determine the price of a company's stock. We use only some of those earnings. What determines the price of the stock is merely the cash that goes into investor's pockets, now or in the future. Or, as John Burr Williams, inventor of intrinsic-value theory, wrote sixty years ago:

> Earnings are only a means to an end, and the means should not be mistaken for the end. Therefore, we must say that a stock derives its value from its dividends, not its earnings. In short, a stock is worth only what you can get out of it.

For now, let's be extremely conservative and concentrate only on the earnings that are used for actual quarterly cash dividends—even though a company like McDonald's pays out only $1 of every $7 it earns to its shareholders in this way. Wouldn't it be reassuring if the traditional dividend flow, all by itself, marked stocks as a great investment?

It does.

ETERNAL TRUTH NO. 5: GROWTH MAKES ALL THE DIFFERENCE

The value of a stock depends on payments that it will make now and on payments investors expect it to make in the distant future. This connection to the future is crucial: As time passes, differences in growth rates become magnified exponentially.

For example, if dividends grow at a rate of 5 percent a year, they will increase fourfold in thirty years. If they grow at a rate of 10 percent a year, they will increase by a factor of 17 in the same time. If they grow at a rate of 20 percent, they will increase by a factor of 237.

Here is what growth means in a more practical sense

Suppose that your brother-in-law tells you about an Internet stock he bought a few months ago. Since then, the price has doubled. "I've missed the boat!" you tell him. But have you really? How can you decide if it is too late to buy?

First, take a look at the company's history and see if it warrants recent price movements. A fictional company—Fido.com, Inc.—sells veterinary supplies over the Internet at a fraction of the cost that old-line distributors charge, and unlike most Web companies, it is very profitable.

In addition, the founder insists on paying out all of the profits of the firm as dividends every quarter. The price of the company has doubled this year, and the dividend has doubled as well since profits have been far above expectations. Indeed, Fido's dividend has doubled four years in a row. It is now $5, with shares trading at $100.

Should you buy? Examine the alternatives. If a bank is paying 5 percent interest, then Fido looks like a great deal, because its dividends are growing. A bank pays the same $5 per $100 each year, but Fido pays $5 this year and then a likely $10 next year.

There are no guarantees, of course, but it seems there is an excellent chance that if you buy stock in Fido.com, you will end up with more money in your pockets than if you just keep your funds in the bank. So it's not too late to buy.

When you purchase a 30-year government bond, you are making a loan to Uncle Sam. The Treasury promises your money back in 30 years, plus twice-yearly interest payments.

A stock is different in three ways: First, the payment you receive is uncertain; it will go up and down with the fortunes of the company. Second, the payment is likely to grow, dividends having a venerable history of rising. Third, the payment does not necessarily end in 30 years; Merck & Co., for example, the giant pharmaceutical house, was founded in 1887.

The growth of dividends provides fabulous rewards to patient investors. Here is a simple example—a slower-growing company called Old-Fashioned Dog Food, Inc. You buy the stock at $100 a share, and it is paying a 3 percent dividend, or $3. But the dividend is growing at 5 percent a year, since that's the modest growth rate of its profits. At the end of 30 years, the dividend will have increased to $12.97, so the return on your original investment will be 13 percent that year—and rising. By contrast, a 30-year government bond that pays 6 percent interest is still paying $6 on your original $100 investment. Over thirty years, the Treasury bond will make total interest payments of $180 while Old-Fashioned Dog Food will make total dividend payments of $209, even at a relatively low growth rate of 5 percent annually.

Both of these examples show how dividends—much-scorned these days—can provide ample justification, all by themselves, for the soaring stock prices of the past two decades. Remember that since stocks and bonds are equally risky, they should produce the same returns over time. But even Old-Fashioned Dog Food, with its dividends growing at just 5 percent, outstrips bonds.

Of course, the two dog food makers are made-up companies. In fact, it's hard to find a company whose dividends have been growing at the sluggish pace of 5 percent. So let's look in closer detail at some real-life examples.

ETERNAL TRUTH NO. 6: DIVIDEND GROWTH IN THE UNITED STATES HAS BEEN AMAZING!

Over and over today, you hear people saying that the stock market has gone up so much that it is too late to get in. By the way, they were saying the same thing in 1995, in 1986, in 1976, in 1960, and back into the dim past.

As with Fido.com, the best way to judge the claim about stocks being overvalued is to see if prices have gone up more than would have been justified by the facts—the essential fact being how much money stocks put in your pockets.

To simplify matters, examine only mature companies that pay dividends. The most famous source of such stocks is the Dow Jones industrial average. Assume you go back to January 1977, to buy each of the thirty stocks that comprised the Dow back then. The Dow changes its composition every few years, so starting with today's Dow and working back would be cheating—that is, operating with a favorable bias since the people at Dow Jones & Co., who oversee the index, take companies like Woolworth off the Dow when their fortunes turn down.

In fact, when you look at the specific companies in the Dow, vintage 1977, they appear to be a bad-news bunch. Many had obvious problems even then. Later, troubles blossomed for such firms as Philip Morris and American Brands (tobacco), Owens-Illinois (asbestos), Bethlehem Steel and Navistar (outdated facilities), and Woolworth and American Can (bad management decisions). The average rate of return on these stocks over the past twenty years has been about 12 percent, including both price appreciation and dividends, compared with a return of 15 percent for the Standard & Poor's 500-stock index, which reflects the performance of the broader market.

Instead of looking at big winners like Coke and GE, let's examine three typical and boring Dow firms from 1977: Exxon, Chrysler, and American Brands. Each experienced significant challenges over the next two decades. Exxon saw the price of oil soar, then plummet, and it was the perpetrator of the highly publicized *Valdez* oil spill in Alaska, for which it paid billions in cleanup costs and fines. Chrysler nearly went out of business, requiring a humiliating rescue by the federal government. The value of the tobacco holdings of American Brands fell sharply, as politicians and the courts turned against cigarette makers. These three stocks hardly constitute a corporate beauty pageant.

But look what happened to investors who purchased them in 1977 and held on through thick and thin.

EXXON

Adjusting for stock splits, you could have bought a share of Exxon in 1977 for $6.02. The dividend was 37.5 cents a year, for a yield of about 6 percent. At the time, the yield on long-term Treasury bonds was about 7.5 percent, so Exxon's yield, in 1977 terms, was not ridiculously high. But, unlike the bond's annual interest payment, Exxon's dividend grew. By 1987, it was almost $1 a share. By 1997, it was $1.63. That's a yield on your original $6.02 investment of 27 percent in 1997 alone ($1.63 ÷ $6.02 = .27)—and the yield continued to rise even as oil prices fell.

An investor who put $1,000 in a thirty-year Treasury bond in 1977 got checks that year totaling $75. Twenty years later, the checks were still $75 annually. An investor who bought $1,000 worth of Exxon shares in 1977 got checks that year totaling about $60. For the year 1997 alone, the checks totaled $270. Over the entire period, the money in the investor's pockets from the Treasury bond added up to $1,500; from the Exxon dividends, $3,585.

Meanwhile, the price of Exxon stock increased from $6.01 in 1977 to $61.19 in 1997. A good way to understand why it rose so much is to look at the dividend yield. If Exxon's price had remained constant over those twenty years, then the stock would have been yielding a 27 percent dividend to investors buying at the end of 1997. If the stock had tripled, the yield would have been 9 percent in 1997. Obviously, 27 percent, or even 9 percent, was far higher than any sensible alternative (T-bonds in 1997 were yielding 6 percent). So investors naturally bid up the price of the stock.

CHRYSLER

In 1977, the price of a share of the automaker, adjusted for splits, was $2.81. The dividend was 20 cents a share, so the yield was about 7 percent—again, less than Treasury bonds. The yield was higher than Exxon's mainly because Chrysler was a company with problems; investors wouldn't buy the stock unless they received a sizeable quarterly check as compensation.

Things turned sour for Chrysler very quickly. By 1980, the company stopped paying dividends altogether and didn't start again until 1984. From then on, the dividend grew in robust fashion, climbing all the way to $1.60 in 1997. Thus, twenty years later, the yield on the original 1977 stake was an incredible 57 percent—per year!

Investors who bought $1,000 worth of Chrysler in 1977 received dividends of $570 in 1997—compared with interest of $75 for a Treasury bond that year. Chrysler's dividend grew over that twenty-year period at an average rate of about 11 percent annually, even taking into account the suspension in payouts in the early 1980s.

Forget Chrysler's 1998 merger with Daimler-Benz for a second. Assume that dividends grow between 1998 and 2007 at just 7 percent a year. Then, the annual dividend in that thirtieth year will be about $1,100, or more than the entire principal returned when the Treasury bond purchased in 1977 matures.

Again, Chrysler's price rose as its dividend rose—and no wonder. Investors would hardly be buying Chrysler for just $2.81 a share if it paid a dividend of $1.60. They were willing to pay far more—$35.19 at the end of 1997, to be exact.

AMERICAN BRANDS

Adjusted for splits, a share of American Brands traded at about $6 in 1977. By 1996, the attack on cigarettes had become so intense that the company decided to split in two. The tobacco business was put into a firm called Gallaher and other lines of business—Master Lock padlocks, Moen faucets, Titleist golf equipment, Jim Beam whisky—into a new company called Fortune Brands.

In 1977, American Brands paid a dividend of 35 cents a share, for a yield of 5.8 percent—well below the Treasury rate of 7.5 percent. In 1997, Fortune Brands paid a dividend of $1.41 and Gallaher paid 80 cents, for a combined dividend of $2.21. Thus, an investment of $1,000 in American Brands stock in 1977 provided its buyer with dividend checks totaling $411.98 in 1997 alone.

Over the twenty years, the total value of all dividends mailed to shareholders who owned $1,000 worth of American Brands in 1977 was $4,696.75, compared with just $1,500 for the Treasury bond. In addition, the stock itself octupled in value. That's not bad for a company that was tossed off the Dow.

THROUGH DIVIDENDS ALONE

These examples are not unusual. We found that if you had invested $1,000 in each of the thirty Dow stocks in 1977, your cumulative dividend checks over twenty years would have exceeded interest payments from an equal $30,000 investment in Treasury bonds by 50 percent. In addition, thanks to stock-price increases, your $30,000 Dow investment would have grown to $176,698.

But forget the capital appreciation. The Dow stocks would have provided a great deal, compared with other investments, through dividends alone.

The point is that the share price grew—in large measure—because the dividends grew. But the share price grew roughly twice as fast. Remember that Exxon's dividend grew four-fold in twenty years, but Exxon's price grew ten-fold.

Why the difference? One reason was that interest rates on other investments—mainly Treasury bonds—fell. But that decline was just a few percentage points. It doesn't tell the whole story.

No, the main factor in rising stock prices was that it gradually became clear to investors that stocks were giving more money to shareholders than bonds were delivering to bondholders. In other words, dividends were far too *cheap* in 1977. You could buy $6 worth of dividends from Exxon for just $100. And that $6 was likely to become $6.60 the next year and $7.26 the year after that.

As this incredible bargain began to dawn on investors, they became willing to pay more for the dividend stream. They bid up the prices of stocks to more reasonable levels. They became *rationally* exuberant.

In 1977, a typical stock had a dividend yield that was about two-thirds' the interest rate on a thirty-year Treasury bond—even though dividends had a habit of growing and T-bond payouts could not. But twenty years later, after investors raised share prices, yields were only about one-third of the bond interest rate. Is that about right?

We think not. Just as stocks in 1977 look ridiculously cheap today—since the cash they generated was so much greater than the cash generated by bonds—stocks today look cheap as well. And for the same reason.

But we don't expect you to believe us yet. First, we have to look more closely at two things—how fast companies can grow and how much risk is really involved in stocks.

CHAPTER 4

A Conservative Look at How High the Stock Market Can Go

Contemporary events differ from history in that we do not know the results they will produce.
—Friedrich von Hayek, *The Road to Serfdom*

WHEN WE LOOK back, the great bull market that began in 1982 seems only logical, considering the bushels of cash that stocks delivered to shareholders through the astonishing growth of dividends. Up was the only direction that stocks could go.

But did stocks go up *enough?* Looking ahead, can we expect stocks to deliver more cash than bonds again? And by how much? In this chapter, we will present evidence that up is the direction stocks will continue. At the end of the twentieth century, stocks are still undervalued. Their prices could double, triple, or quadruple immediately and still be reasonable.

That statement still shocks people, but we make it in the confidence that our assumptions are cautious. In fact, in this chapter, we take the most conservative case—looking only at the dividends that firms distribute to their shareholders. In the next chapter, we will become slightly (but only slightly) more aggressive, using earnings to value firms. When we do, the news will be even better.

SAME RISK, DIFFERENT RETURNS. WEIRD.

In the past, the stock market made millions of people rich. That sounds reassuring, but what we care about is the future, and the future is unknowable. Still, history is the best we have to go on, and by looking at the history of stocks, we are confronted with a puzzle: Stocks have been about as risky as bonds, but they have produced annual returns more than twice as high. Two kinds of investments. Same risk. Wildly different returns. Weird.

Consider a small town with a single bank. Accounts are covered by the Federal Deposit Insurance Corporation up to $100,000, so they are perfectly safe. What happens when a new bank sets up shop a few blocks away from the old one, a bank that is covered by the same insurance?

At first, the two banks will look strikingly different from each other. Even with the federal insurance, customers will be a little wary of the newcomer, wondering if the proprietors will head to Brazil with their money a few weeks after opening. Partly because of this caution, the new bank will start out with just a few customers. It might then try to lure new deposits by offering special, higher interest rates on savings accounts. It might even give you a new toaster.

After a while, citizens will grow comfortable with the new bank and recognize that it is just as safe and convenient as the old one. Folks might move accounts to the new bank because it is closer to their homes or offices. People enticed by toasters might find that the service is excellent, and the old bank would be forced to shape up or lose business.

Fast-forward a couple of years. Now, you would expect to see the two banks offering roughly the same services and paying roughly the same interest rates. In order to coexist, they would have to. If one bank tried paying lower interest than the other, nearly all its customers would move.

History shows that bonds and stocks are assets that have very similar risk characteristics—just as the two banks have. One would expect that they should—again like the two banks—pay people about the same amount of money on their investments. But stocks have paid a lot more.

It is as if we visited the town twenty years after the second bank opened and found that the first bank was paying its customers 5 percent interest while the second was paying 11 percent. Why would anyone *not* keep his money in the second bank? Why would anyone *not* buy stocks?

The answer lies in the confusion many people have about stocks— what they are, what risk they carry, what they return. And, unfortunately, financial professionals have not been much help. Most analysts were completely mystified by the huge increase in stock prices during the 1980s and 1990s, screaming "Overvalued!" at virtually every turn. Typical was a cover story in *Business Week* on September 14, 1998. Most investment professionals, worried about high P/E ratios, believe "that stocks will not hit new highs in 1998 and that there's a good chance that the market has not yet hit bottom." In fact, the bottom that year occurred on August 31, and the Dow rose 23 percent to a new high within eleven weeks after the piece was written.

But, lacking an adequate understanding of the true risks and returns of stocks, tens of millions of Americans who could afford to invest in equities have instead chosen to stay out of the market.

Certainly, viewed from a conventional perspective, stocks seem far too high. The doomsayers argue that the average P/E ratio since 1872 has been 14, and, because shares should revert to that mean, the Dow will soon be lopped in half. "That is unobjectionable," wrote newsletter editor Mark Hulbert in *The New York Times*. Really? The only problem is that the experts have been making this case for years, and stocks have kept rising. The idea that a historic P/E ratio acts as a ceiling on stock prices is nonsense if stocks have perenially been undervalued.

Viewed from our perspective, the increase in stock prices makes lots of sense. They have put a lot more money into the pockets of investors—in just dividends—than bonds. If stocks can *still* be expected to put more money into shareholder's pockets than bonds, then the market remains oddly out of balance.

To know whether the stock market is too high or too low, we need to discover what we call the "perfectly reasonable price" (or PRP) of stocks. The PRP is the price a sensible investor with a long time horizon should be willing to pay.

This long-term perspective is important. In the short term, stocks are far more volatile, or risky, than bonds. Their prices jump up and down in scary fashion. But in the long term, the volatility smooths out significantly. As a result, the only reasonable period for holding stocks is the long term—at least five years and, better, twenty years or more. That is why stocks are the perfect retirement vehicles. Shorter periods are fine for gamblers, but not for rational investors.

But let's get one thing straight: The evidence does *not* suggest that stocks aren't risky, only that they are about as risky as bonds. Risk is a relative term. You are always comparing the chances that something bad will happen with Asset A or Action A against the chances that something bad will happen with Asset B or Action B.

Stocks will certainly go down in the future if earnings disappoint, just as the value of your capital will dwindle if you place it in bonds and interest rates rise. Between 1977 and 1980, for example, the inflation-adjusted value of an investment in long-term Treasury bonds fell 24 percent. Bonds can fall, and stocks can fall. Our point is that the risks for both have, historically, been about the same for the long term.

Perhaps investors will never become "perfectly reasonable." Perhaps they will always worry more than they should about the short-term volatility, or ups and downs, of stock prices. For that reason, the price targets that we discuss in this chapter should be regarded as the upper level of a comfort zone between today's low prices and the PRP.

If you find a stock that is priced significantly lower than the PRP, then it can still rise without causing concern—certainly without the worry that it is being artifically puffed up, like a bubble.

But it is undeniable that investors are becoming more sophisticated. Taxi drivers and schoolteachers know that they should try to stay invested for the long run. They also recognize many other stock market truths, such as the value of buying indexed mutual funds (which we will discuss in Chapter 11).

For example, a study by Peter D. Hart Research Associates in 1997 asked what investors would do "if stock prices were generally to go down significantly in the next year." Of the respondents, 54 percent said they would "make no major changes," 31 percent would "buy more stocks or mutual funds shares, to take advantage of lower prices," and only 8 percent said they would "sell . . . to avoid further losses." More important, this is exactly the way they behaved in 1998, when stocks fell 20 percent in six weeks. They did not bail out.

Thanks in part to this increased sophistication, the market is evolving toward the target of the PRP. Irrational fears about risk are dissipating—just as they dissipated for the customers who decided to move their money into a new bank in town.

So the movement toward the PRP provides a sound explanation for the amazing bull market of 1990s. But we still can't discard the possibility that the past two decades comprised a period of unusual growth—an anomaly.

Also, the more pressing question is whether stocks are *still* cheap. Or has the gap been closed? Did a number of lucky draws make dividend growth unusually high over the past twenty years, or was it a normal run? Have investors gradually learned to be less wary of stocks, or have they become irrationally euphoric? One way to find out is by analyzing specific stocks to see whether their PRPs are higher than their recent prices. Then, we'll look at the market as a whole.

SAMPLING SOME GOOD STOCKS

We value stocks by looking at how much cash they put in your pocket—not by their historic P/E ratio or some gut feeling about the market being too high. So we need to construct a method to determine the likely flow of cash that stocks will deliver over time. Then, we need to put a present value on that flow—what it's worth today to own an asset that will give you, say, $50,000 over the next fifty years. This second part is easy; we can use a simple financial formula. The first part—estimating the cash flow—is a little tougher.

WELLS FARGO & COMPANY

With antecedents in the famous stagecoach line of the Old West, this San Francisco–based bank merged in 1998 with Norwest Corporation, with headquarters in Minneapolis and tentacles throughout the country. The new company kept the Wells Fargo name and became the seventh-largest bank in the United States, with more than twenty-eight hundred conventional branches and three thousand mini-branches inside retail stores in twenty-one states. It finished the year with $137 billion in deposits and nearly $2 billion in after-tax profits. Wells Fargo also happens to be one of the better investments of Berkshire Hathaway, Inc., the holding company chaired by superinvestor Warren Buffett. At the end of 1998, Berkshire owned 67 million shares of Wells, worth $2.9 billion—stock that had originally cost Buffett just $392 million. Berkshire is the largest shareholder in the bank.

In April 1999, a share of Wells Fargo stock cost $40 and paid an annual dividend of 75 cents, for a yield of 1.9 percent. If you took your $40 and put it in a long-term Treasury bond at that time, then it would pay you 5.5 percent interest, or $2.20 a year for thirty years. The gap between the interest payment of $2.20 and the dividend payment of 75 cents seems very large—at $1.45. Can Wells really increase its dividends so much in the future that it will put more money in your pockets than the bond?

The answer depends on how much that dividend grows. Let's look first at the past. Between 1993 and 1998, Wells Fargo increased its dividends per share at a rate of 16.5 percent annually; between 1988 and 1998, at 14.5 percent. Those growth rates are solid, but Wells Fargo's story is not unusual. There are hundreds of firms that have posted similarly successful records.

If Wells Fargo can sustain similar growth in the future (and we will discuss in Chapter 13 the sort of companies that are most likely to accomplish such a feat), then the dividend payments will become very big, very fast.

Growing at 16.5 percent per year, that 75-cent dividend becomes a $1.61 dividend in the fifth year. In the tenth year, the dividend becomes $3.45. In the twentieth year, it is $15.91. In the thirtieth year, the dividend rises to $73 while the payment from the Treasury bond is still $2.20. In other words, in that single year, the dividend payment to a shareholder from Wells Fargo is more than 10 percent greater than the total of all the payments from the bond over thirty years—and almost twice as great as the bond's $40 principal.

But, of course, growth at 16.5 percent cannot go on forever; indeed, if a firm constantly grew faster than the economy as a whole, the firm would ultimately swallow the whole thing up. Sooner or later, a company will mature, and just keep up with the growth rate of the nation's goods and services, the Gross Domestic Product (if that).

Yes, 16.5 percent is probably unrealistic, but, if we are willing to make some assumptions about the growth that the company will be able to post in the future, we can predict the amount of cash it will generate in dividends—and from that figure, we can compute its proper value today.

Let's break a company's life cycle up into two stages: "adolescence" and "adulthood." During adolescence (which can describe even a venerable firm like Wells Fargo), a company grows at a rate that is higher than the growth rate of the economy as a whole. Once it becomes an adult, the firm grows at a rate below that of the economy. More detailed and realistic growth patterns, which allow firms to enter maturity gradually, generally increase the PRPs of companies, but we like this simpler approach, given our cautious inclinations.

The value of a company depends on the amount of its dividend today, how fast the dividend will grow during adolescence, how long adolescence will last, and how fast the dividend will grow during adulthood. (The best firms, like the best people, are those that keep their adolescent energies even as they reach advanced ages.) Once we have made our judgments, we can construct a present value for the firm using a simple spreadsheet calculation. (Later in this chapter, we show you a simple way to do the calculations in your head).

Wells Fargo is hardly an adolescent, but a reinvigorated management and the merger with Norwest give it a teenage vitality. So, let's start by assuming that Wells Fargo will maintain the 16.5 percent rate of dividend growth of the past five years for *another* five years. Then, let's assume it will abruptly mature and, after that, grow about one-half of a percentage point *slower* than the economy as a whole (our own definition of normal adulthood), or 4.5 percent, including inflation. Let's also assume that the prevailing long-term Treasury bond rate is 5.5 percent, as it was in the spring of 1998. (This rate is really not so vital, as we'll see.)

Under these assumptions, we can easily estimate the total of all of the bank's future dividends and, from that figure, calculate what those dividends are worth today—their present value, discounted by the bond rate. The answer: $128 a share. Let's call that our first estimate of the PRP for Wells Fargo. If, in May 1999, the market smartened up and correctly priced the stock immediately, the share price would have to rise from $40 to $128. The P/E ratio, which at the time was 33, would jump to 105.

But this is just one scenario. Let's try some others. If the company can stay adolescent for ten years, that is, maintain the 16.5 percent growth rate of the past five years for a full decade before trailing off, then the PRP becomes $214.

On the other hand, slower growth can reduce the numbers—although not enough to make the company look like a bad investment. Say that Wells Fargo grows at a rate of only 14.5 percent during adolescence. If that high-growth period lasts five years before reverting to low-growth adulthood, then the May 1999 PRP is $117; if adolescence lasts ten years, $156 if it lasts 20 years, $181.

Now assume that the company's dividends in adulthood rise only with the level of inflation (say, 2.5 percent) rather than slightly below the rate of GDP growth. In that case, with a five-year adolescence growing at 16.5 percent, the PRP would be $45 (roughly the stock price in April 1999); or, with a ten-year adolescence, $79, for a P/E ratio of 65.

Which is the most likely scenario? The choice is yours—which is why you should study the stock. Our own guess would be a ten-year adolescence at a growth rate of 14.5 percent, then a slowdown to growth at 0.5 percent below the GDP rate. That would cause the price of Wells Fargo to quadruple and the P/E to rise to about 150.

Is Wells Fargo special? Not at all! The stock market universe is filled with companies that have stories that are at least as compelling.

CAMPBELL SOUP CO.

Selling soup may not sound as exciting as selling microchips, but when you have a 75 percent share of the U.S. market, as Campbell's does, you can make a pots of money. The company was started in 1869 by an icebox maker and fruit merchant named, appropriately, Joseph Campbell. Around the turn of the century, a young chemist, working for the firm, figured out a way to condense soup by taking out most of the water. That cut distribution costs. Products quickly spread across the country, with the help of Campbell Kids characters, who were introduced in 1904. Today, the company also owns Pepperidge Farm cookies and crackers (including those addictive Goldfish), Godiva chocolates, Prego sauces, Pace salsa and Fresh Start Bakeries, which makes buns for McDonald's. Campbell's has expanded aggressively abroad. In Britain, for example, the firm owns Homepride, the number-one cooking sauce. Foreign sales now account for more than one-fourth of revenues. The company has a solid balance sheet, with an A+ rating for financial strength from Value Line, the highly regarded research firm.

In May 1999, Campbell's was trading at $41 per share and paying a dividend of 90 cents, for a yield of 2.2 percent. With one of the most powerful brand names in the world, Campbell's has increased its dividend for the ten past years (and for the past five as well) at an average of 15.5 percent annually. What is Campbell's PRP?

Assume that the company will maintain that 15.5 percent growth rate for a five-year adolescence, then drop to a growth rate of 2 percent in real (after-inflation) terms—again, about 0.5 percent below the likely growth rate of real GDP—then the perfectly reasonable price for Campbell's is $147—or about three and a half times its level of May 1999, for a P/E of 78. If adolescence lasts ten years, the PRP is $236, or more than five times the 1999 price.

Again, it is sensible to explore alternative assumptions. If the company stops posting real growth in dividends after it matures, the numbers are again lower, but not startlingly so. If adolescence lasts five years and growth reverts to the inflation rate (that is, a zero rate of real growth), the PRP is $52; if it lasts ten years, the PRP is $87; if it lasts twenty years, the PRP is $230.

Both Wells Fargo and Campbell Soup are well-known, but relatively boring, companies. Now, look at a true star.

FANNIE MAE

Many stars don't pay dividends, and we will wait until the next chapter to look at them. But a great dividend-paying stock over the past ten years has been Fannie Mae, now the official name of the Federal National Mortgage Association, which was created by Franklin Roosevelt as a government institution in 1938 but became a private corporation trading on the New York Stock Exchange in 1970. Fannie Mae is the nation's largest financial services company, with $485 billion in assets. Its main business is buying home mortgages from the banks, savings and loan associations, and other institutions that originate them and then repackaging the mortgages as securities (essentially bonds) to sell all over the world. Fannie Mae serves an important function by creating liquidity—that is, a ready market—for mortgages, so that smaller lenders don't have to take the risk of holding them. The company has a special status (as does Freddie Mac, another mortgage funder) as a for-profit corporation with the federal government implicitly (though not in strict legal terms) standing behind its debt, which totals $260 billion. Fannie Mae borrows at a low rate and then uses the money to acquire mortgages that pay a higher rate—a very nice way to make a living. And you can become a partner just by buying the stock.

In May 1999, Fannie Mae was trading at $67 a share and paying an annual dividend of $1.08, for a yield of 1.6 percent. Between 1988 and 1998, according to the *Value Line Investment Survey,* Fannie Mae increased its dividend at an astounding annual rate of 47 percent; between 1993 and 1998, at 30 percent. Let's look at what would happen if the 30 percent rate continued for a little while.

The $1.08 dividend would become $4 in five years, $14.89 in ten years, $205 in twenty years, and $537,764 in fifty years—for one share! If the dividend grows at 30 percent for the next five years and then grows at 0.5 percent less than the real GDP growth rate, we calculate that Fannie Mae's perfectly reasonable price should be $315. If the stock jumped immediately to this PRP, the P/E ratio would climb from 20 to 94. If Fannie Mae can manage to keep up its recent adolescent growth rate for ten years, the PRP will hit $903, or more than ten times the current price, at a P/E of 269.

If adolescence lasts five years and then Fannie Mae's real dividend growth falls to zero, then the PRP is $110, still a jump of 64 percent over the May 1999 price. The PRP climbs to $322 (with a P/E of 96) if maturity is ten years off.

Remember that the statistics that support the view that stocks are not riskier than bonds apply not to a handful of companies but to the market as a whole. Putting all of your money in three good stocks could be very risky.

So let's move beyond anecdote and assess the market. There are two ways we could do it: (1) look at the more than seven thousand stocks one-by-one and calculate the PRP of each or (2) try a more intuitive, back-of-the-envelope approach, which will actually give us a better view of the key forces that are driving the market higher. Let's take this tack.

A VALUE FOR THE WHOLE MARKET

To set the stage, we need to go back to the yardstick against which stock prices are measured: our friend, the U.S. Treasury bond, the main alternative for many investors thinking about buying stocks.

A bond is an IOU, a piece of paper that shows that the borrower promises to pay the lender back, with interest. The longest maturity for a Treasury bond you can buy today is thirty years. In early 1999, that bond was paying interest of about 5.5 percent. In other words, if you lent the U.S. government $1,000, it would send you checks of $55 per year for the next thirty years and then hand you the $1,000 back. In the past, there have been bonds with even longer maturities—issued by companies, not the U.S. government. The Walt Disney Co., Coca-Cola Co., and IBM have all sold 100-year bonds.

If you are considering a long-term bond, you are probably thinking more about how much interest it will pay you than about the money you will get back thirty years from now. That is perfectly reasonable. A claim today on $1,000 in another thirty years is not worth very much. By the time you get the $1,000, its purchasing power will be reduced significantly. At an inflation rate of 2.5 percent, $1,000 loses more than half its value in thirty years and about nine-tenths of its value in one hundred years.

A stock has no definite maturity, certainly no promise to repay your original investment down the road. Sure, if a company is bought out or dissolved, the shareholders might get paid off, but if the company is successful, that event could be decades, or even a century, away. The General Electric Co., for example, traces its beginnings to the Edison Electric Light Co. in 1878 and continues to increase its profits at a rapid clip. GE's earnings were $9 billion in 1998, up from $4 billion in 1993.

So one way to think of a stock is as a bond with a really, really far-off maturity, similar to those Disney century bonds. While no stock will last forever, a strategy of keeping your funds in the market as a whole through a mutual fund can be sustained for quite a long time. Extending the maturity toward a far-off horizon actually makes our analysis easier since we can ignore the repayment of your original investment and focus only on the cash flow.

That, after all, is the key question in investing: how much money goes into your pockets?

Now, suppose the government decided to offer a bond that lasted forever—something called a perpetuity. If the interest rate on this bond were constant over time, then it would be easy to price—just like current long-term Treasuries.

Let's say that the rate on comparable investments, such as insured bank certificates of deposit, is 10 percent. Then, a bond that paid $1 per year forever would cost $10—since that is how much you would have to invest elsewhere to get the same cash flow ($10 × 0.10 = $1).

If the interest rate on comparable investments were 5 percent, then the perpetuity that pays $1 per year forever would cost $20, since that is how much you would have to invest elsewhere to get that same $1 per year ($20 × .05 = $1).

Now, suppose that, in addition to the 5 percent "normal" bond, the government introduced another kind of perpetuity that made an annual payment that increased every year at some growth rate—say, 2 percent. Let's call this a "growth bond."

Remember that the government's promise to pay is the same in both cases. Now, what interest rate should the growth bond pay *today* in order to pay exactly as much over its *lifetime,* in present value, as the 5 percent rate on that normal, fixed-rate bond?

Clearly, the initial rate on the growth bond should be lower than 5 percent—since growth will make payments higher in the future. But how much lower?

That seems like a difficult math problem, but actually the solution is simple—and it's treated in nearly every finance textbook. A normal bond and a growth bond are equivalent in present value if the sum of the growth bond's interest rate plus its growth rate is equal to the normal bond's interest rate.

So, if the normal bond is paying 5 percent and the growth bond's payments will rise at 2 percent a year, then the Growth Bond should start off today paying 3 percent interest. It's that easy.

Of course, the timing of the payments is different. In the first year, a $1,000 normal bond will pay $50 in interest while the growth bond will pay $30. In the second year, the growth bond will pay $30.60 and in the tenth year, $35.85. And so on. If the sum of the growth bond's interest rate and growth rate is *bigger* than the interest rate of the normal bond, then the growth bond is paying its holders too much money. What does "paying too much" mean? Simply that the growth bond would be underpriced, too cheap.

Now, let's bring these mathematical calculations back to the world of stocks:

- First, think of a stock as being the same thing as a growth bond.
- Second, think of a stock's dividend yield as being the same thing as the growth bond's interest rate.
- Third, think of the growth rate of the stock's annual dividend as the same thing as the growth rate of the growth bond's annual interest payment.

Remember that we want the stock to provide the same flow of cash as a normal long-term Treasury bond. The stock will do so if the sum of its dividend yield and the growth rate of its dividends is equal to the interest rate on that normal Treasury bond. If the sum is greater than the Treasury rate, then the stock is paying too much.

Just like a growth bond, a stock that pays too much is *underpriced*. Again, think of a bond. If one bond that costs $1,000 is paying interest of $100 per year while all other similar bonds that cost $1,000 are paying interest of $50 per year, then, obviously, the bond that is paying $100 per year is too cheap at $1,000. Its price should rise to $2,000, where its return would be the same 5 percent ($100 ÷ $2,000 = 0.05).

Now, think of the stock market, as represented by the S&P 500 index. When the sum of the S&P's dividend yield and the growth rate of dividends (how much they increase, on average, per year) exceeds the rate on a normal Treasury bond, then the market has not reached the target of fair pricing—the PRP. The market is too cheap. It needs to rise some more.

Let's get down to the real numbers. We need only look at three things: the interest rate on long-term Treasury bonds, the dividend yield on stocks, and the expected long-term growth rate of those dividends.

The first two numbers are easy to find in any newspaper. In the spring of 1999, the rate on a thirty-year T-bond was roughly 5.5 percent and the dividend yield for the average stock in the Dow Jones industrial average was 1.5 percent—both rates low by traditional standards.

The third rate—the growth of dividends per share—is not listed in newspapers or magazines, but its history is easy to discover, using statistics developed by economist Robert Shiller of Yale. (If you would like to see the data yourself, they are available on his website at www.econ.yale.edu/~shiller/index.html.)

The figures are compelling. Over the past twenty years, the growth rate for dividends has been 6.1 percent. Since 1946, the rate has been 6.2 percent.

The consistency of these numbers is important. There are two possible explanations for the apparent undervaluation of stocks back in the late 1970s. Either dividends grew far more than could possibly be expected, or people were too cautious about the risks of stocks. As it happens, dividend growth over the past twenty years is almost precisely the same as over the past fifty years. So the growth should have come as no big surprise. That leaves the exaggerated worry about risk—a critical issue to which we will return.

But back to the calculations.

To start, assume that dividends will grow in the future at the same fairly steady rate as over the past half-century—about 6.1 percent. You can see that stocks are paying too much since, when you add the yield of dividends (about 1.5 percent in 1998) to the growth rate (6.1 percent), you get 7.6 percent, or 2.1 percentage points more than the T-bond rate (5.5 percent). Thus, stocks put more money in your pockets than bonds even though both stocks and bonds carry about the same risk over long periods.

Now, use the simple model we used for Wells Fargo, Campbell Soup, and Fannie Mae—breaking up a firm's life into adolescence and adulthood.

Suppose, for example, that the dividends of all the companies in the market will grow at 6 percent a year for the next ten years and then grow a half-percentage point slower than GDP after that. With those numbers, the present value of dividends that you purchase when you buy $100 worth of a diversified portfolio of stocks that represents the entire Standard & Poor's 500 index is $172. In other words, the market would have to rise immediately by 72 percent under these extremely modest assumptions to reach the PRP.

If the growth rate that has prevailed since 1946 continues for another fifty years before tailing off, then when you buy $100 worth of stock today, you get dividends worth $270 in present value. But dividends have grown faster than GDP for some time, so perhaps we should be more aggressive. If the dividends just keep up with GDP (rather than falling behind by a half-point) after ten more years of 6 percent growth, then the present value of dividends climbs to $329; to

$360 if the 6 percent growth lasts twenty years; to $460 if this period of adolescence lasts fifty years.

After weighing the historical evidence, we support an estimate based on one of the last two numbers. The PRP for the entire market, then, should be at least three times as high as it is now.

The current yield for the Dow is about 1.5 percent. In other words, if you invest $1,000, you'll get dividends of $15. But if stock prices triple, your investment will be worth $3,000. Dividends will remain $15, so the yield will fall to 0.5 percent ($15 ÷ $3,000 = 0.005).

It is easy to pull the same answer out of the growth bond relationship. If the dividend yield is 0.5 percent and the Treasury bond yield is 5.5 percent, then the equation (cash returns from bonds = dividend yield + g) balances if g, the growth rate of dividends, is 5 percent (5.5 = 0.5 + 5). That growth rate is more than one percentage point below the average growth rate of dividends since 1946, so it seems to us perfectly reasonable.

CORRECTING FOR INFLATION

But wait. These calculations have been based on numbers that don't account for inflation, or the year-to-year rise in the prices of the things we buy. Inflation makes saving for tomorrow less attractive, since one dollar tomorrow can't buy as much as one dollar today. Although your dividends are higher ten years from now, a new car or a trip to Europe will cost more.

Since the interest payment on the normal T-bond is the same every year, the bond's future payments are worth less and less as inflation erodes the value of the dollar. To account for this degradation, economists talk about the "real yield" of a bond, which is the nominal (or stated) interest rate minus the inflation rate.

So let's look at some numbers that correct for inflation.

In its forecast at the beginning of 1999, the Congressional Budget Office predicted that inflation would rise at an average of about 2.6 percent per year through 2009. That means that the real yield on long-term Treasuries paying 5.5 percent was about 2.9 percent.

For stocks, the dividend yield, remember, is 1.5 percent. We don't need to adjust it for inflation since it is a starting point. Instead, we adjust the *growth rate* for inflation.

How do you find the real growth rate for dividends? One source is the data developed by Professor Shiller. From 1946 to 1998, dividends per share grew at an inflation-adjusted annual rate of 2.2 percent. For the past twenty years, the real rate was 2.3 percent. For the past ten years, 3 percent.

Add the middle real growth rate to the dividend yield of 1.5 percent, and you get a total of 3.8 percent, or nine-tenths of a percentage point more than the 2.9 percent real interest rate on bonds. Use the more recent figure for real growth, and the difference is even larger.

If we assume that the real growth of dividends will continue at 2 to 3 percent, then stocks are, once again, paying too much money. The only way this imbalance can be corrected is for stocks to rise in price.

But there is a serious problem with these numbers! The dividend payouts are far, far too *low* when you compare them with earnings that companies are cranking out. Why?

Two reasons. First, when a firm pays out dividends to its shareholders, the shareholders are forced to pay tax immediately on the payment. When the firm retains its earnings, the shareholders pay no tax. Firms have gradually learned in recent years that shareholders prefer not to pay taxes, and the fraction of earnings that is paid out in dividends has dropped dramatically—from about 70 percent in the 1950s to less than 40 percent today. This downward trend absolutely does not reflect a decline in firms' *ability* to pay dividends—an issue we'll explore in the next chapter.

Second, the data we have used so far are based on the dividends of the S&P 500 index. One of the intriguing characteristics of the recent bull market is that many of the firms that have done the best are computer and Internet companies that do not pay dividends. This change in the composition of the S&P 500 means that dividend statistics are currently biased downward. A better measure might correct for this big-firm, low-dividend bias by looking at the market as a whole.

To accomplish this, we constructed an aggregate measure of dividend yield and dividend growth for all companies from the Federal Reserve's Flow of Funds tables. These numbers make the market look even better.

The dividend yield for U.S. companies in 1998, based on calculations from the Fed data, was 2 percent, and the rate of dividend growth for the twenty preceding years averaged 9.4 percent. Adding those two numbers, we get 11.4 percent, compared with the 7.6 percent we derived by adding a yield of 1.5 percent to the Shiller data's growth rate of 6.1 percent.

STOCKS NEED TO TRIPLE (AT LEAST)

How much will prices have to rise?

Until they reach our PRP, or perfectly reasonable price.

And where, precisely, is that?

Let's step back. If a stock's dividend payout in dollars stays the same and the stock rises in price, then its yield will decline. Take AT&T Corp. Say it pays a dividend of $1.50 a share while shares are trading at $100. Its yield is 1.5 percent ($1.50 ÷ $100 = .015). Now assume that AT&T triples in price but that its dividend stays the same. Its yield falls to one-half of 1 percent, or 0.5 percent ($1.50 ÷ $300 = .005).

Now, let's suppose that the entire market is represented by that single share of AT&T. After all, at the start of 1999, the stocks in the Dow Jones industrial average were offering a dividend yield of about 1.5 percent. If the entire market triples in price and the market's dividend payout in dollars stays the same, then the yield will drop to 0.5 percent.

Add that yield (0.5 percent) to our conservative real growth rate of dividends (2.3 percent), and you get 2.8 percent—approximately the same figure as the real T-bond rate (2.9 percent). The equation balances.

At the start of 1999, the Dow Jones industrial average was about 9000. If the Dow, representing the entire market, were to triple—to 27,000—then dividend yields would decline to their "perfectly reasonable" level, the level where stocks put the same amount into your pockets as bonds.

Recognize that our assumptions are modest. First, we are looking just at dividends—even though we know that dividends are merely a lower boundary for true cash flow. Second, we are using a conservative estimate—2.3 percent—for real dividend growth. It could easily be 3 percent or higher.

Give this powerful idea some time to sink in: Stocks, by our simple, logical calculation may be undervalued by as much as two-thirds. They need to triple to get to where they should be: the PRP.

But firms earn far more than they pay out in dividends, and those earnings count, too in figuring out the money that ends up in an investor's pockets. How much do they count? A lot—as we'll see in the next chapter.

CHAPTER 5

A More Reasonable Look at How High the Market Can Go

In an old legend the wise men finally boiled down the history of mortal affairs into the single phrase, "This too will pass." Confronted with a like challenge to distill the secret of sound investment into three words, we venture the motto, "MARGIN OF SAFETY."

—Benjamin Graham, *The Intelligent Investor*

I F YOU OWN a restaurant or a dry cleaning shop, you really aren't picky about what the profits are *called*. What's important is that the cash that comes in is greater than the cash that goes out, and that you have actual money to put into your bank account.

This positive flow of cash is the reason to invest.

But, so far, we have been using just one kind of cash flow—dividends—as the measure for all cash flow. This is a very conservative approach since, in recent years, the total profits (official after-tax earnings, as reported to the Securities and Exchange Commission) of the average company have been nearly three times the dividends it pays to shareholders.

Earnings are much higher than dividends since many firms keep part (or all) of that money to make investments which, they expect, will deliver more profits in the future. In addition, businesses recognize that there's a tax advantage to retaining earnings since the tax rates that shareholders pay on dividends are higher than the rates they pay on capital gains—in the case of rich shareholders, roughly twice as high.

Certainly, earnings are real money, but in most circumstances, it would be an egregious error to apply the analysis we just used for dividends to *all* earnings for *all* companies.

But, for most companies, some of the earnings beyond dividends will certainly flow to shareholders. In this chapter, we calculate how much—and, from that, make a less cautious but more reasonable estimate of how stocks should be priced than we did in Chapter 4. We also explain why price-to-earnings ratios in the triple digits are justified for the market as a whole and how, when we factor in taxes, stocks look even better. We show how investing today in a diversified portfolio offers what Benjamin Graham, one of the greatest minds in financial history, called the "margin of safety."

But, first, listen to Warren Buffett, America's most successful investor and a disciple of Graham's, explain to shareholders at the 1998 annual meeting of the company he chairs, Berkshire Hathaway, Inc., why all earnings aren't created equal. He defines what he calls a "wonderful business":

> The business is wonderful if it gives you more and more money every year without putting up anything—or [by putting up] very little. And we have some businesses like that. . . . The worst business of all is the one that grows a lot, where you're forced to grow just to stay in the game at all, and where you're reinvesting the capital at a very low rate of return. And sometimes people are in those businesses without knowing it.

In other words, the fact that a company's earnings are rising each year doesn't mean that its long-run prospects are improving. Those rising earnings may have to go straight into the business to pay for vital capital investments just for it to stay on an even keel.

Consider, for example, a limousine company that has to use all of its profits each year to buy new cars just to keep up with the competition. If it does not buy the cars and its rivals do, then the limo company will lose customers and eventually go bankrupt.

So, even if its profits are growing at 20 percent a year, they never go into the pockets of the owners. They are sunk into new cars. In the end, the limo company is an asset with no value since it has no cash flow.

Now consider another company that owns a seaside hotel that requires almost no upkeep. As people get richer, demand for rooms increases, so the hotel raises its rates. But very little money has to go back into the business. If the hotel distributes the cash that is left over to its shareholders, then we can do our usual calculations—dividend rate plus growth rate of dividends should equal or exceed the T-bond rate—and everything is fine.

But if the hotel decides to retain all those earnings and stash the cash in, say, a savings account paying 5 percent interest, then we have a problem. The earnings will be inflated in subsequent years by the interest the company is paid by the bank—interest shareholders could have earned themselves if the hotel had paid the dividends to them.

These are the two reasons why cash flow to shareholders is rarely equal to reported earnings: (1) huge reinvestments may be necessary just in order to maintain a firm's competitive position in the future, as in the case of the limo business, and (2) there's the potential for double-counting, as in the case of the hotel.

For most companies, reported earnings, clearly, are greater than the cash that flows into your pockets over the time you own a stock. But, just as clearly, quarterly dividends are *less* than that cash flow. After all, many of today's greatest success stories—Microsoft, Amgen, Dell Computer, to name a few—do not pay conventional dividends at all. Yet their stock prices have risen sharply, a reflection that investors believe that they will see cash in their pockets in the future.

Is there any way we can value a company that has earnings but no regular dividend?

THREE MORE GOOD COMPANIES

Actually, there are several. One way is to use the two stages we introduced in Chapter 4—adolescence and adulthood—but with a subtle change. Now we will assume that during adolescence, as a company pours its earnings back into the firm, rather than handing them out to shareholders as dividends, the company will increase its earnings at a high rate. Then, at maturity, the firm starts *paying* dividends and increases those dividends at a low rate. Historically, mature firms have paid about 70 percent of earnings out as dividends each year, so we will use that assumption. Let's see how much cash can be expected to go into your pocket if you put your money in three popular firms that had very high P/Es in the spring of 1999 but that don't pay dividends.

CISCO SYSTEMS, INC.

Founded in 1984 by a small group including Leonard Bosack and Sandra Lerner, a husband-wife team from Stanford University who mortgaged their house to raise money and built prototypes in their garage, Cisco Systems has become the largest manufacturer of computer networking products in the world. Specifically, Cisco controls two-thirds of the market for routers, which move data between networks—an essential function of the Internet—and is a big maker of LAN (local area network) switches. It also makes the dial-up servers that give computer users access to the Web. Cisco, in short, provides the Internet's infrastructure.

Cisco's sales rose from $28 million in 1989 to $8.5 billion in 1998. Over those years, the firm increased in its earnings by an annual average of 115 percent. Growth has slowed recently, but it is still torrid. Over the five years ending in 1998, average annual earnings increases were 59 percent. The company has a fabulous balance sheet, with no debt, $1.6 billion in cash and marketable securities, and another $1.3 billion in notes due from others. Much of its profits Cisco puts to work back in the business, but not all.

In June 1999, Cisco was selling at a price of $64 and with earnings per share of 74 cents, it had a P/E of 85. Pretty expensive stock? Not really. If Cisco increases its earnings at the same rate over the *next* five years that it has over the past five, then they will increase by a factor of 10, to $7.50 per share. Say Cisco's price doubles over that five years. Its P/E at that time will be 17—hardly outrageous.

Now, suppose that Cisco has five years of adolescence, with earnings continuing to grow at 59 percent, and then, hitting maturity, starts paying 70 percent of earnings out as dividends. Let's use our old assumption that dividends per share grow about a half a percentage point slower than GDP after the firm reaches maturity.

Using the standard formula for calculating a stock's present value based on its flow of cash over time, you will find that Cisco's perfectly reasonable price should be $399 per share. In other words, to reach its PRP from its June 1999 level, Cisco would need to sextuple. Its P/E would rise to 530 (no, that's not a misprint).

But even with the Internet boom, it may be stretching credulity to project 59 percent growth for Cisco. Value Line's analysts project earnings growth for the company of 25.5 percent for the next five years. So let's use that figure—and again assume that, when adolescence ends, dividend payouts of 70 percent of earnings begin, with dividends growing slightly slower than the U.S. economy. In that case, with a five-year adolescence, the PRP for Cisco should be $122, for a P/E of 162. If the 25.5 percent rate continues for a ten-year adolescence, then the PRP is $291, or five times the 1999 price for the stock; with a 20-year adolescence, $1,652.

The point is that, at its current levels, Cisco is not an overvalued stock. Whether it should rise by a factor of 2 or a factor of 45 to reach its PRP depends on your assumptions. We think a factor of 4 or 5 is reasonable.

MICROSOFT CORP.

The most famous non-dividend-paying stock, Microsoft, tells a similar story. In 1988, the company was earning $124 million in after-tax profits on $591 million in sales. In 1998, earnings were $4.5 billion on $14.5 billion in sales, an even higher profit margin. (See Chapter 13 for a more detailed analysis of Microsoft and its history.) For the ten years ending in 1998, Microsoft increased its earnings at an annual rate of 41.5 percent. Between 1993 and 1998, the growth rate was 34.5 percent. According to Value Line's analysts, Microsoft should increase its earnings at an annual rate of 30.5 percent from 1999 to 2004. The stock in May 1999 was trading at $80 a share with a P/E—believed to be high by most analysts (and about twice the market average)—of 64.

Say that Microsoft's earnings do meet Value Line's estimates. Then, with a five-year adolescence growing by 30.5 percent, followed by dividend payouts growing 0.5 percent slower than real GDP, Microsoft's perfectly reasonable price in 1999 was $251—or more than triple its actual price in May of that year. Its P/E ratio, using this PRP, would be 201. If adolescence lasts ten years, then the PRP should be $727; if it lasts twenty years, $6,095.

Do these figures sound hopelessly optimstic? Then, let's go *back* five years and try a similar analysis with Microsoft. In April 1994, the stock, adjusted for splits, was trading at $5.50 a share; the company's earnings were 22 cents a share, for a P/E of 25. Using perfect hindsight, let's say that Microsoft's earnings over the next five years—through April 1999—would grow 34.5 percent annually. Now, if we had projected Microsoft's adolescence to last five years, then its PRP, as calculated in 1994, would have been $51 per share; if we had posited a ten-year adolescence, the PRP would have been $173. The actual price of Microsoft in May 1999, remember, was $80—which is nestled between these two figures.

Anyone claiming in 1994 that Microsoft stock would rise from $5.50 to $80 in just five years would have been classified as nuts. But such growth would have been absolutely sensible under our analysis.

BIOGEN, INC.

Computer companies are not the only ones that grow quickly and don't pay dividends. So do pharmaceutical firms engaged in biotechnology—the search for ways to cure diseases and improve health through the manipulation of genes. Started in 1978 by a group of scientists led by Nobel laureate Walter Gilbert, Biogen, based in Cambridge, Massachusetts, went public in 1983. Its cash cow in 1999 was Avonex, a drug that helps stop the progression of multiple sclerosis and which patients must take indefinitely. Biogen is also concentrating on drugs to treat inflammatory and cardiovascular diseases.

Like many biotech companies, Biogen lost money for years as it spent heavily on research before coming up with drugs that generate revenues. In 1987, for instance, the firm lost $23 million on sales of just $9 million. Profits appeared in 1989 and, after some rocky years, accelerated. For the five years ending in 1998, Biogen's earnings grew at an annual rate of 20 percent. But Value Line's analysts expect this growth to increase to 38.5 percent over the next five years as Avonex captures more of the international market and other products in the pipeline begin to deliver cash.

If Biogen can achieve this growth over a five-year adolescence, then by our standard assumptions, its PRP will be $546 per share and the price-to-earnings ratio, 270. That compares with a price of $105 in May

1999 and a P/E of 52. If Biogen grows at 38.5 percent for a ten-year adolescence, the PRP is $2,130. But let's be more cautious. What if Biogen boosts earnings at 20 percent—the same rate as the past five years? Then, the PRP for a five-year adolescence is $267, or a little less than triple the 1999 price, putting the P/E ratio at 132; for a ten-year adolescence, $507, for a P/E of 251.

THE MARKET AS A WHOLE

Again, it is not difficult to find firms that logically should have prices and P/E ratios well above the historical averages. But what about the market as a whole? One approach is to try to value a firm without making assumptions about future dividend payouts. This is what smart analysts like Warren Buffett do when they look at companies. Buffett comes up with a number he calls "instrinsic value," which he defines as "the discounted value of the cash that can be taken out of a business [not necessarily as quarterly dividends] during its remaining life." But even with individual companies, "The calculation of intrinsic value . . . is not so simple."

One common method for deriving what could be called intrinsic value involves controlling for reinvestment and double-counting (as in our limo and hotel examples)—an exercise that has occupied a number of smart academics for years. The idea is that you can constuct a reasonable value for a company if you can identify the current and future "free-cash flow" that the firm can generate and then discount that back to today with the appropriate interest rate.

FREE-CASH FLOW: METHOD 1

Making adjustments to earnings in order to derive free-cash flow can be very complicated, but a fairly easy-to-read reference is the book *Valuation, Measuring, and Managing the Value of Companies,* by Tom Copeland, Tim Koller, and Jack Murrin. There is also a rapidly expanding literature on the topic, started by a brilliant theoretical accountant (bet you didn't know those existed) named Jim Ohlson.

These folks have narrowed down the earnings-based calculation to three possible methods, which should all yield the same answer. We will discuss here the two that are easiest to apply.

When firms calculate their earnings, they don't subtract the investments that they make in a given year, but they do subtract a phantom, noncash accounting charge called "depreciation," which is supposed to represent the wear and tear on a company's machines. The basic idea of the first measure of free-cash flow is to add back in the phantom charge and then subtract out the actual investment a firm makes. (The approach requires a few other adjustments, but this is the big one.) Do the calculation for several years, and you will have a measure of free-cash flow that you can use to construct a value for the firm, a measure that doesn't depend on dividend-payout policy.

The surprise is that this measure of cash flow often turns out to be fairly close to earnings. But this makes intuitive sense. If a firm introduces new machines at roughly the same rate as the old machines are written off for tax purposes, then depreciation and new-investment requirements nearly cancel each other out. As Buffett said at the Berkshire Hathaway annual meeting in 1998, in response to a question from a shareholder: "By and large, in most companies, the depreciation charge is not inappropriate to use as a proxy for required capital expenditures."

Take the example of Johnson & Johnson, the giant health products company. In 1997, J&J's official reported after-tax earnings were $3.3 billion. Which part of those earnings goes to the shareholders and which part has to be reinvested in the business for J&J simply to keep running in place?

In 1997, J&J made what its annual report calls "additions to property, plant and equipment" totaling $1.4 billion. That was the company's new capital investment that year—needed to keep the profits flowing in the future. But, at the same time, the company wrote off $1.1 billion in depreciation of old property, plant, and equipment—a deduction that was taken into account in the earnings figure. Thus, net cash shelled out for capital investment was $300 million, the difference between the two.

In other words, out of $3.3 billion in profits, $3 billion was left for the owners. Of the $3 billion, $1.1 billion went out directly as dividends. The rest was kept in the firm to build up J&J's cash hoard, which would ultimately benefit shareholders.

Here's another example. Ford Motor Co. has two businesses—making automobiles, which is straightforward, and providing financial services, which is too specialized for our purposes. But looking at the auto business, you find that in 1997, Ford had net income of $4.7 billion, capital investment of $8.1 billion and depreciation of $6 billion. So total cash available to shareholders was about $2.6 billion [$4.7 − ($8.1 − $6)]. Of that, $2.2 billion was paid in dividends and $400 million went into the corporate treasury on behalf of its owners.

The best place to find figures on a company's capital investments is in the Statement of Consolidated Cash Flows in its annual report—often reprinted on corporate Internet sites. But these reports aren't easy to interpret, especially since companies frequently buy back stock, take on new debt, and repay old. As we said, there are other things which, while usually not nearly as significant as depreciation and investment, need to be taken into account if you use this approach. Most important, you have figure out the change in working capital, which requires a bit more digging into annual reports. Because of such details, we usually don't attempt to calculate free-cash flow this way—especially if we are trying to think about the stock market as a whole.

FREE-CASH FLOW: METHOD 2

The second approach to approximate free-cash flow, and the one we use most often, is to examine a firm's *financial* flows. If a company earns money, it can do only four things with it: put it in the bank, pay it out as a dividend, repurchase some of its own shares, or repay debt.

Thus, you can also approximate free-cash flow by adding together dividends and repurchases and then subtracting (or adding) the change in debt. Repurchases and debt are both "net" variables. If a firm repurchases and issues shares in the same year, for example, you need to subtract the amount issued from the amount repurchased. "Net debt" is debt outstanding minus money in the bank.

Copeland and his coauthors recommend constructing the value of the firm by calculating the present value of this measure of free-cash flow. Before actually making the calculations for the market as a whole, let's look more carefully at the key elements:

• **Dividends you should know well.** They are just the checks mailed to shareholders four times a year.

• **A share repurchase occurs when a firm buys some of its stock back from shareholders.** It is really just another way of paying dividends—often an attractive way since the tax bill can be lowered significantly. Suppose, for example, that you owned 100 percent of the stock of a company and it decided to buy 10 percent of that stock back from you. Why? Perhaps the stock price is low and the company itself is a great investment. The firm gives you some money; you give the firm some shares. After that happens, you still own 100 percent of the firm (you own the firm, so you also own the shares that the firm owns). But now, you have some cash as well. If the firm had decided to pay out 10 percent of its value as a dividend, you would be in the same circumstance, but the tax consequences would be very different: In the case of a repurchase, you pay a capital gains tax; in the case of dividends, you pay taxes on ordinary income, which can be twice as much. Of course, it's rare that anyone owns 100 percent of a company. Instead, when repurchases occur, most shareholders hold onto their stock. But the effect is the same. Say you own 100 shares of a company with a total of 10,000 shares outstanding. You own 1 percent of the stock (100 ÷ 10,000 = .01) and have a claim on 1 percent of the future earnings. Suppose the company uses its cash to repurchase 2,000 shares of stock. Now you own 1.25 percent of the stock (100 ÷ 8,000 = 0.0125) and have a claim on 1.25 percent of the future earnings. In effect, your stock is worth 25 percent more than it would be of the firm had paid a dividend, but you don't have to pay taxes on that gain. In 1997, for example, Johnson & Johnson repurchased $628 million worth of its stock, in addition to paying $1.1 million in quarterly cash dividends. At the end of that year, the dividend yield on J&J stock was 1.4 percent while the repurchase amounted to an extra dividend yield of 0.8 percent—a total of 2.2 percent. Between 1996 and 1998, Alcoa, the aluminum company, repurchased $1.3 billion worth of stock, while paying out only $800 million in dividends to shareholders. In fact, during 1998, the value of stock repurchases by U.S. corporations was about equal to the dividends they paid. In other words, instead of figuring dividend yields as 1.5 percent, they should be 3 percent. In the analysis in the last chapter, we found that reasonable dividend yields for the market should be 0.5 percent. Since yields were about 1.5 percent, stocks should triple. But if true yields are 3 percent, then stocks should sextuple.

• **The third component, the change in net debt, can also be important, especially when firms are not paying dividends or repurchasing**

stock. For example, when Biogen earns $100 million and puts it in the bank, net debt (the amount of money owed to bondholders and other creditors minus the amount of money in the bank) goes down by $100 million. If a firm has no debt, but lots of money piling up in the bank, then net debt is negative (which is the case with Microsoft) and the debt correction can make free-cash flow much higher.

We like this method for measuring free-cash flow. It is easy to calculate not only for individual firms, but for the stock market as a whole, using data from the Federal Reserve Board. And the story one discovers is very striking, for three reasons:

1. When we do the arithmetic, we find that, for the market as a whole since World War II, the correct measure of cash flow is about 68 percent of earnings. This is a useful fact, since it allows you to look at earnings and make a quick guess at the PRP without doing any further digging.

2. Free-cash flow growth has been even greater than earnings growth by the measure we have been using. The earnings measure came from the Shiller data, which looked only at the five hundred stocks of the S&P, the usual proxy for the market as a whole. But, when an Internet company with minuscule current earnings but a large market capitalization and great promise replaces a manufacturer on the S&P, earnings for the index as a whole can drop significantly. In our examination of the aggregate cash flow figures, we look at the Fed data for *all* corporations, and there's a big difference.

3. The "cash yield" from these numbers is much higher than the dividend yield for the market as a whole, confirming the intuition that our previous, dividends-only calculations were extremely cautious.

Let's get specific: For the market as a whole, the growth rate of free-cash flow has been about 10 percent annually since World War II, compared with 7.3 percent for the growth of earnings (using the Shiller data) over this period; for the past twenty years, cash flow has grown at 8 percent, compared with 6.7 percent for earnings.

More impressively, if we look at all corporations, the average cash-flow *yield* in 1998 was 3.3 percent, as opposed to the 1.5 percent dividend yield we found in Chapter 4.

So let's do some PRP calculations, assuming that the current cash-flow yield for the market as a whole is the starting point and then trying out some different growth scenarios. To keep it simple, let's break up the hypothetical aggregate company's life into two stages once again: adolescence and maturity.

If firms increase their free-cash flow through adolescence at the same rate that has held for the past ten years (8 percent, or 2 percentage points below the long-run average) and increase it in maturity at 0.5 percent below long-run GDP growth, then $100 invested in the market today buys you a cash flow that has a present value of $387, (again using a bond rate of 5.5 percent). The market would nearly have to quadruple immediately to reach the PRP. If adolescence lasted ten years, the present value of cash bought for $100 would equal $452; if it lasted twenty years, $606.

If firms post *no* real growth in cash flow once they reach maturity, then the present value of cash delivered for a $100 investment is $140 after a five-year adolescence, $174 after a ten-year adolescence, and $255 after a twenty-year adolescence.

By even the most cautious estimate, the market still looks awfully cheap.

EARNINGS AND DOW 36,000

Remember that free-cash flow has been about 70 percent of earnings, according to the Fed data. But let's double-check this calculation using another common-sense approach: looking at the historical relationship between earnings and dividends.

Over time, companies have gradually cut the percentage of earnings that they pay out to shareholders, probably because managers have come to recognize that most shareholders, for tax reasons, would prefer not to receive dividends but, instead, have them reinvested by the company, boosting its value and its stock price.

But tax concerns were not always so important to managers, and high dividend payouts had a strong attraction for investors. In fact, from 1871 to 1900, U.S. companies paid out an average of about 75 percent of their earnings as dividends. That rate persisted through World World II, and even as late as the 1950s—when economic conditions last resembled current ones—the payout ratio was still 70 percent. So our measure of free-cash flow has the same ratio to earnings as dividends did, before firms paid close attention to the tax bills of their shareholders.

The proportion has dropped consistently since then and is now only 38 percent. In other words, for every dollar a firm earns, 62 cents are retained in its bank account or reinvested in capital improvements and 38 cents are paid to shareholders in dividends.

Unless a company is growing very fast—and, therefore, has to use its annual profits to make heavy capital investments in new machines—this rule of thumb works well. Yes, certain individual companies with capital needs devouring all their earnings will resemble the limo company. Others, such as Coca-Cola, get such phenomenal returns from the capital they invest that, in a typical year, capital investments are twice annual depreciation. But, for most companies, the depreciation of old capital investments is pretty close to the cost of new ones.

The evidence indicates strongly that companies *could* pay out 70 percent of their earnings if they wanted to. Therefore, the cash that investors will put in their pockets—in dividends both now and down the road—should be roughly 70 percent of reported earnings. But, as with all of our assumptions, we lean toward caution. We're believers in Graham's "margin of safety." So let's say that the dividend flowing to shareholders is 50 percent of earnings, not 70 percent. Still, 50 percent is considerably higher than the dividend payout rate of 38 percent. In fact, it boosts cash-flow assumptions—above quarterly dividends alone—by one-third.

If you make such an adjustment, then how high could the market go?

For an answer, you need to examine the growth of *earnings* per share—rather than dividends per share. Remember that, since 1946, earnings growth has averaged 7.3 percent; for the past twenty years, it has been 6.7 percent; for the past ten years, 8.5 percent. Real earnings growth has been 3.3 percent since World War II, about 2.9 percent over the past twenty years, and 5.8 percent over the past ten years.

With such a history, it is difficult to make a guess about the future. Also, earnings per share might have grown in part because of retained earnings increasing; and profits may have been boosted by bank interest. We want to be careful not to double-count, as we would if we allowed the bank interest payments in our hotel example to enter the earnings and growth calculations.

So, to be extra cautious, let's simply use the same growth rate we used for dividends in the last chapter: 5 percent.

Next, we need the earnings equivalent of the dividend yield. Remember the P/E, or price-to-earnings, ratio? The inverse—the E/P, or earnings-to-price, ratio—is a company's earnings per share divided by its market price.

You rarely see this figure presented, but it indicates the percentage of its market price that the company throws off in earnings. The best way to calculate it is to flip the P/E ratio upside down, that is, divide it into 1.

In early 1999, the P/E ratio (using year-ahead earnings) for the broad market was about 26. The E/P, or earnings yield, was 1/26, or 0.038—which is to say, 3.8 percent. In other words, a stock that cost $100 was producing $3.80 in after-tax earnings.

Our conservative estimate is that the flow of cash into your pockets equals half of earnings, so the *cash* yield comes to 1.9 percent.

So, using these more precise measures, we find that stocks are vastly cheaper than they should be. For stocks to produce the same cash flow as bonds, the *cash* yield on stocks would have to drop to 0.5 percent (5.5 − 5 = 0.5), so the *earnings* yield would have to drop to 1 percent. If that happened, the P/E would be 100 (1 ÷ 0.01 = 100).

In other words, by this analysis, a P/E ratio of 100—more than four times current levels and eight times historic averages—is fully justified.

TAXES AND THE PRP

So far, we have ignored the question of taxes altogether. (Wouldn't it be nice if we could always do that?) When you earn a dollar, you don't get to keep the dollar because federal, state, and sometimes local governments want their share. Most Americans with enough income to be investors face a total tax rate on income of around 40 percent. Bond interest counts as ordinary income—although interest checks from Treasury bonds are not subject to state tax. Interest on municipal bonds, issued by state and local governments, is not subject to federal tax. But the rate on munis is lower than on T-bonds.

Assume you are in the top tax bracket (which in 1999 was 39.6 percent, federal) and that you own only T-bonds. Out of every dollar you receive in interest from your bonds, you will see only 60 cents. The feds get the rest.

For stocks, calculations are more complicated. If a company pays all of its profits out in dividends, then federal and state governments treat the money just like interest, so the tax effect is the same as for bonds. But if a firm, like Microsoft, pays no dividends, then most of the return you receive will be in the form of capital gains—your profit when you sell a stock at a higher price than what you paid for it.

Capital gains are taxed at a lower rate than dividends—20 percent was the top rate in 1999 on capital gains at the federal level for stocks held for at least a year—so a stock whose earnings translate into capital gains will put more after-tax money into your pocket than a bond or a stock that pays hefty dividends.

But it gets better. You don't have to pay tax on your capital gains until you sell the stock.

If you plan to put your certificates under your bed for many, many years, then the tax payment is way off in the future, so, if you take the long view, and if you buy stocks that don't pay dividends, then you are choosing a highly "tax-advantaged" strategy.

When we cranked the numbers, we found that the appropriate tax adjustment for capital gains and dividends on stocks reduces their returns—and thus, their fair prices—by about 10 percent, as opposed to a 40 percent reduction in the top bracket and a 28 percent reduction in the average bracket for bonds.

Thus, taxes are the friend of the Dow 36,000 Theory. If you account for them, then the argument that stocks are currently undervalued becomes even stronger.

THE BEAUTY OF SKEWNESS

To construct our measures of the PRP for the market, we applied conservative assumptions to statistics for the market as a whole. One reason we say the figures are cautious is that the PRP can be very large for some fast-growing firms, as we saw in the case of Microsoft and Cisco, and that such firms can have a big effect on indexes that are supposed to reflect the market.

If a firm falls out of favor, its P/E can get very low, but it can never go below zero. This means that the effect of a real dog on the market averages can never get too big, since the largest conceivable gap between the P/E for the market and the P/E for a dog is the P/E for the market. A P/E of zero is 26 points below the market P/E, and that's it. But if a firm has great growth prospects and a little bit of earnings, then the P/E can climb into the stratosphere, hundreds of points above the market average. The distribution of P/Es is very skewed, with lots of big P/Es, but none that is far below average. America Online, example, had a P/E of 436 in May 1999. Such large P/Es have a disproportionate effect, a point that analysts who complain that stocks are overvalued rarely acknowledge.

In May 1999, the P/E for the S&P 500 was about 26.7 (based on earnings estimates for the full year). Remove Microsoft and the market P/E drops to about 25.2. Remove the ten biggest firms, most of which, like Cisco, have great growth prospects and sensibly high P/Es, and the market P/E-drops to about 22.3. Remove the twenty largest firms (AOL, by the way, was number 17) and the market P/E drops all the way to 18.5.

As an alternative to the aggregate calculations presented above, we also constructed estimates of the likely path of the market from the bottom up, using free-cash flow and dividends as a measure of the money in your pockets delivered by stock. That is, we looked at the PRP for each firm in the index and used these figures to construct a PRP for the index as a whole. This exercise, once again, makes Dow 36,000 look very conservative.

To see why, think about what would happen if only one firm, Microsoft, jumped to its PRP. Take the ten-year-adolescence PRP of $727. If Microsoft climbs to this level, then its P/E would jump to 582. Suppose that every other firm stays exactly where it is when that happens. Then Microsoft climbs from about 3 percent to about 19 percent of the entire market. At that point, 19 percent of the market has a P/E of 582, and the P/E for the market as a whole climbs to 130—even though Microsoft was the only firm to reach its PRP!

The effects of this skewness in PRPs are so dramatic that it is easy to crank down our growth and cash-flow assumptions considerably and still pull out the prediction that the PRP for the market implies an average P/E of 100.

SUMMING UP

Our circumspect assumptions show that the PRP is much higher than the valuation of the overall market today, but it cannot be pinpointed precisely. For that reason, we like to think of the perfectly rational price as defining the upper boundary of a "comfort zone." As a long-term investor with a diversified portfolio, you should not be concerned about warnings of overvaluation or manias or bubbles—as long as P/Es are under 100. You're within the margin of safety.

We can't know for sure whether the PRP for the Dow is 27,000 or 54,000. However, we are sure of two things: (1) thinking about stocks in the way we have described in this chapter forces investors to ask the right questions, and (2) anyone who claims that the market is too high today is viewing history from an outdated and flawed perspective.

When we take into account growth, dividends, and interest rates—the factors behind the money that goes into your pockets—the market is at least as good a buy as it has ever been. And, in the long run, it has always been undervalued.

But the circle is not quite closed. Remember that at the start of this chapter, we made some assumptions about risk in order to simplify our analysis. We said that the long-term investor viewed the riskiness of stocks as equivalent to the riskiness of bonds. This assumption lies at the heart of the Dow 36,000 Theory, and it can't be treated lightly. In the next chapter, we look more closely at risk—for too many investors, the forgotten fact of financial life.

CHAPTER 6

Unrisky Business

All Nature is but Art, unknown to thee;
All Chance, Direction, which thou canst not see . . .
—Alexander Pope, *An Essay on Man*

H OW RISKY IS the stock market? In the short run—a month, a year, three years—it is very risky. In the long run, it is no more risky than the market for Treasury bonds. That undeniable, historical fact forms the foundation of the Dow 36,000 Theory.

Investors in recent years have begun to understand this secret about the riskiness of stocks. As a result, they have bid up prices—a process that will continue until shares reach their PRP. Another way to describe what's happening is that investors, acting rationally at last, are requiring a lower "risk premium"—a smaller bonus—in return for taking the chances involved in investing in stocks.

Not only are investors becoming more enlightened about the riskiness of stocks, the real-life riskiness is actually going down—for reasons we'll describe in this chapter.

But before all that, let's take a closer look at what risk is.

THE MANY FLAVORS

We face risks every day. Some are accepted eagerly. Millions of Americans buy lottery tickets, for example, even if the payoff is $1 million for a dollar ticket and the true chances of winning are 2 million-to-1.

Other risks are incorporated into our everyday lives so that we hardly notice them. When we cross the street, for instance, we face a chance (even a slight one) of being hit by a runaway car.

In general, we think of taking a risk as exposing ourselves to something bad. If you skydive, there's a possibility that your parachute won't open. If you hire a person whose background you don't know, there's a chance he will steal you blind.

Risk has many flavors. Sometimes, notions of risk reflect ignorance. We might think that there is a 50-50 chance that it will rain tomorrow, but, really, the uncertainty results from an inability to model meteorological phenomena with accuracy. If there were a perfect model—a computer program drawn from history and based on the circulation of air masses around the globe—then you would know for sure (or, anyway, within a 99 percent chance of accuracy) whether it would rain. But since you have to make do with an imperfect model, you take a risk when you go out without a raincoat.

Other risks exist even when we fully understand the odds. If you wager $5 on the flip of a coin, there is a 50 percent chance you will win. No amount of additional information gathering or fancy computer modeling can change those odds.

Every asset that is traded in a financial market also carries the risk that the returns that you will get on your investment cannot be known with precision. With a stock, you might lose all your money or earn 20 times what you put up (or more—Amazon.com, the online retailer, rose from $6 to $200 a share in its first eighteen months of trading).

Even with a large basket of stocks from dozens of companies, the return is uncertain—mainly for two reasons. First, there is much about the economy (and its effect on corporate profits) that is still not understood. And, second, truly unpredictable outside (or "exogenous") events, like a war in East Asia, can influence the success of all investments, at least in the short term.

When we say *all* investments, we really mean it. Take U.S. Treasury bonds, which are often called "riskless." If you buy a $1,000 T-bond, you are lending $1,000 to the federal government. The Treasury promises to pay you interest for a fixed number of years and then return your $1,000 in full. So long as the Treasury remains solvent, Cuba doesn't conquer the United States, and the earth isn't hit by a meteor, your payments are safe—that is, essentially riskless. You'll definitely get your checks.

But, as a bondholder, you face another kind of risk. If inflation soars, the $1,000 that the government gives back to you at maturity will be worth far less—in terms of what it can buy—than the $1,000 you turned over in the first place. And the interest payments, which were fixed when you bought the bond (that is, made the loan), might not make up for the decline.

For example, at the beginning of 1977, a $10,000 Treasury note maturing at the end of 1981 was paying 7 percent interest, but over the next five years inflation totaled 60 percent, so that it cost $16,000 in 1982 to buy what cost $10,000 in 1977. Over those years, interest payments totaled only $3,500. Even if you had been smart enough to reinvest the interest checks in short-term deposits at a 10 percent rate, you would still have been a loser to inflation.

Nevertheless, at any point in time, the interest rate on a Treasury bond is considered the benchmark, the *nearly* riskless rate against which all other investments are measured.

Now consider a corporate bond. Like a Treasury security, it is an IOU that pays fixed interest and then matures, giving you your money back. Again, you are exposed to the risk of inflation. But with corporates, there is another risk: Unlike the federal government, a private company doesn't have taxing power. If it can't sell enough of its products at a good price, it can go broke, and creditors who bought bonds are left holding the bag.

The market has a way to handle this "credit" risk, as it's called. It requires firms that are less likely to repay their debts, to pay a higher interest rate on their bonds. In other words, investors won't be attracted to buy corporate bonds unless the firms that issue them offer to pay a premium (an extra amount of interest) over the Treasury rate. A highly risky corporation that insists on selling its bonds at the government rate will simply find no buyers—no one to lend it money.

In the movie *Rocky*, Sylvester Stallone plays an aspiring boxer who makes ends meet by helping a loan shark collect debts. The shark specializes in lending to people who are desperately in need of cash but who are unusually high risks—unlikely to get a Visa card or a loan at the bank. The shark charges a high risk premium for his loans—and, of course, uses strong-arm tactics to ensure the safety of his capital. In the U.S. financial markets, there are companies like General Electric that are perceived as barely more risky than the federal government, but other firms are not too far removed from the circumstances that would make them customers of Rocky's boss.

At the start of 1999, for instance, an AT&T bond, maturing in eight years, paid an interest rate of 6.7 percent while a similar bond issued by Chesapeake Energy, a more shaky company, paid 12.3 percent. Investors worried that Chesapeake might not be able to give them their money back in 2007, so they demanded higher interest payments along the way.

For bonds, the difference between the nearly risk-free interest rate—that is, the Treasury rate—and the actual interest rate is called the risk premium. Since the Treasury rate on eight-year maturities was about 5 percent at the start of 1999, the risk premium on the AT&T bonds was 1.7 percent, but the risk premium on the Chesapeake bonds was a hefty 7.3 percent. The risk premium isn't set by the Federal Reserve Board or by a large bank. It is set by the market—that is, by the tastes and forecasts of investors.

IT'S NOT THE HEAT, IT'S THE VOLATILITY

How do individual attitudes toward risk—those tastes, hopes, and fears—affect the prices of stocks and bonds?

To get an understanding, try a thought experiment. Suppose that the Treasury offered "coin-flip" bonds. At the start of each year, just before the government mails its interest checks to bondholders, imagine that the Secretary of the Treasury flips a coin in a big ceremony on television. If it's heads, the interest rate is boosted by one percentage point. If it's tails, the rate is reduced by one percentage point. Over the years, of course, heads and tails average out, and these coin-flip bonds would end up paying the same interest as regular bonds. But which would you rather have?

If you are like most people, you would choose regular bonds—since you know what you are getting, guaranteed, ahead of time. Research, as well as intuition, shows that most folks are more unhappy about losing money than they are happy about gaining the same amount. So the risk of loss—even if it is precisely the same as the chance of gain—would deter investors from buying coin-flip bonds. In order to sell them, the Treasury would have to offer higher interest rates.

How much higher? That depends on the risk aversion of the bond buyers—and also on the amount of risk, the range of the results from flip to flip. In this coin-flip example, the gain or loss each year is just one percentage point. But imagine a bond that gave investors an extra 5 percent for heads and subtracted 5 percent for tails. Or imagine one that exacted a $100,000 penalty for tails and a similar bonus for heads.

Again, on average, bondholders would probably end up with the same amount of interest at the end of twenty or thirty years. But the extra risk would induce them to demand higher interest rates—that is, a bigger risk premium. The penalty also points to the difference in risk perception between rich and poor. A $100,000 penalty might mean little to a rich investor, but it would send a poor family into debt. It's no surprise, then, that research shows lower-income people are more risk-averse when it comes to investments than the wealthy.

So, while we usually think of risk as the chance of losing lots of money—or your health or your life—risk is something else in financial terms. It is the *volatility*—that is, the extremes of the ups and downs—of the returns you get from investments. Increase the volatility (as with the coin-flip bonds), and accordingly, you increase the risk as it is perceived by an investor, who will then demand a higher premium for plunking down his money.

Exactly how much increased risk *should* raise the yield of a risky stock or bond is impossible to say—since the markup depends on individual preferences. Still, it is easy to observe how big a markup has been demanded by the market as a whole in exchange for taking on risk—as with the risk premium between corporate bonds and Treasuries—and that observation is a window into investors' preferences.

HOW RISK CHANGES PRICES

Earlier, we presented evidence that stocks are no riskier than bonds in the long run. For example, Jeremy Siegel uses data back to 1802 to show that there has *never* been a period of 17 years or longer in which stocks have not produced positive returns after inflation; for bonds, however, there have been negative returns as great as 3 percent.

If we assume that stocks and bonds are equally risky, then the perfectly reasonable price (PRP) of a stock is the one that produces a flow of cash over time that should equal the flow of cash from a Treasury bond.

But we have also shown that, in the past, investors who have owned stocks have received much *more* cash in their pockets than those who have owned bonds.

Remember that to find out the returns you can expect from a stock, you simply add the dividend yield to the anticipated rate of dividend growth. That number has typically been higher than the yield on a Treasury bond, which makes interest payments that don't rise over time.

In early 1999, the stock of AlliedSignal, Inc., a diversified manufacturer that makes aerospace and automotive products, was paying a dividend of 68 cents a year and traded at $45 a share, for a yield of about 1.5 percent. The company's dividend growth rate was projected at 6 percent—at the minimum. Add 1.5 percent and 6 percent and get the expected cash return over time from the stock—7.5 percent. Meanwhile, a long-term Treasury bond was yielding 5.5 percent. The difference between the two returns was being 2 percentage points.

Think of the 7.5 percent dividend return on AlliedSignal stock as being exactly comparable to the payments from a risky bond paying a fixed rate of 7.5 percent. For the risky bond, that extra 2 points over the Treasury rate is called the risk premium, and so it is for the risky stock. It is the extra cash flow that investors demand to compensate them for the extra risk of owning stocks instead of Treasury bonds.

But, wait! In truth, there is no extra risk, at least not for a diversified basket of stocks. On average, stocks and bonds are equally risky over long horizons. Yes, the chance that the U.S. government will fail to meet its obligations is minuscule, but in a large, diversified portfolio of stocks, only a tiny number of companies will go bankrupt. Investors run major risks, too, when they buy long-term T-bonds because their after-inflation returns could be negative. Stocks carry risks as well but over time those risks dissipate significantly. And the numbers don't lie: Using the established indicators of volatility, such as standard deviation, stocks are no more risky than bonds and may, in fact, be less risky.

But investors don't believe it. They perceive additional risk even if it doesn't exist, so they demand higher returns.

But what happens if these investors wake up to reality? What happens if their preferences and perceptions shift as they learn the truth about stocks?

To put it simply: Prices will move toward the PRP and rates of return will fall.

Say you own a house in northern California that's in a neighborhood that everyone believes is an earthquake zone. You rent out the house for $500 a month, or $6,000 per year—the going rate in that part of the country. The market value of the house is $60,000—a relatively low figure because of the threat of quakes and the risk of losing the entire investment (let's assume that you can't get the house insured and that you, as owner, are responsible for any of the tenant's losses). Therefore, the annual return on your investment, based on the value of the house, is 10 percent annually ($6,000 ÷ $60,000 = 0.10).

Suddenly, a new seismological study is released which shows that, in fact, the neighborhood is not in an earthquake zone, so the risk of losing your house in a catastrophe plummets to practically zero. The value of the house soars to $100,000 (you know this because someone just bought an identical house next door for that amount). The income from the tenant, however, remains the same since it was set by the market (the tenant could always move to another neighborhood and he was insured by you). Therefore, your return is now 6 percent annually ($6,000 ÷ $100,000 = 0.06).

This is a good illustration of what happens when the risk premium undergoes a perception shift. The risk-free rate of return on the house turned out to be 6 percent, but you were getting a return of 10 percent when it appeared you were in an earthquake zone. So you were receiving a risk premium of four percentage points. But, as the risk was unmasked as an illusion, the premium vanished. The value (or price) of the house rose, and the return fell.

This is precisely what we believe has been happening in the stock market, and will continue to happen until the risk premium disappears completely: Prices will rise and, eventually, returns will fall.

Similar swings have happened elsewhere. Bonds of companies that received low (or no) ratings from Moody's and other credit services used to pay about eight percentage points more than bonds issued by AAA-rated companies. This 8 percent risk premium for junk, or high-yield, bonds was illogically high when one actually looked at the historic default rates of the two different kinds of companies. As more information about the true riskiness of the bonds came out, the risk premium for junk gradually decreased. As that premium fell, the prices of junk bonds rose and bondholders made enormous profits.

Think of it this way: Stock prices are inversely related to the risk premium. As the risk premium falls, the price of a stock rises. As the price of a stock rises its dividend yield falls. And vice versa.

With a specific interest rate on Treasuries and a specific rate of dividend growth, it is the risk premium that determines how big a dividend yield is required to entice investors into stocks instead of bonds.

If the risk premium rises, then investors are demanding more dollars in dividends for every $100 they invest in stocks. Since a firm can't immediately boost its cash flow and raise its dividends, the price of its stock must go down in order to meet investors' needs.

Consider Glimcher Realty Trust—based in Columbus, Ohio—a real estate investment trust, or REIT, that owns and manages regional malls and shopping centers. Starting in 1995, Glimcher paid a consistent dividend of $1.92 annually. In March 1997, the stock price was $22, so Glimcher's yield was 8.7 percent ($1.92 ÷ $22 = 0.087). But later that year, after the Russian default and worries of a slowdown at home, investors became wary of mortgage lenders and real estate companies. They demanded a higher dividend yield in return for holding the stock of a firm like Glimcher—specifically, a risk premium that was about four percentage points greater. Since the company could not raise its payout beyond $1.92—it wasn't making enough money—the stock price had to fall to satisfy investors' needs. By March 1998, the price had dropped to $15, and the yield rose to 12.8 percent.

The same process works in the opposite direction. If the risk premium *falls*, investors are willing to accept a smaller dividend yield. In September 1998, the annual dividend payout for Procter & Gamble Co., the giant consumer-products firm, was $1.14 and the stock traded at $70, for a yield of 1.6 percent. But as 1999 unfolded, with the dividend the same, investors felt more secure about the company's prospects. The yield dropped to 1.1 percent—a decline in the risk premium of one-half of 1 percent—as the stock price rose above $100.

This is the Dow 36,000 Theory's case for stocks: They should rise in price as investors squeeze out the risk premium. If stocks and bonds are equally risky (as history shows they are), then the risk premium, which was roughly 2.5 percent in 1999, should be zero, and stocks will increase until they reach the PRP.

WHY A RISK PREMIUM?

There is no official risk premium figure that's reported every year, but as long as we make some assumptions, we can construct a series (a historical record). Once again using the raw data compiled by Robert Shiller of Yale University, we can go all the way back to 1871. The risk premium is the number of percentage points you have to add to the Treasury bond interest rate in order to make it equal the dividend yield for stocks plus their dividend growth rate.

It's easy to find the bond rate and the dividend yield, but we have to guess what people expected the growth rate of dividends would be each year. For simplicity, we made the assumption that the expected growth rate was a consistent 6 percent—the average over the entire period.

Take a year when the dividend yield was 3 percent and the bond rate was 5 percent. Yield (3 percent) plus dividend growth rate (6 percent) equals 9 percent. Subtract the bond rate (5 percent) from 9 percent, and you get the risk premium: 4 percent.

OK. Now, look at the actual results. From 1871 to 1929, the risk premium averaged 7 percent per year. The 1929 crash scared investors so badly that they boosted the premium even higher. From 1930 to 1950, it stayed at a plateau of 11 percent. As World War II ended and the economy picked up, fears began to diminish, and during the 1950s, the premium dropped to about 9.5 percent. In the 1960s, it continued to fall. The rate then fluctuated wildly as Paul Volcker, the Fed chairman, launched a war against inflation by hiking interest rates and creating enormous uncertainties. This measure of the risk premium fell all the way to around 2.5 percent by the late 1990s. That is less than one-fourth its value in the 1950s.

On average, the risk premium was about 7 percent, and its sharp decline was what propelled stocks higher in the bull market of the late twentieth century. Changes in other elements in the equation have been slight. While many analysts talk about the growth in corporate profits, the truth is that dividend increases have been remarkably steady. Earnings growth has been regular as well, and while nominal bond rates have gone up and down, the real rate has been notably consistent. No, it is the declining risk premium that explains the market's boom.

But what explains the risk premium?

THE THEORY OF RISK AVERSION

The risk premium has posed a major intellectual challenge to financial scholars for a long time. Hundreds of academic papers have offered explanations but none has received wide acceptance.

The most plausible story is that people are very averse to losing their hard-earned money—as in the case of our coin-flip bonds—and that, throughout history, they have had very short time horizons. Without a doubt, stocks are riskier than bonds over short periods. So, perhaps investors are scared out of their wits by the sharp fluctuations of stocks over one- or two-year periods and then irrationally project that fear into longer periods, like someone who watches three inches of snow fall and immediately starts shovelling for his life, thinking he'll be buried in an avalanche.

To account for the high risk premium, investors must be very, very frightened of short-term volatility. How frightened? In a recent paper published by the National Bureau of Economic Research, John Cochrane of the University of Chicago tried an experiment to find out. Using a computer model, he took a family with annual income of $50,000 that is exactly as risk-averse as shareholders have demonstrated themselves to be. He then asked a simple question: How much money would this family be willing to pay each year in order to avoid having to take a bet on a coin flip that would increase or decrease their lifetime annual income by $1,000? The answer was $863!

It is hard to believe that shareholders can be so risk-averse. But, if they are, then why have stocks soared in recent years? In other words, why has the risk premium fallen? Scholars are at a complete loss.

Without a theory, the experts have to fall back on the argument that the 457 percent run-up in the market from June 1989 to June 1999 reflected a temporary euphoria over stocks and that the historical risk premium accurately reflects people's preferences. As irrational as they may appear, investors are naturally scared to death by stocks, goes the reasoning from this view, so a huge correction is coming, with the risk premium reverting to the mean—its historic norm.

If the risk premium did return to normal, the carnage would be devastating. Add a 7 percent risk premium to a 5 percent Treasury yield and you get a 12 percent target for the sum of the dividend yield and the growth rate of dividends. Assume that growth is 6 percent. Then the yield would have to quadruple from its current 1.5 percent to 6 percent. For that to happen, stock prices would have to fall by 75 percent. For example, a $100 stock paying a $1.50 dividend would drop to $25 a share ($1.50 ÷ .06 = 25). Ouch.

In this example, we used dividends as the measure of cash flowing into your pockets. But even if we used earnings instead, the market would have to drop by about one-third.

A NEW UNDERSTANDING OF INVESTMENT RISK

We aren't worried about a return to an absurdly high risk premium, however, because we have a different explanation for what has happened over the past few decades. We see the decline in the risk premium as reasonable and long-lasting, not as insane and transitory. Investors have gradually learned about stocks and how they move over time. The prices that held in the past reflected an irrationally high aversion to risk as we measure it today, but in the past, our understanding of risk and its calculation was in its infancy.

Investors relied more on theory than practice. For example, in legal terms, bondholders have priority over stockholders when a firm dissolves and its assets are distributed. So bonds, the experts and their clients concluded, must be far less risky than stocks. But, in fact, very few firms listed on stock exchanges end their lives in bankruptcy or dissolution, so this little legalism is far less important than the actual performance of bonds and stocks over long periods of time—statistics that are now widely available.

As stock ownership expands, so does education—by mutual funds, banks, more consumer-friendly brokerage firms, journalists, and scholars. There is far better research today, and it is easily disseminated on the Internet. Seventy years ago, most investors did not understand that excessive trading undermines profits; that stock-price fluctuations tend to cancel themselves out over time, making stocks less risky than they would appear at first glance; and that it is extremely difficult to outperform the market averages. American investors have learned to buy and hold and to purchase shares when prices dip. They don't always act on this knowledge, but at least they have it in their grasp.

Over the past few decades, investors have entered the stock market the way a cautious child enters cold water. First, he puts in a toe and pulls back. Then a tentative foot submerges and is left there. Then the child wades in to his knees, to his waist. At last, he dives in. Americans are now diving into the stock market, having found that the water's fine. They feel the risks are not nearly so great as they feared, having survived a 508-point decline in the Dow in a single day in 1987, a 554-point decline in a single day in 1997, and a 1,800-point decline in just six weeks in 1998. They are using their resources and energy to learn about stocks and the best strategies for owning them. It makes good sense that such efforts would push the price of stocks toward the PRP.

As the information arrived, investors brought their prior beliefs up to date and became more willing to hold on to stocks. This willingness has still not advanced as far as it should, and prices will rise a good deal more.

To believe that the market is overvalued, you have to believe that the risk premium, once so irrationally large and getting rationally small, will move back to that irrationally large state again. It is our strong belief—and the linchpin of our theory—that the risk premium will continue to shrink, and for good reasons. The best reason is the one that has prevailed for the past two hundred years: Stocks are no more risky, in the aggregate and over the long term, than bonds.

Every time an analyst says that P/E ratios are too high today compared with historical experience, she is implicitly saying that the risk premium is too low today compared with historical experience. In other words, she expects investors to go back to the days when they were so irrationally risk-averse. Maybe they will, but we strongly doubt that such a profitable lesson, once learned, will quickly be unlearned.

WHY RISK HAS DROPPED

Besides better information and education, there are at least nine other arguments for a smaller risk premium, for a nice round total of ten:

1. The depression generation is dying out. The crash of 1929 and the Great Depression permanently scarred those who lived through it. In a 1995 study, the Federal Reserve asked participants in its Survey of

Consumer Finances to describe their willingness to take chances with investments. Almost 40 percent of Americans over age sixty-five said they were unwilling to take on *any* risk. Nearly all of them experienced the 1929 crash or its aftermath personally, and it's not surprising they would assign a large risk premium to stocks. But only about 20 percent of Americans between twenty-one and sixty-five say they are unwilling to take risks. Part of the difference is simply the conservatism of the old, but most, we believe, is the result of a specific event in history. As younger, less risk-averse investors move into the markets, they will change the way stocks are priced. Barring another catastrophe, this is a change that is here to stay.

2. American investors have become longer-term investors, in part because of the growth of 401(k) plans, retirement accounts that require employees to decide themselves how much and where they want to put their money. One feature of 401(k) plans and their predecessors, individual retirement accounts, is that investors generally can't touch these investments without incurring an onerous penalty, until age 59 1/2. In other words, the money is locked up. Another kind of locking-up, meanwhile, has been occurring with taxable accounts. As the risk premium falls and stock prices rise, Americans accumulate huge unrealized capital gains. If you bought $5,000 worth of Microsoft stock in 1993, its market value was $80,000 in 1999. To sell would mean paying Uncle Sam $15,000 in taxes—a good incentive to continue to take the long view.

3. U.S. businesses have restructured and are now better-run and better-prepared for tough times. The renovation of companies in the 1980s was, to a great degree, the work of takeover artists like Michael Milken and other investors who frightened corporate managements into becoming leaner, more profitable, and more shareholder-oriented. In addition, technology—especially the advent of the personal computer—has reduced corporate expenses and increased productivity. In other words, firms need fewer inputs (people and machines) to get the same outputs (goods and services).

4. The White House and Congress have generally adopted benign fiscal policies. Ronald Reagan brought the top tax rate down from 70 percent to 28 percent, and while it rose to 39.6 percent by the end of the century, it was still low enough to encourage more working and

saving. In addition, the rate on capital gains was cut from 28 percent to 20 percent in 1997. Meanwhile, the federal budget went from deficit to surplus, so the Treasury was no longer competing heatedly with private businesses for capital, a practice that pushes up interest rates and lowers profits. When the government runs a deficit, it needs to borrow in order to raise cash to cover its expenses. When its borrowing needs are heavy, as they were, for example, in the early 1990s, with deficits of $200 billion or more, the government has to raise interest rates to attract buyers. With a surplus, the government is actually retiring debt.

5. Monetary management has improved. For the past two decades, under Paul Volcker and Alan Greenspan, the Fed has learned to handle the supply of money in a way that avoids the kind of mistakes and shocks that previously led to recessions. The result is not just growth, but stability. The period from 1982 to 1999 marked the first time the United States went for seventeen years with only a shallow, brief recession. The consistency of interest rates, GDP growth, and inflation has been unprecedented. Of course, the business cycle has not been repealed, but it is safe to believe that the downward portions will be less severe and prolonged. It is no wonder investors are reducing the risk premium for stocks: The economy itself is less risky.

6. Capitalism has been spreading abroad, with the fall of the Berlin Wall, the advent of democracy throughout Latin America and most of Asia, and the strengthening of European economies following the Maastricht treaty. Meanwhile, free trade, which has been expanding since the end of World II, is helping U.S. companies in two ways: (*a*) removing barriers to reaching hundreds of millions of new customers for their goods and services and (*b*) providing cheaper raw materials and parts for manufacturing here at home. Of course, the spread of capitalism and free trade has also increased competition, but that too has been beneficial, forcing American firms to trim costs and become more productive. Just look at the auto industry. Over the past ten years, with fierce competition from Japan, Korea, and Europe, Ford Motor Co. has increased its dividends at an annual rate of 9.5 percent.

7. The world is less threatening. National security is vital to shareholders. After all, one atomic bomb can ruin your whole investment portfolio. It is hardly surprising, then, that during the forty-plus years

of the Cold War, the risk premium reflected the possibility of nuclear or conventional war with the Soviet Union. In fact, from 1917 through 1989, history was dominated by world war, depression, and strife between capitalism and Communism. Since the fall of the Soviet Union, the risk premium for the U.S. stock market has been cut in half, and the risk of widespread, devastating war has been reduced by at least as much.

8. People are richer. The enormous increase in the wealth and incomes of ordinary Americans makes them less worried about losing money—less risk averse. A hungry person can't afford to risk what little he has. A wealthy person can sleep soundly even if the market turns against him in the short run. Extensive research confirms what we know through common sense: The richer you are, the more financial risk you are willing to take. So, as wealth rises, the risk premium falls.

9. The fundamentals are less volatile. One of the most amazing changes in recent years has been the sharp, dramatic decline in the volatility of cash flows from corporations into their shareholders' pockets. From 1871 to 1945, the dividend growth rate averaged 5.1 percent, but the standard deviation of the growth rate was almost 7 percent. In other words, two-thirds of the time, the rate was swinging between minus-2 percent and plus-12 percent. That's risky. But since 1945, the standard deviation of dividend growth has dropped to 3 percent. Earnings volatility has dropped even more. In a world in which businesses can make more predictable profits, a steep risk premium is unnecessary.

THE PLAGUE LIFTS

The stock market has been laboring under a misapprehension. It is nonsense to say that P/Es are high and will revert to the mean if P/Es were irrationally low in the first place.

Suppose there are two types of Treasury securities—normal bonds and "plague" bonds. The latter, according to superstition, sometimes cause the bubonic plague in people who own them. Now, suppose that the superstition is incorrect but that you are the only person to know it. What happens?

Since most Americans are reluctant to buy plague bonds, the Treasury has to pay a significantly higher rate of interest to induce people to purchase them. But since you know that the bonds *don't* cause the plague, you are happy to buy them since you get higher interest payments without bearing any extra risk. In other words, you benefit from an exaggerated risk premium.

As people watch the performance of plague bonds over time, they too realize that the holders of these bonds don't get sick. So they become willing to buy the bonds at lower interest rates. Eventually, the rate on the plague bonds will descend until it is the same as on normal bonds.

Now, remember that as interest rates fall, prices rise. You may have bought a plague bond for $1,000 that pays $100 in interest a year—a yield of 10 percent. But over time, new plague bonds are being issued that pay just $50 in interest for every $1,000 invested, a yield of 5 percent. Your old plague bond, with the $100-a-year obligation from the government, becomes much more valuable. You could probably sell it for $2,000, which, with that $100 interest payment, would mean a yield of 5 percent, the same as normal bonds.

The plague-bond example shows what is happening now in the stock market. Dividend and earnings yields are dropping as the risk premium is exposed as superstition. Stock prices are rising, and they will continue to rise until the risk premium reaches zero—a process that could easily lead to the tripling or quadrupling of the market in a very short time. Hence, Dow 36,000 or even 40,000 or 50,000.

It is unlikely that the risk premium will go straight down. It could rebound if investors are suddenly frightened by short-term setbacks in the economy or by exogenous shocks like war. And it could stay stuck at about 2.5 percent. To a long-term investor, however, the future movements of the risk premium won't really matter that much.

Why? Well, suppose you purchased just enough plague bonds to finance your retirement, calculating that interest on the bonds would provide you with what you need to live comfortably. Say you bought $300,000 worth of plague bonds paying 10 percent interest (or $30,000 annually) until they mature, thirty years from now. Assume also that normal bonds pay 5 percent interest.

If everyone wakes up one day and realizes plague bonds don't cause plague, the price of the bonds will double and their yield will go down to 5 percent. You are rich, right?

Not really. Say you sell your plague bonds for $600,000. You will need that entire $600,000 to reinvest in new bonds at 5 percent in order to get $30,000 a year to live on. So you are back where you started as far as annual income is concerned.

This is a vital lesson for investors in stocks under the Dow 36,000 Theory. With eyes on the prize—the money flowing into your pockets—long-term investors should be completely indifferent to others wising up to the undervaluation of the market.

If you buy shares today, you are buying a stream of cash that has the same value to you—no matter what others decide to pay for stocks later. That stream of cash is extremely generous. Only if you want to cash out, do you care what the market is paying for stocks. If you are in for the long haul, and if dividends—and the flow of cash in general—continue to rise at historic rates, then you can ignore prices and enjoy a delicious retirement, or do whatever you want with your hoard.

But if you wait too long, stocks will rise in price and returns will drop. The benefits of the ascent to Dow 36,000 will pass you by.

CHAPTER 7

The Jungle Stocks Live In

*Observing that the market was frequently efficient, they went on
to conclude incorrectly that the market was always efficient. The
difference between the propositions is night and day.*
    —Warren Buffett, letter to the shareholders of Berkshire
                                        Hathaway, Inc., 1988

IN THE SPRING of 1998, after we first aired our views about the undervalued stock market in *The Wall Street Journal,* a reporter from *Fortune* magazine called.

"You are so sure that stocks are cheap," she said. "I want to know
how sure. Do you have all of your money invested in stocks?"

Neither of us did. We still don't. Despite our strong opinions, we
think that putting every last dime in the stock market is reckless. We
each have about 80 percent in stocks and 20 percent in bonds and cash.
We'll talk more about such distributions—called asset allocation—in
Chapter 14.

But one reason we don't put all our money in the market—and
haven't mortgaged our houses to the hilt to buy stocks—is that no theory is 100 percent foolproof.

The list of things that could go wrong is long. If bond rates soar to
10 percent, if earnings growth slows to 1 percent, or if government and
monetary authorities unlearn the lessons of the past two decades, then
stocks will more likely creep up slowly—or even fall—than rise.

But there is a more important and far more subtle reason for our
lack of fanaticism. Up until now we have explained in great detail what
a stock is and how it should be valued. We have not, however, discussed the market in which stocks are traded. This is a serious omis-

sion, a little like studying everything about a wild animal except its habitat. The market is the jungle that stocks live in. To know why we don't have all our money in stocks—and why you shouldn't either—requires a better understanding of that environment: an ecology of the market.

A LITTLE RESPECT

One of the misconceptions about investing is that money "flows into" and "flows out of" the stock market. Nothing of the sort can happen. For every buyer, there is a seller. When you call your broker to purchase 100 shares of a company's stock, you are relying on the fact that at the current price someone, somewhere, has convinced herself that the same company's stock is worth unloading. In other words, the transaction works only if there is someone who believes you are dead wrong! That person sells her stock to you.

When the trade occurs, you write a $1,000 check from your bank account and give it to your broker, who uses a trader on the floor of the New York Stock Exchange to match you up with the seller. The broker then gives the stock to you and the cash to the seller. The flow of money into the market is precisely zero. The $1,000 simply moved from one checking account (the buyer's) to another checking account (the seller's).

Of course, this does not mean that the market value (which is the same thing as saying the price) of stocks always stays the same.

Suppose that you decide to buy a share of IBM stock for $100 and another investor wants to buy the share as well. A seller would pit the two of you against each other in a mini-auction. In the end, suppose you prevail, but at a price of $101. At that point you give your broker $101, which she gives to the seller, while handing you an IBM stock certificate. This is precisely the process that plays out every working day on the floors of stock exchanges. But, again, the money moves from your bank account to the seller's. There is no net flow of cash into the market.

So the swings in the prices of stocks depend on demand and supply. If an investor really wants to buy 1,000 shares of Cisco Systems at $150, but just 100 shares are being offered at that price, then he'll have to raise his bid to $151 to attract more supply—another 900 shares. In other words, the market is driven, not so much by inflows and outflows of cash as by opinions of what shares are worth.

But what drives those opinions? Information.

Everyone is trying to get an edge on everyone else by gathering as much information as possible and acting on it. Each day, news hits the market, and players have to decide how it affects the stocks they own—or want to buy.

A terrorist bombing in the Middle East? Perhaps it will boost the earnings of oil companies.

Unusually good weather for corn in the Midwest? Breakfast cereals could be cheaper to make, a boon to Kellogg's.

Hints that the Fed will reduce short-term interest rates? Auto companies that depend on consumer loans could benefit.

Notice such events before everyone else catches on, and you can make short-term profits. It is the lust for an edge that creates the drive for information, which in turn determines the prices in the market. Since millions of investors are trying to get an advantage, information travels fast—so fast that some say the stock market is the most powerful and efficient computing device in the world. At any instant in time, the price of a stock reflects the balance of all opinion about a company. (Insiders, such as a company's top managers or lawyers, may have additional information, but the law prevents them from capitalizing on it.)

It's true that not everyone knows every bit of information about a company. And it's also true that some investors act from purely personal motives; they may have to sell quickly, for instance, to raise cash in an emergency. Still, when you buy, you should recognize that the person selling to you is probably acting in a reasonable way. He may even have noticed something you didn't and decided to bail out before the stock tumbles. A healthy regard for the opinions of others is an important attribute of a prudent investor.

We divide investors into two types: outsmarters, who think they are more clever than the sum of wisdom in the market, and partakers, who want merely to participate in the profits that companies make. Yes, some outsmarters succeed in beating the market, but very few. They usually get outsmarted themselves. Partakers are almost always winners.

In other words, respect the market. Millions of people around the world—some brilliant, some not—are trying to figure out what each company is worth. Their collective judgment is what determines prices. Is your own judgment really so much better?

THE RANDOM WALK

Now, how does this giant computing mechanism that determines stock prices work?

Suppose that one morning, a genie popped out of your sugar bowl and told you that, without a doubt, the price of Microsoft was going to double tomorrow. You would run out and buy Microsoft like mad and cash in the next day.

Now, suppose the genie appeared over Manhattan with the same news—the way that a vision of Woody Allen's mother appeared in the movie *New York Stories.* Thousands of investors would rush to call their brokers, and the price of Microsoft would double immediately—not tomorrow but today—in anticipation of what would happen. All but the very fastest investors would reap little or nothing in the way of profit from the genie's advice.

In the real world, information doesn't travel quite so fast. But if the genie told you alone about Microsoft, you might tell some of your friends, and the sight of all of you buying like crazy would alert traders to the fact that something funny was going on. Other traders might dig hard enough to find out the facts underlying the genie's prediction.

For that reason, it is rare that a small investor can cash in on a hot tip about a stock. By the time you learn the news—that a new product is coming or that a competitor is leaving the field—you can be sure that lots of other people already have heard it and have acted on it. For that reason, we never buy stocks simply on tips from other people. Never. The information has almost certainly been "discounted"—or already reflected in the price of the stock.

If markets fully incorporate all available information rationally into stock prices, then the best forecast for tomorrow's price is today's. In other words, we may know everything we can possibly know up to this minute about a stock, but we can't know what will move its price tomorrow. Since the change in the price between today and tomorrow is completely unknowable, it will seem random, or irrational, from the vantage point of today.

Thus, prices move from day to day according to a "random walk"—a view that has spread among ordinary investors thanks to an influential book, published in 1973, called *A Random Walk down Wall Street*, by Princeton professor Burton Malkiel. He wrote:

> A random walk is one in which future steps or directions cannot be predicted on the basis of past actions. When the term is applied to the stock market, it means that short-run changes cannot be predicted. . . . It means that a blindfolded monkey throwing darts at a newspaper's financial pages could select a portfolio that would do just as well as one carefully selected by the experts.

The random walk theory has been exposed to hundreds of scientific tests. *The Wall Street Journal*, for instance, regularly shows that a selection of stocks picked by humans (not monkeys) tossing darts does about as well as those chosen by analysts.

In the short run, the hypothesis that Malkiel made popular is certainly correct. No one can tell, based on today's price for IBM, what tomorrow's price for IBM will be. In the short run, the random walk is the overwhelming force influencing stock prices. As a result, quick-and-easy money is not available to those hoping to dart in and out of the market, as many online day traders have learned to their chagrin. Since no one can tell what will happen tomorrow, betting on whether prices will rise or fall is roughly an even-money proposition, and in the end, the transaction costs will eat you up—the way that the house advantage does in a casino.

BUT CAN YOU BEAT THE MARKET?

The random walk can also be called a "no-arbitrage" condition. Arbitrage is the practice of trying to capitalize on tiny price discrepancies—buying a U.S. stock, for instance, on the Tokyo exchange because it might be a half-dollar cheaper and then immediately selling it on the New York exchange.

But with the random walk, no one can make money for very long off a new system or a new revelation that tries to exploit glitches. As soon as investors find that a strategy produces extraordinary returns, the market incorporates that information into the price of stocks, boosting their prices. This property of markets is poorly understood, and it is as paradoxical as the most abstruse quantum physics: As soon as everyone accepts that some strategy works, the strategy no longer works!

A good example is the Dogs of the Dow system, first propounded by Michael O'Higgins, who in 1978 set up a money-management firm to help clients profit from it. The system calls for investing equal amounts in the ten stocks with the highest dividend yields among the thirty stocks in the Dow Jones industrial average, then selling those ten and repeating the process at the start of each year with the new ten top yielders.

When James O'Shaughnessy, a Connecticut money manager and quantitative analyst, tested the system against actual results from 1952 to 1996, he found it outperformed the S&P 500 by an average of 3.5 percentage points a year—an extraordinary achievement. After the system received wide coverage in the press in the early 1990s, investors responded with enthusiasm. Brokerage firms set up unit trusts—similar to mutual funds, but with fixed portfolios rather than continually changing ones—to put the strategy into action, and by early 1998, they had $14 billion in assets.

The problem was that suddenly the system stopped working—just like most systems that try to outsmart the market. Why? Because the market learns.

The system worked in the past because stocks with high dividend yields are likely to be undervalued compared with other stocks. The yield is a percentage derived by dividing a stock's annual dividend payout by its price. The yield can be high for two reasons—a high dividend payout or a low price. So, often, the highest Dow yielders are those with prices that are inordinately low—which is why they are called Dogs.

But the popularity of the Dogs system highlighted the potential of these undervalued stocks, so investors bought them up, and they were no longer undervalued.

Here's how the market defeats clever schemes to outperform the averages. Assume you know that two or three new stocks will join the Dogs of the Dow in early January. That information is easily available since it reflects published dividend yields. What should you do? Buy the stocks in December before they are bid up by eager Dogs buyers in January. Similarly, you can dump stocks in December that will exit the list. If enough investors take these steps in December—or perhaps even earlier—they can practically guarantee that the new owners in January will get stocks at bad (that is, too high) prices.

The Dogs of the Dow story used to work as a value-stock play, but it flopped in 1996, 1997, and 1998. Why? Because enough people began to believe it to spoil the arbitrage, as O'Higgins admitted in an interview with us—shortly after the publication of his new book, based on *another* system: *Beating the Dow with Bonds.*

This does not mean, however, that the Dogs strategy is particularly bad; indeed, we are fond of it, but as a *discipline* rather than as a system that makes big profits. Market efficiency, which is at the root of the random walk theory, requires that, over a long period, no known strategy can make profits that exceed those you could make by buying the market as a whole. Aside from strategies that devour your money with transaction costs, the flip side of this idea is that almost any random selection of stocks should perform about as well as the market. If the Dogs strategy induces people to buy stocks and stay in them, then it serves a very useful function. Market efficiency requires that if you buy and hold a diversified portfolio of stocks, you won't lose out.

Wayne Nelson, a Merrill Lynch & Co. senior vice president in Washington, told us that selling his clients a unit trust based on the Dogs of the Dow was the only way to induce some of them to buy good companies whose stock was depressed. At the time—in 1997—he cited AT&T Corp., which had fallen in a year from $45 to $32. "They wouldn't buy AT&T alone," he said, "but as part of a Dogs of the Dow package, they would." AT&T was paying a 3 percent dividend, which qualified it as one of the Dogs. Over the next year, the stock doubled.

But AT&T was an anomaly. The Dogs were dragging in the late 1990s. Of course, if you *knew* that the Dogs strategy would underperform the market, you might be able to profit from that approach as well by shorting the ten stocks. When you sell a stock short, you borrow the stock from someone else, pay interest on the loan, and eventually return the stock.

Say you want to short Coca-Cola because you think its price will fall. You go to any broker, who arranges for you to borrow it. Then you sell it right away into the market, collecting $60 in cash. Assume the price falls—as you hoped. You buy a share in the market at $50 and then return that share to repay your debt. Total profit for you: $10, minus borrowing and transaction costs.

You could take advantage of the Dogs' lackluster performance by shorting them today, waiting for their prices to drop, buying them back, and returning them to the lender at a healthy profit. But if other investors caught on to this strategy, they too would short the Dogs, driving down their prices before your short could occur. So, once again, the short trade would no longer be profitable.

The lesson here is that trying to score short-term profits in stocks by outsmarting other investors is a fool's errand. The market is too efficient. It is like a giant river. A strong swimmer may overpower the current for a short time, but ultimately, every swimmer tires and goes the same speed and direction as the river.

IN THE SHORT RUN ONLY

While the random walk theory works, it is useful only over shorter periods. Over longer periods, the volatility of stocks decreases sharply—far more than would be predicted under the random walk. If stock prices were truly the result of a random walk, then we would expect that there would be some disastrous lengthy stretches in market history, but there haven't been any. Never, according to Jeremy Siegel's research, which goes back to 1802, has a basket of large-cap stocks (the S&P 500 or a similar index) failed to make a profit, after inflation, in any seventeen-year stretch (that is, 1802–1818, 1803–1819, etc.).

In other words, something *besides* today's price has helped predict tomorrow's—perhaps a reversion to the mean caused by an attraction that keeps the prices from wandering too far away from something fundamental, such as the cash flows of corporations. Certainly, for stocks to be less volatile over long time frames than over short, it must be the case that stocks have tended to go up more than average in periods following higher-than-average declines—and to go up less than average in periods following higher-than-average advances. That is precisely what has happened throughout most of the past.

Still, even if you believe that stock prices return toward the averages, you can't tell for sure *when* that reversal will happen. Thus, it is doubtful that an arbitrage opportunity exists. Borrow a lot to buy stocks after a big decline, and you may find yourself wiped out after further declines.

For practical purposes, then, it is useful to assume that stock prices do move in a random walk—but that they can be affected, in the long term, by powerful forces that are not random at all.

Our explanation for the dramatic increase in stock prices since the early 1980s is the gradual decline in the equity risk premium. That's a powerful force. But could the decline have been predicted? If so, then investors would have bought stocks immediately, bringing their prices to appropriate levels, from which they would not have surged further. In other words, a predictable decline in the risk premium would demonstrate that the market has been seriously "inefficient"—that it makes big mistakes from which observant investors could prosper.

But we don't think the market's essential nature is inefficiency. Yes, the risk premium was falling, but at no point could someone have known that a further decline would occur. While the overall decline makes sense in retrospect, it was never a certainty while it was happening.

That is an important lesson. We have been arguing that a further decline in the equity premium will lead to a huge increase in stock prices. But we admit that we cannot know for sure. Such uncertainty is healthy. Its opposite, a kind of know-it-all hubris, is what leads to disaster, not just in personal life, but in the stock market.

NOBODY OUTSMARTS THE MARKET

Irving Fisher, who is widely regarded as one of the brightest and most influential economists of the twentieth century, also made one of the worst predictions. After studying stock valuation in the 1920s, Fisher, a professor of economics at Yale, became convinced that equities were a great buy. On October 14, 1929, he gave a widely reported speech in which he claimed, "Stocks have reached a permanently high plateau." Two weeks later came the worst crash in history, which eventually destroyed three-quarters of the value of the market.

In fact, Fisher was right about everything but timing. As we showed in Chapter 2, if you had bought $10,000 worth of stocks at the beginning of October 1929, on the brink of the crash, the investment would have been worth $8.4 million at the end of 1998. Still, Fisher's statement has gone down with other terrible predictions—the Titanic is unsinkable, the Maginot Line invincible.

A steadfast believer in stocks, Fisher accumulated more than $10 million in assets by 1928—the equivalent of about $100 million in today's dollars. He invested heavily in small- and medium-sized companies. Even after trouble began, he continued to reinvest through the first dips in the market, when other economists were predicting sharp declines. He kept on buying after Black Thursday and Black Tuesday.

As the market continued to fall, Fisher's personal finances worsened. To pay his bills and meet his margin calls, he borrowed from Caroline Hazard, his wife's sister, who had received a substantial inheritance. His debt to her exceeded $1 million. By 1935, Fisher was forced to sell his house to Yale, with the agreement that he could rent it for life. Although he lived modestly, the huge losses made it apparent that he could not even pay the rent. With a few pieces of furniture, he and his wife moved to a small apartment, also owned by Yale.

After Fisher's wife died, his sister-in-law reduced the interest on her loan to one percent, but he still could not meet the payments. When Fisher himself died in 1947, his total assets had shrunk to less than $60,000, a decline of more than 90 percent. While the events of the past seventy years have vindicated the professor, he might have been saved if he possessed a healthy respect for the intelligence of the market. He was so sure that he was correct, and that the market was wrong, that he bet everything—and lost.

Now, fast-forward the tape several generations. In December 1996, Robert Shiller, also a professor of economics at Yale University, is giving a talk to governors and staff members of the Federal Reserve Board in Washington. Shiller—a charming man, a bright light in modern financial economics, and a candidate to win the Nobel Prize—is giving a terrifying talk, summarizing work that he and his associate, John Campbell of Harvard, had just completed. They had looked at the long history of the stock market and found that whenever dividend yields had dropped as low as they had in 1996 (to below 2.5 percent), a big correction was in order. How big? Shiller and Campbell warned in a manuscript they later circulated that the market might lose as much as two-thirds of its value.

Shortly after Shiller's talk, Alan Greenspan, the Fed chairman, gave his speech at the annual American Enterprise Institute dinner, warning of "irrational exuberance" in the stock market.

Shiller and Campbell concluded their presentation with this admonition: "There may be special circumstances now that will change the historical relations between the valuation ratios and subsequent stock market performance. But there have always been special circumstances, circumstances that are adduced every time the ratios have been extreme, and that have in the past allowed people to fail to heed the message of the ratios."

In other words, the two economists argued that traditional valuation measures rule. When investors forget the "ceilings" that P/E ratios and dividend yields impose, they will suffer.

Shiller and Campbell have something in common with Fisher. They both talked—and in the case of Fisher, at least, acted—as though they were smarter than the market. Investors listening to Fisher, impressed by his credentials and convinced by his logic, might have run out and put all of their money in stocks. Over the long run, that was a good idea, but in the short run, the losses were astonishing. Investors who listened to Shiller and Campbell, equally impressive, might have run out and *sold* their stock holdings—or worse, shorted the market. That was a terrible idea. Investors lost almost as much money, in terms of what they missed in the market's rise, as Fisher's followers did. Between Greenspan's talk and July 2, 1999, the S&P 500 returned 96 percent. By selling at the time, an investor with a $100,000 portfolio would have missed an $88,000 appreciation in her holdings from stocks while earning about $12,000 from short-term Treasury bonds.

The lesson is simple: No one knows for sure what the market will do tomorrow or the next day. Any prudent strategy for investing needs to account for the random walk—and to respect the market.

COMPUTER FAILURE

But if people can't outsmart the market, what about computers?

When the partners of Long-Term Capital Management, L.P., set up shop in suburban Connecticut as a high-powered hedge fund in 1994, they said they would use sophisticated computer models to exploit little anomalies in bond markets and make lots of money. How could anyone doubt them? The partners included John Meriwether, who had been a legendary bond trader at Salomon Brothers; Robert Merton and Myron Scholes, both Nobel Prize winners; and David Mullins, a former Fed vice chairman.

The partners recruited Ph.D.s in mathematics, physics, and finance to concoct complicated computer models to predict the movements of security prices and interest rates. Their precise niche was an arbitrage strategy called "convergence trading"—finding thin spreads between the prices of different types of bonds, then speculating that those spreads would narrow or disappear over time.

For example, suppose a ten-year Treasury bond was yielding 6 percent interest when a certain kind of sliced-and-diced mortgage security was yielding 9 percent. That spread, the firm's computers might conclude, was too large. The proper, historical relationship might have been a difference of just two percentage points, not three. So the firm would speculate that rates on the T-bond would rise and rates on the mortgage security would fall.

What matters is not whether market conditions pushed all rates up or down, but whether the relationship between the two securities returned to normal. Such a strategy, Meriwether believed, would reduce risk, and, he told *Business Week,* "Risk management is the key to success."

But exploiting glitches required huge bets on very small price or rate movements—which, in turn, required heavy leverage, or borrowing. At one point, the firm's positions exceeded $100 billion, or as much as 50 times its capital. The rest of the money represented loans, with the interest meter running. So, even if Long-Term's computers were right, the relationships had to return to normal quickly, or borrowing costs would lead to bankruptcy.

But the partners thought they had cracked the code. By the summer of 1998, their self-confidence had already become legendary. They turned down the proffered capital of some investors who wanted to renew their positions, so that the partners themselves could take their shares. They wouldn't reveal their investments to their clients. Their attitude was, "We are so smart you should trust us."

At the start, the strategies worked, and the firm nearly tripled the money of investors between 1994 and 1997. But soon, the partners were investing heavily on margin, vastly increasing their risk. Imagine, for example, buying $100 worth of stock by putting up only $2 and borrowing $98. If the stock rises to just $102, you will make a 100 percent profit on your original investment (minus borrowing costs), but if the stock falls slightly, to $98, your original investment is wiped out.

By the fall of 1998, the scheme collapsed. Events that their models said were practically impossible began unfolding, as investors, spooked by the currency collapse in Asia, stampeded into the safest securities. Instead of disappearing by reverting to the mean, the gap between T-bonds and more risky bonds actually widened.

A hasty bailout was arranged in September 1998 at a meeting called at the New York Federal Reserve. The nation's leading banks and brokerage firms attempted to unwind the Long-Term Capital positions in a manner that would minimize harm to the many big institutions (i.e., themselves) that had loaned the firm money.

But the firm's failure hasn't stopped techno wizards from trying to crack the stock market code—if there is one. They use computers to create a model, or mini-universe, using variables such as short-term bond rates and growth in GDP. The model is supposed to predict the future behavior of individuals, stocks, or sectors.

As computers have grown faster and more powerful, you would think that they could supplant the brains of humble humans, especially in a game such as investing, where data are copious and the interplay of different factors—say, interest rates and stock prices—can be backtested against history. The fact, however, is that the market has continually outsmarted the most sophisticated modelers.

Money managers, like those at Long-Term Capital, who rely upon computer models are called "quants," short for "quantitative analysts." Public mutual funds using this approach have a distinctively unimpressive record. Fidelity Stock Selector, for example, the largest of the quant funds, scored an average annual return for the three years ending in June 1999 that was more than one-fourth below the performance of the S&P 500.

Does that mean computers are useless? Not at all. A standard personal computer is excellent at "screening." It can, for instance, in a universe of ten thousand stocks, find only those with, say, a market capitalization of at least $500 million and a P/E ratio of less than 15 that have increased their dividends for the past five years. Such screening is a simple exercise for a computer, but it would take even a smart person weeks or months.

But using a computer to predict short-term price swings is folly. The market is too complex and too efficient. Today's price reflects all known information, and tomorrow's will reflect information no one can yet know. How do you beat a system like that? It is not easy, and if it can be done, it will require a new paradigm—a new vantage point for understanding—rather than a faster computer.

WHEN THE BULL AND BEAR ARE DEAD

Now, we can return to the question from the *Fortune* reporter. Are we so sure that the market is cheap that we are betting everything on a big advance? In other words, are we saying that the market is incorrectly pricing stocks and that the random walk hypothesis is wrong?

Not at all. In fact, our entire premise rests, in the end, on a rational market. There are two ways of viewing this connection.

Pessimists might say that a corollary of the random walk theory is that, at any point in time, the arguments for stocks going up should be about as good as the arguments for the market going down. The Dow 36,000 Theory is, then, at the very least, a counterweight to the continual negative speculation of the financial establishment. Under this view, the PRP provides a logical upper boundary for the value of stocks, and the distance between today's price and the PRP defines a zone within which investors should be comfortable that there is no stock market bubble.

But optimists (like us) would go further. We believe the work of many students of the market over the past century—and especially the past twenty years—has added successive pieces to a puzzle, and now a view of the solution is finally in sight. As this new picture of valuation becomes universally accepted, prices must rise, just as the price of Microsoft would rise almost immediately if that genie appeared over New York.

But unlike a stock tip, this new information really has not become fully discounted, or incorporated, into the prices of stocks. There are still too many doubters. Investors who act now, before the news has spread far and wide, should score significant gains. Afterwards, however, stocks will no longer provide the kind of amazing returns they once did. At that point, the random walk hypothesis will look good in both the short run and the long run.

If you accept the arguments in this book, then the PRP for stocks will be reached when the Dow hits 36,000. But when that happens, does it mean you should dump your stocks?

No, but it means that stocks will merely become as good a buy as bonds. Long-term investors will no longer care much whether they own one asset or the other. Most firms will probably continue to retain most of their earnings, and barring massive positive surprises about profitability, the market will return about 5 percent or 6 percent annually. There could be dislocations from exogenous events, but the bull and bear will both be dead.

So why keep stocks at all? Three reasons: First, for most investors, stocks will continue to provide a significant tax advantage because capital gains are taxed only when you realize them, while interest from bonds is taxed every year. Second, as we approach the heights described in this book, it will be important to remember that the assumptions that produced the prediction were *cautious*. The U.S. economy grew, for example, at a real rate of 4 percent for the three years ending in March 1999, compared with our own projection of just 2.5 percent growth for corporate profits. A few more years of growth in the 3 percent to 4 percent range may well make higher growth assumptions seem sensible. Our hunch is, that will be the case. Dow 36,000 could be too modest. Third, while the stock market as a whole will level off, some stocks will continue to perform much better than others, and smart investors may be able to identify them.

PICK UP THE TEN SPOT

While the random walk determines short-term price movements, something else—a kind of North Pole magnetism—is affecting prices in the long term, reducing risk and pulling values upward. One likely force is the consistency of earnings and dividends of American firms.

But what if the force is the risk premium itself?

Suppose that investors have observed the tendency of the market to revert to the mean. Suppose they believe that the market is due for a correction whenever there has been a big increase in prices. At that point, investors would demand a large risk premium in order to hold stocks. This makes some sense: fearing an imminent correction, they would not want to buy stocks unless they were given a special incentive. Their demand for more risk insurance would, of course, drive down prices.

Now, suppose that stocks are depressed for a while. In this case, the same investors might well believe that stocks were due for an *increase*— a reversion to the mean in the other direction. This anticipation drives down the risk premium, and it drives stock prices back up.

If investors have acted this way in the past—and there is evidence that they have—then the risk premium itself has provided an important "governor" on the volatility of stock prices. Over time, prices cannot become too extreme in either direction.

Now, suppose that students of financial markets conclude that stocks are clearly no more risky than bonds—but stocks pay a huge risk premium anyway.

Investors, convinced by the overwhelming data and by arguments such as those made in this book, rush to purchase stocks, driving the risk premium to zero and the Dow to 36,000.

Now, suddenly, there is no risk premium—and, thus, no governor. It may be that stock prices become riskier when the risk premium is no longer present—expanding and contracting to meet the fears and hopes of investors. So the worst enemy of the zero risk premium may well be the presence of a zero risk premium!

The world of Dow 36,000 could be a stable place, with a diversified basket of stocks throwing off decent, but unspectacular, returns, varying a little, year by year, almost like short-term bonds. But it could also become an unpleasant environment of fierce storms followed quickly by sunshine and then by storms again. If the latter happens, expect the risk premium to go back up.

We can't be sure what this new world will look like—whether it will be a jungle or a placid meadowland. But we do believe that there are spectacular profits to be made on the road to the destination. The odds strongly favor keeping your money in the stock market for the long haul.

Remember that there are two kinds of risk. A coin flip is risky, but in a way we can understand and measure. The weather is risky too—

mainly because we lack sufficient knowledge of a complex process that is, deep down, deterministic but (at this point in history) not fully understood.

The study of financial data has led us to understand some of the basic properties of stocks. But this insight is useful only if the data have, like a coin flip, been generated by some mechanism that does not change over time. Unfortunately, we don't know enough about the mechanism to predict stock prices—and probably never will. Always, the forces that comprise the mechanism that moves stock prices— profit growth, the equity risk premium, inflation, and interest rates— will be sources of uncertainty even as the ability to measure and calculate has honed our knowledge of stock-price volatility to near perfection.

We are left with a paradox. On the one hand, we see investors becoming more rational and bidding up stock prices to the PRP. But on the other hand, we see the market as efficient; in that case, why hasn't the PRP been achieved already?

In his book, Malkiel tackled a similar paradox.

There is a well-known academic story about the random walk of a finance professor and two of his students. The finance professor, a proponent of the strong form of the random walk theory, was convinced that markets were always perfectly efficient. When he and the students spotted a ten-dollar bill lying on the street, he told them to ignore it.

"If it was really a ten-dollar bill," he reasoned out loud, "someone would have already picked it up."

In other words, in a perfect market, opportunities for arbitrage—for picking up ten-dollar bills—simply don't exist. The same could be said for our prediction that the Dow will go to 36,000.

But completing the anecdote, Malkiel, the great advocate of the random walk hypothesis, suggested a better response for the professor to make. "You had better pick that ten-dollar bill up quickly," he should tell the students, "because if it is really there, someone else will surely take it."

For that same reason, you should seize the opportunity now to profit from the rise of the Dow to 36,000. Pick up the ten-spot before someone else gets it.

CHAPTER 8

Today, When Stocks
Were Still Cheap

Don't pay any attention to the critics—don't even ignore them!
—Samuel Goldwyn (1882–1974)

AFTER A DECADE in which stocks rose very far very fast, most people have a hard time believing that shares are still undervalued. When we began to give our ideas an airing in early 1998, the reaction was incredulity and even anger. That wasn't surprising. We didn't expect the Dow 36,000 Theory to be immediately embraced, and some of the arguments we heard in opposition were good ones.

In this chapter, we raise these tough questions and answer them. Then, before summarizing the first part of the book, we tell you what bothers *us*—what could go wrong on the road to Dow 36,000. But, first, the five toughest criticisms.

Question: Your theory rests on the notion that people are long-term investors. You say that, in the long term, stocks aren't as risky as bonds. OK, but, in the short term, stocks are *very* risky, and there are lots of short-term investors out there. So what about them?

Answer: The Dow 36,000 Theory depends on the risk premium for stocks disappearing. People demand that premium because they believe stocks are more risky than bonds. Stocks aren't so risky in the long term, but they are in the short. In other words, we assumed that the person with the long time horizon would determine the price of the stock.

But there are millions of investors in the market, and each one of them has a story. Some expect to live another fifty years and to hold their stocks until retirement or pass them on to their children. Some are day traders who expect to sell most of their holdings in a few hours.

The short-term investors look at the market and see wildly volatile prices. (On April 6, 1999, Gillette, a very solid company, lost 13 percent of its value in a single day.) They need to be compensated for the real chances they are running, so they naturally want a bonus in order to risk their money. They don't care that the risk diminishes over five or ten or twenty years. They can't wait that long.

The PRP, or perfectly reasonable price, is what a person with a long time horizon should be willing to pay—the price without the risk premium. In other words, a much higher price. So why do we believe that the market will rise to the PRP rather than stay at lower levels required by buyers with short horizons?

The market, remember, is an auction. A seller looks out over the sea of possible buyers and picks the one who is willing to pay the highest price—certainly not the lowest. If Sotheby's is selling a Van Gogh, the painting goes to the person who bids $20 million, not the person who bids $10 million. In other words, the winner is the bidder who places the *highest* value on what's for sale.

Back to stocks: Say a seller of one hundred shares of Cisco faces two potential buyers. The first wants to hold the stock for no more than a year and then sell it. He looks at the high annual volatility of Cisco and gets nervous—and demands a healthy risk premium. In effect, he is saying, "I won't buy this stock from you unless the price is low enough to compensate me for that chance that, a year from now, it will be 50 percent lower." (And it certainly could be. In 1998, Cisco dropped from $103 to $44 in just six weeks.) "So I'll bid $100."

The second buyer takes the long view, recognizes that the stock is not very risky over time—and demands no risk premium. She is saying, "I am holding this stock for at least twenty years, and I know that never in the history of the market have stocks lost money, even to inflation, over such a long period. In fact, the chances are excellent that I will get an eight-fold return on my investment with no more risk than if I bought a bond. So I'll bid $120." The stock is worth more to her since it doesn't make her nervous.

The seller, obviously, will take the *higher* bid.

As time passes, we believe that stocks will increasingly flow into the hands of people who take the long view since, increasingly, they will be the high bidders. When the new equilibrium is reached, at about Dow 36,000, short-horizon investors will be priced out of the market for stocks (just as people who don't appreciate the lasting quality of Van Gogh are priced out of the market for his paintings). Instead, the short-termers will probably have all of their holdings in debt securities—bonds, CDs, money-market funds—since the risk premium, which produced the low prices that attracted them to stocks, has disappeared.

Question: You say your Dow 36,000 Theory assumptions are "modest"—that earnings and dividends, for example, will rise at a rate of 5 percent annually, or about 2 percent after inflation. But how modest is that? Why should earnings rise at all, given the vicious competition and price-cutting that mark the world economy?

Answer: This is a question we hear from economists. In the simplest textbook examples of companies—the foundations of introductory economics courses—firms don't earn any profits from their operations beyond the interest rate that they pay on investments.

Remember the vending machines? One firm buys a machine and starts making lots of money. So another firm buys a machine and cuts into the profits of the first firm. Machines proliferate until each firm is just able to stay in business, paying the borrowing expenses for the machines it buys but not earning anything more.

Mimicry is as American as apple pie. Just check out the differences between the Amazon and Barnes & Noble websites, or the differences between the food at McDonald's and Burger King. Mimicking continues, at least in theory, until every firm is just scraping by.

From such a vantage point, what should be the growth rate of the cash generated by a company? In real terms, zero. In nominal terms, the inflation rate. In other words, the vending company can raise its prices only if the general level of prices goes up (that's the definition of inflation). But if that happens, the owners of the vending company won't be able to buy anything more with their inflationary gains—since everything else costs more too.

This view of the world, which claims that firms can earn no excess profits in the long run, is often called the "classical model." If it prevails, then Dow 36,000 is a pipe dream. With 3 percent growth (or zero real growth) in earnings, stock prices should come crashing down.

In theory, the classical model seems to make sense, but in practice it is dead wrong. Earnings have grown at 7.3 percent annually for the past fifty years. The assumptions that generate Dow 36,000 are actually well below the historical averages.

The world, quite simply, is a more complicated place than the one depicted in a simple economists' model. How many firms do you know that earn no profits beyond inflation? How many firms do you know that operate in a market that is open to all comers?

Look at the soft-drink business. In 1998, Coke earned returns of 42 percent on its stockholders' equity (their investment in the company); PepsiCo earned 31 percent. In theory, other soft-drink makers should be entering the field and should be content with returns of, say, 20 percent, undercutting Coke and Pepsi on price and driving down the profits of the entire industry. In practice, that hasn't happened.

The classical model fails to describe our world because products are more than simple commodities. Most are differentiated; they have something special. Coke and Pepsi are both soft drinks, but they aren't the *same* soft drink.

When you buy a car, for instance, you are purchasing more than a means of transportation. Among other things, you are buying a reputation and an image. Some companies, like Volvo, emphasize safety. Others, like Jaguar, put expensive wood and fine fittings inside, attracting drivers who want to be seen in a luxurious automobile (and who enjoy the feel of buttery leather seats). With advertising and public relations, companies manipulate their reputations continually over decades. Once a firm has established such an image, it can milk the image for profits because it will have few, if any, *direct* competitors. Only Jaguar makes a Jaguar.

In 1999, the top three public-stock holdings of Warren Buffett's company, Berkshire Hathaway, Inc., were Coke, Gillette, and American Express. Each has a solid identity that precludes direct competition—a franchise. Also, each is in a business with high barriers to entry. Gillette spent six years and nearly $1 billion developing its Mach3 shaver. The company controls 70 percent of the U.S. razor market, and it has a broad distribution system, established over more than a century, to get its products into every drugstore and grocery. How can a start-up, or even an established company, compete? Of course, Gillette cannot charge whatever it wants. People will shift to inferior razors if prices go too high—or to electric razors, or even beards. But simply undercutting Gillette on price is not enough because a Gillette razor, as opposed to a generic disposable, is not a mere commodity.

Find a successful firm, and you will find a similar story. Microsoft makes the operating system that runs the world's personal computers—and, more and more, its business computers as well. In 1998, Microsoft's profit margin (its after-tax earnings divided by its revenues) was more than 30 percent. Under the classical model, that would be impossible.

In the end, however, the answer to theory is reality. History is not a perfect guide to the future, but it is a powerful argument. Over the past fifty years, after accounting for inflation, earnings have risen 3.3 percent; over the past twenty years, 2.9 percent. Zero is nowhere in sight.

Question: You are double-counting earnings. You say that your theory is based on the cash that flows into shareholders' pockets. Fine. But companies need their earnings to keep growing—and that growth is a requirement for Dow 36,000. How can you have it both ways?

Answer: We don't double-count. Since we began developing our theory, we have been aware of the problem of defining cash flow, and we have been very conservative in our definition.

Let's go back to the start: What's important in any investment is the cash that goes into your pockets. When you buy rental property, what you look for is the rental income it generates. Yes, you hope you'll be able to sell the property for a lot of money some day, but if you hold it long enough, that payoff is dwarfed by the income you earn along the way. The same with stocks.

But what goes into your pockets with a stock? Dividends, certainly. For example, in 1998, Merck & Co., the pharmaceutical house, paid stockholders dividends amounting to 95 cents for every share they owned. But Merck's officially reported after-tax earnings were $2.15. Can we count the other $1.20 in our analysis of cash flow?

No. Emphatically, unequivocally, we cannot. Earnings do not equal cash in pockets, and nowhere in this book do we say they do.

Some portion of earnings has to be used by Merck to build new plants and buy new machines just to replace old ones and to keep profits growing. Merck spent about 80 cents on such capital expenditures in 1998, but offsetting those cash outlays were about 40 cents' worth of non-cash depreciation.

Thus, Merck used $1.35 of its $2.15 in earnings for dividends and for investment in plant and equipment. In other words, it has something left over. In fact, Merck has $3.5 billion in cash, built out of the earnings that it didn't pay in dividends and didn't use for capital investments. It is, in effect, keeping those earnings for shareholders to give them later. At some point down the road, shareholders will get that cash in the form of dividends. Or Merck will be bought out, or will use its assets to buy other companies that pay higher dividends.

In Chapter 5, we addressed the thorny question of how to determine what part of officially reported earnings go to investors, in the present or in the future. We found that a perfectly good rule of thumb is that for the average company at least half of all earnings flow to shareholders.

But the Dow 36,000 calculations work perfectly well with companies like Merck by using dividends *alone*. For instance, Merck's dividend yield in early 1999 was 1.3 percent, and the growth rate of dividends for the past five years has been 13 percent. Add the two figures, and you get 14.3 percent—at a time when long-term bond rates were 5.5 percent. Under our theory, Merck, trading at a P/E of about 35, still has plenty of room to grow.

Companies do not need to retain all their earnings in order to grow. Just look at real estate investment trusts, or REITs, which are companies that own portfolios of properties. REITs are required by law to pay out 95 percent of their earnings each year to shareholders as dividends. They retain no more than five cents of every dollar. Yet most of them increase their profits from year to year. Vornado Realty Trust, for instance, one of the largest REITs, boosted dividends an average of 15 percent and earnings an average of 11 percent annually from 1994 to 1998.

But the Dow 36,000 Theory is *not* built on the notion that every penny of earnings—or even 51 cents' worth of earnings—will eventually reach the pockets of shareholders. That notion is erroneous and mischievous.

Question: Throughout this book you have glossed over the question of bond interest rates. Isn't it true that the big reason stock prices have risen is that bond rates have fallen? Won't your theory disintegrate if they rise again?

Answer: There are three elements to the equation that leads us to Dow 36,000: the dividend or earnings yield for stocks, the growth rate of those dividends or earnings, and the interest rate for bonds. Add a stock's yield to the growth rate, and you should get the bond rate.

Our assumption is that the growth rate for earnings will continue at about the same pace as the gross domestic product. So, if growth stays the same as now and bond rates stay the same as now, then the earnings (or dividend) yield has to fall. The only way for that to happen is for stock prices to rise. Thus, Dow 36,000.

But why, as the question above asks, should bond rates stay roughly the same? If they rise, then our equation can balance without any increase in stock prices.

The answer comes from Irving Fisher—yes, the same Irving Fisher who, unfortunately, earned his fame by predicting, just before the 1929 crash, that stocks were reaching a "permanent high plateau."

Fisher, a Yale economist, discovered that since inflation eats into the value of your cash holdings, the amount of interest you demand when you buy a bond should increase one-for-one with inflation. Recall that when we incorporated inflation into our analysis, we used the *real* interest rate, which is the stated (or "nominal") interest rate minus what you expect inflation to be.

As it turns out, the real interest rate is something that depends on fundamental characteristics of the economy, and these don't change very often. Thus, a shorthand way to express the Fisher theory is that the real interest rate should be about constant. Economists have written scores of papers on the subject and have concluded that the theory appears to be correct and that the real rate hovers between 2 percent and 3 percent. Deviations tend to be temporary.

If the nominal interest rate on T-bonds shoots up to 8 percent, the reason is almost certain to be that investors are worried about higher inflation and they are demanding compensation for lending their money to the government. But higher interest rates can close the cash-flow gap between stocks and bonds only if they are higher real rates, and history teaches us that real rates don't go up very much. In the case of 8 percent bond rates, inflation will probably be in the 6 percent range, so the real bond rate will be about 2 percent. For example, in the spring of 1999, Treasury rates climbed from below 5 percent to 5.8 percent as reports indicated inflation was heading from 2 percent to 3 percent.

As for the notion that stocks have risen in recent years simply because bond rates have fallen: Consider that at the start of 1999, the thirty-year bond rate was about 5 percent and the expected inflation rate was about 2 percent. At a real rate of 3 percent, bonds actually yield slightly *more* than their historic averages.

Question: You continually talk about very tiny numbers—a half of a percentage point, three-tenths, etc. But how can you be so precise? Your calculations could be off by a little bit, and the results would be very different.

Answer: It's true that small changes, especially in growth rates, can be a big deal, since the changes are compounded over time. In their excellent textbook *Economic Growth*, Robert Barro and Xavier Sala-i-Martin provide a vivid illustration. They point out that between 1870 and 1990 real GDP in the United States grew at an annual real rate of 1.75 percent; as a result, per capita income increased by a factor of 8, to about $18,000 (in 1990 dollars). But, they write, if the GDP had risen over this period one percentage point more slowly, U.S. incomes would have increased to only $5,500. They would be about the same level as those in Mexico and $1,000 below those in Greece!

If real growth rates for earnings and dividends turn out to be only 1 percent in the future—instead of the 2.5 percent we expect—then stocks are only slightly undervalued today, rather than undervalued by a factor of three or four.

Because tiny differences can mean a lot, we have been cautious in the assumptions we have used to develop the PRP.

WHAT WORRIES US

In determining the price of a stock, the market acts like an efficient computer. Using every scrap of available information, the market weighs the probability of good news against bad. It's a balancing act.

The bad news is out there, but we think it is far outweighed by the good. Still, it would be misleading to deny we have worries.

THE RISK PREMIUM COULD RISE

Our calculations show that over the past 120 years, by accepting the risks of investing in stocks, investors have reaped a premium of 7 percent a year. In other words, returns have been an average of seven points higher than they would have been if stocks were rationally priced—that is, if they were valued so that they would return as much as bonds.

Today, the equity premium is around 2.5 percent and falling, we believe, toward zero—which is where it should be if investors with long horizons set the price of stocks.

But let's assume that the risk premium goes back up—reverts to the mean. Once more, investors will demand much higher returns from stocks than from Treasury bonds. Instead of a flow of cash into their pockets of roughly 1 or 2 percent of the price of a stock, they will need, to pick a round number, 6 percent. Dividend yields will rise, and P/E ratios will fall. The market could lose more than half its value.

But why would the risk premium rise?

Perhaps, deep down, investors are as short-sighted and risk-averse as history suggests. No wonder. They are constantly besieged in the media with warnings of gloom and doom—both because threats get attention and because the financial models that identify those threats are wrong.

Consider a typical television program: ABC's *Nightline*, March 7, 1997. The thrust of the show—titled "When You Retire, How Much Are You Willing to Gamble?"—was that millions of Americans are going to be in big trouble because they are making bad decisions about where to put their 401(k) pension money.

The problem, said Robert Krulwich, the ABC economics reporter, was not that they invest too conservatively (which truly *is* the problem) but that they have too much in stocks and are headed for losses in a wildly risky market.

Krulwich offered a tour of bear markets and concluded: "So if you add up all these years, of 107 years, seventy-seven of them were kind of yucky for investors."

In other words, three out of four years have been "yucky." How could he come to such a conclusion?

His chronology: "In 1890, there was a 64 percent drop on the New York Stock Exchange, and it took fifteen years to recover. In 1906, a 48 percent drop, and ten years to wait till recovery. In 1916, a 56 percent drop and a nine-year wait. Here's the Great Depression, twenty-six years, and on and on until 1973, which was a ten-year plateau. So if you add up. . . ."

Krulwich made two mistakes. The first is that he did not take dividends into account, and they are a huge factor, compounding smartly over time. Since 1920, dividends have averaged 4.5 percent annually. Krulwich is right, for example, when he says that it took about twenty-six years for the S&P 500 (roughly the same as the NYSE) to get back to the same level it reached in 1929. But an investor who stayed with the S&P stocks and reinvested dividends would have recovered his losses in just *seven* years. After 1936, the market took another drop, but it bounced back again by 1943.

Thanks to dividends, an investor who put $1,000 into the S&P stocks at the start of 1929 would have had $6,400—not $1,000—at the end of Krulwich's twenty-six years. As for the bear market of the 1970s: An investor who put $1,000 into large-cap stocks at the end of 1972, just as stocks were tanking, would have $1,900 by 1982. An investor who split his money between large-caps and small-caps would have seen his account quadruple.

Krulwich's second mistake is that he added up all the years in the bad periods and pronounced each and every one of those years "yucky." That's nonsense. Yes, the market crashed in 1929 and didn't get back to the same number on the Dow for twenty-six years, but that doesn't mean that the *entire* intervening period was terrible. On the contrary. During the five years from 1932 to 1936, large-caps returned 170 percent. In 1935, the Dow went from a low of 97 to a high of 148. This is the equivalent of the Dow rising from 9181 at the start of 1999 to 13,817 at the end of the year.

It is hardly surprising that investors have tended toward fear. Newspapers, magazines, and TV programs dwell on the frightening and the short-term. The effects can be seen in the markets.

In an article titled "Anomalies: The Equity Premium Puzzle," in the *Journal of Economic Perspectives,* Jeremy Siegel of Wharton and Richard H. Thaler of the University of Chicago tried to explain why the difference between the return on stocks and Treasury bills was so "strikingly large."

They could not come up with an answer for the excess return or equity premium—except to cite "myopic risk aversion." In other words, investors are frightened of short-term losses in the market. This behavior may be irrational, say the authors, but it is a fact.

Today, what worries many financial experts is that they see investors erring on the other side. They may simply have been overcome by a euphoria that is temporary. What worries us is not this overenthusiasm; in fact, investors are not enthusiastic *enough* about stocks. No, we worry that they may not have learned, truly and deeply, the lesson that stocks are highly volatile in the short term but less risky than bonds and T-bills in the long term. Perhaps they never will.

In that case, the equity premium, rationally or not, could revert to its old ways. As it goes up, stock prices will go down.

Political unrest around the world could also boost the risk premium. The world has enjoyed a period of relative calm since the end of World War II, and the risk of nuclear war diminished when the Berlin Wall fell in 1989. But aggressive, unpredictable nations like Iraq and Iran now have greater access to weapons of mass destruction. The Balkans remain a caldron. The era of Pax Americana could end tomorrow, and it is not hard to imagine investors becoming more nervous about their stocks, not to mention their own survival.

The benign domestic climate for investors could also get nasty. The federal surplus could lead to more government spending, higher inflation, and higher taxes. Fears of foreign competition could lead to higher trade barriers. A new regime at the Federal Reserve Board could produce less stable monetary policy. And a mere cyclical downturn in the economy, after nearly two decades of growth, could shock investors who have become used to good times. They could overreact to only slightly higher real risks by demanding a much higher risk premium—sending the prices of stocks down sharply.

These are worries. Investors should be aware of them, but not paralyzed with fear over them. We have a very short response to the concerns over a rising risk premium: Since stocks and bonds are equally risky over the long run, it is *reasonable* for the returns of stocks and bonds to be equal over the long run. The idea that stocks should return more than bonds is based on a fallacy—that stocks are more risky than they are. Over the past two decades, investors have become more and more aware of this fallacy, so they are doing the *reasonable* thing—bidding up the prices of stocks. The risk premium is falling to zero because that is where it *reasonably* belongs. For investors to demand a higher risk premium is to behave *unreasonably*. It could happen, certainly, but we prefer to place our bets on reason rather than on unreason.

PROFITS COULD FALL

Even if the risk premium stays low, however, earnings and dividend growth could decline in the future—and the result would be lower prices for stocks.

Throughout this century, profits have risen because firms have been able to earn significantly more on a dollar of investment than it cost them to acquire that dollar—either by borrowing it or by issuing stock. Why? One reason is market power. Another is efficiency.

Are there limits to both?

Consider newspapers. They used to be among the best "franchise" businesses—in Buffett's terms. With huge barriers to entry, strong brand names, and long traditions, they did not have to worry about start-up competition. But the Internet has changed all that. Anyone can start an e-publication, and circulation for many papers has fallen. Newspaper managers cannot sit back and reap profits from their franchise alone. They have lost their market power. They have to go into new businesses (many have launched extensive websites), which may succeed or may not.

It is clear that the staples of newspaper profits—sales to subscribers and help-wanted classifieds—will diminish, or even vanish, over time. It is easier to browse the paper occasionally and to find a job on the Web. Of course, tradition dies hard, and newspapers have time to adjust. They have been feeling the pinch for at least a decade and have responded by cutting costs and becoming more efficient. But they can cut costs only so far.

A similar revolution has hit retailing, with cyberspace replacing bricks and mortar as a shopping venue. And it is not only the Internet that is challenging market power. Think of the power business itself: New laws are deregulating electric utilities, and their status as dividend machines for investors has changed with competition.

On the other hand, new technology could help firms cut their costs enough to increase their profit margins—even if raising prices is difficult. In fact, the Internet may make brand names more important since consumers will need to trust any company whose stores it cannot actually enter or goods it cannot actually see. Still, it is only prudent to worry that increasing profits won't be as easy in an electronic age.

Profit growth is another factor in the Dow 36,000 equation that could be affected by a change in government policies. In recent years, governments around the world have become less intrusive, reducing tax rates and, if not actually lightening the burdens of regulation, at least not increasing them much. But there is no guarantee this trend will continue. Nothing would lower profits faster than a big increase in taxes, since they immediately reduce the flow of cash into investors' pockets.

Still, while the nature of the future is that it is unknowable, a good guess is that the human imagination will find new products and new ways of providing services, much as in the past.

As for fears that governments will throttle earnings: The opposite is more likely. With the growth in stock ownership, a new "investor class," in the words of economist Lawrence Kudlow, has arisen—a voting bloc with interests more closely aligned with those of the companies whose stocks people own (see Chapter 15 for a closer examination). At the very least, the investor class should serve as a deterrent to politicians who want to raise taxes and increase regulations and thus depress profits.

THE PROBLEM WITH BAD NEWS

A decisive problem with these bad-news arguments is that they remain the same, year after year. Financial analysts are consistently saying that the market is overvalued, and they have consistently been wrong.

Somehow, it seems, the stock market is *perpetually* overvalued. Yet it keeps returning an average of 11 percent per year.

Something is out of whack, and it requires a different view of the market from the traditional view of the worriers to see the derangement. Warren Buffett has just that view. He wrote shareholders in a March 14, 1998, letter that "there is no reason to think of stocks as generally overvalued" as long as interest rates remain low and businesses continue to operate as profitably as they have in recent years.

Yes. With long-term Treasury bond rates of around 5.5 percent and annual profit increases of around 5 percent, stocks are not overvalued. In fact, they are significantly undervalued. Here is why:

• **Over the long run, stocks are as safe an investment as any other, including Treasury bonds and even very short-term T-bills.** That is the conclusion of solid research, looking at market data going all the way back to 1802.

• **Stocks have historically paid shareholders a significant premium, an average of about 7 percent, over bonds.** This equity premium has been studied for years, but no one can come up with a good explanation—other than to say that investors operate on the erroneous assumption that the market is so risky that anyone who invests in it must be paid extra to compensate for that alleged volatility. In other words, stocks give investors a delightful unearned bonus.

• **Evidence abounds that investors are figuring out that the equity premium is unnecessary.** They are enthusiastically bidding up the prices of stocks—or, to put it another way, they are driving down the risk premium. If there is no risk premium, then, over time, stocks and bonds should put about the same amount of money into the pockets of people who buy them.

• **Therefore, the correct valuation for the stock market—the PRP—would be one that equalizes the flow of cash between stocks and bonds in the long run.**

• **Where is that point of equilibrium?** Using a variety of techniques, we found that the P/E (the price of a stock divided by its annual earnings per share) that would accomplish this aim is about 100 and the dividend yield is about one-half of 1 percent.

• **By this measure, the stock market is undervalued by a factor of about 4.** In 1998, when we began writing this book, the Dow Jones industrial average was about 9000 and P/E ratios were around 25. If P/Es should be 100 then the Dow needs to rise to 36,000. How soon? The rational time frame is this afternoon. But the process will probably take longer as understanding spreads about the true risks of stocks. A sensible target date for Dow 36,000 is early 2005, but it could be reached much earlier. After that, stocks will continue to rise, but at a slower pace.

This means that stocks, right now, are an extraordinary investment. They are just as safe as bonds over long periods of time, and the returns are significantly higher. Between here and Dow 36,000, stock prices remain in a comfort zone for investors who build the kinds of portfolios we will describe in the next part of this book.

Remember that our assumption in predicting Dow 36,000 was that earnings would grow at the same rate as the gross domestic product, or about 5 percent per year including inflation. Our hunch is that our assumptions are far too conservative, and that the U.S. economy will grow much more rapidly in the next forty years than it has in the past forty—mainly because of the computer and Internet revolutions and the opening of vast new markets in Asia, Latin America, and Africa. But we don't need those "New Economy" changes for our predictions to come true. Indeed, all we need is for the history of earnings growth to keep repeating itself.

But if those big changes in the economy do happen, Dow 36,000 itself will be a distant memory—of happier times when stocks were still cheap.

PART II: IN PRACTICE

CHAPTER 9

How to Profit from the Dow 36,000 Theory

We study theory in order to apply it, not for its own sake.
—Ho Chi Minh (1892–1969)

IT'S TIME to move from principle to practice—from telling you why stocks have soared in recent years and why they will soon double, triple, and quadruple to telling you how to build an investment plan to exploit the Dow 36,000 Theory and reap the profits of the historic rise in the market that's ahead.

First, here are two pieces of shorthand. We like to use the word "36er" to describe an investor who believes in the ideas we have laid out in this book, specifically that:

• Stock prices today are drastically undervalued, since . . .

• the way to value a stock is by the cash it puts in your pocket over time, but . . .

• the financial establishment, instead, has concentrated on a misreading of the history of price-to-earnings ratios and dividend yields and, unwittingly, has frightened off investors, but . . .

• the truth is that, over the long-term, stocks are no more risky than bonds or Treasury bills, so . . .

• with this in mind, investors in recent years have begun to act more rationally, bidding up the prices of stocks and driving down the premium they had demanded when they believed stocks were more risky, and . . .

• soon, prices will rise to where they will be "perfectly reasonable"—around 36,000 on the Dow Jones industrial average.

THE ONE-STEP FORMULA

The second bit of shorthand is the perfectly reasonable price, or PRP, itself. We based the PRP on modest assumptions, mainly that the average company will increase its profits and dividends at the same rate as that of the gross domestic product (the sum of goods and services)—or about 5 percent in nominal terms, that is, including inflation. We also assumed that the interest rate on long-term Treasury bonds would be about 5.5 to 6 percent, or about 2.5 to 3 percent in real (inflation-adjusted) terms.

At the time we developed our ideas, the Dow was about 9,000 and the price-to-earnings ratio of the average stock for the year ahead was about 25. Our PRP calculations indicated we could comfortably justify P/E ratios of 100. Thus, the Dow should quadruple to 36,000.

The objective of our analysis was to find the price at which a stock produces returns that put as much money into an investor's pockets over time as a Treasury bond. That stands to reason. Stocks and bonds, since they are equally risky, should produce equal cash returns to investors.

The key equation is this:

$$\text{Cash return} = \text{cash yield} + g$$

where g is the growth rate of the cash flow from the stock. Since a bond's cash flow stays the same each year, g equals 0 for bonds. What about stocks?

Let's look at a particularly unsexy one: Ford Motor Co., the second-largest U.S. automaker. In May 1999, Ford paid a dividend of $1.84 and was trading at $60 a share, for a yield of 3 percent—which, in this case, is the cash yield in the equation above. If you bought a share of Ford, you could expect to get 3 percent of the purchase price back the first year in dividends.

What about g?

Over the ten preceding years, Ford's cash dividend payments had risen at a rate of 9.5 percent annually. For the five years ahead, analysts expect that the growth rate will slow to about 8 percent, not much different from the market as a whole. Let's be even *more* conservative and assume a 5 percent growth rate for dividends far into the future. Add the yield and the growth rate together, and you get 8 percent ($3 + 5 = 8$). That is the cash return an investor can expect over a long period.

The yield on bonds at the time was about 5.5 percent. So Ford, by our 36er reckoning, is a substantially undervalued stock. You really don't have to go any further in your analysis. This is our incredibly simple, one-step formula for determining whether a stock is undervalued:

Find the cash return rate (cash yield + *g*), and make sure that it is comfortably greater than the long-term Treasury rate.

But what if you want to know Ford's precise PRP?

Ford, we project, will produce cash returns of 8 percent while bonds produce cash returns of 5.5 percent. If Ford and bonds are equally risky over time, then they should produce the *same* returns, but for that to happen, Ford stock has to rise.

By how much?

Since Ford's dividends are growing at 5 percent, the stock would need a dividend yield of just 0.5 percent for its cash returns to be the same as bonds (5.5 − 5 = 0.5).

Assume that Ford continues to pay out the same amount in dividends as it pays now—$1.84 a year. How could the yield fall immediately from its current 3 percent down to 0.5 percent? Simple: by the stock price rising by a factor of six. The dividend was $1.84, and the stock was trading at $60, for a 3 percent yield. But if the stock goes to $360, then the dividend yield drops to 0.5 percent ($1.84 ÷ $360 = 0.005).

In other words, the calculation suggests that Ford's stock is undervalued with its current dividend until its price sextuples.

But the dividend yield often underestimates the cash flow of a stock. Our quick-and-dirty rule is that a firm can pay out half of its earnings to shareholders and still increase its future earnings at a healthy rate. Ford's dividend return could equal 0.5 percent and its stock would still return as much cash as a bond. But Ford's *earnings* return would have to equal 1 percent to return as much.

What *was* Ford's earnings return in 1999? Again, the calculation is simple. Ford's P/E ratio was 12:1, or 12. The earnings yield is the E/P ratio (earnings divided by price), or the reciprocal of P/E. So divide 12 into 1, and you get 0.083; call it 8 percent. Also assume that earnings, like dividends, will rise at 5 percent annually. Since Ford's earnings yield is 8 percent, Ford's price would have to rise by a factor of 8 to reduce its yield to 1 percent. The P/E ratio would have to go to nearly 100 ($12 \times 8 = 96$).

Applying a similar approach to the market as a whole, we found that a reasonable P/E is indeed in the neighborhood of 100—a calculation that works pretty much the same with both dividend and earnings yields, as long as you are careful not to double-count.

For companies that have traditionally paid decent dividends, like Ford and AT&T, the cash return rate is simply the dividend rate plus the expected rate of dividend growth—a figure you can get from the *Value Line Investment Survey,* a research service available in most libraries, or through Internet sites such as www.dailystocks.com.

For companies that don't pay dividends or that have yields of 1 percent or less, you simply take the P/E, divide it into 1, then cut that percentage in half. Next, add the result to the earnings growth rate, which is probably close to the dividend growth rate. Then, compare the sum with the rate on a thirty-year T-bond.

Let's take another example: Pfizer, Inc., the pharmaceutical company that makes Viagra and other fine drugs. In May 1999, Pfizer was trading at $130 a share and paying a dividend of 88 cents, for a yield of just 0.8 percent. That's very low, so let's do an earnings analysis.

Pfizer's P/E, which you can find in *The Wall Street Journal,* in many daily newspapers, and on sites such as www.quote.com or www.marketplace.com, was 52. Get the E/P by dividing 52 into 1, and you find Pfizer's earnings yield—just 1.9 percent. But how fast will those earnings grow? For ten preceding years, the annual growth rate had been 12 percent; for the next five years, the estimate by Value Line analysts is a whopping 18 percent.

So, cut Pfizer's earnings yield in half to get an approximation of the *cash* yield for investors: 0.95 percent (which, by the way, is not far from the dividend yield). Now, add a reasonable projection of earnings growth—18 percent seems high, so let's divide it in half. In other words, Pfizer's cash yield plus its growth rate comes to 9.95 percent—far, far ahead of the Treasury bond yield of 5.5 percent.

As we warned in the first part of this book, the earnings growth rate might reflect interest on retained earnings and we don't want to double-count. But, again, a complicated analysis isn't necessary. The gap between the cash return over time for Pfizer and the cash return over time for Treasuries is so large (more than four percentage points) that any reasonable correction would still make the stock a steal. At this point, with the market so underpriced, 36ers don't need to slice the numbers razor-thin. There are so many bargains to be had.

COMPANIES WE LIKE

But a price well below the PRP isn't the only thing we look for in a stock. Here are the basic criteria of the companies that 36ers should own:
- A long history of rising earnings.
- A "moat"—such as powerful patents, a strong brand name, client relationships, a unique distribution system—around the firm's products that helps keep out competition.
- A lack of heavy demands for reinvesting earnings back in the company. In other words, a lot of free-cash flow that can go to shareholders, now or in the future.
- An earnings growth rate for the next five years that is projected to average 8 percent or more.
- A P/E ratio below 100.

As a bonus, we like companies that have:
- A dividend at least as high as the market average (about 1.5 percent) and dividend growth of at least 7.2 percent annually (see page 229) over the past ten years.
- Volatility that is no higher than the market as a whole. (Low volatility makes holding on to your stocks easier.)

A GLORIOUS COMPANY WITHIN OUR COMFORT ZONE

We will go into much deeper detail on these characteristics in Chapters 11, 12, and 13, and we'll discuss the stocks and mutual funds you should consider. But as a preview, let's look briefly at a magnificent company that the market has consistently underpriced: Automatic Data Processing, Inc.

ADP is a wonder. Since 1960, it has annually increased its earnings over the previous year by at least 10 percent—a record unmatched by any large American firm. Between 1988 and 1998, ADP's earnings grew at an average rate of 14.5 percent; its dividends, by 16 percent.

ADP provides payroll accounting and tax-filing services to firms employing 23 million people and processes 625,000 trades a day for Wall Street brokerage houses, but as Babson-United Investment Advisors in Wellesley Hills, Massachusetts, points out, "Over half the major corporations in America and 80 percent of small businesses . . . still process their payrolls in-house." Opportunities, in other words, remain.

In the spring of 1989, you could have bought 100 shares of ADP for $3,900. Dividends on those shares totaled $66 that year, for a yield of 1.7 percent. By 1999, those 100 shares, through splits, had become 800 shares, producing dividends that year of $240. So, in 1999 alone, on that original 1989 investment, the yield was 6.2 percent ($240 ÷ $3,900 = .062), higher than Treasury bond rates—and rising. By 2019, the annual dividend payout, rising at the same pace as the decade before, should be $2,700—for a yield of 69 percent on the initial investment—in just that one year!

But ADP's dividends represent only about one-quarter of its earnings. Remaining profits are reinvested in a booming company. As a result, ADP's stock price has risen by a factor of more than 8. That $3,900 investment became $33,000 just ten years later—not counting the dividends.

What about ADP's future? It certainly has a beautiful balance sheet, with $900 million in cash and just $165 million in long-term debt. But is it a 36er stock?

Absolutely. In early 1999, its P/E was 36, so its earnings yield (E/P) was 2.8 percent. Value Line projects that earnings will grow over the next five years at 15 percent annually. Take half the earnings yield, then add it to the growth rate to get the cash return. The result: 16.4 percent, at a time the thirty-year Treasury bond was yielding 5.5 percent. That's quite a margin of safety!

A dividend analysis leads to similar results. ADP's dividend yield is 0.7 percent, also growing at 15 percent annually (a slight decline from the previous ten years). Total cash return: 15.7 percent. Even if dividend growth and earnings growth fall by half, ADP is substantially undervalued, returning about three full points more than Treasuries. The bond rate would have to rise to more than 8 percent to deter 36ers from buying ADP, even under a superconservative analysis.

What is the PRP—the correct price—for ADP? Again, our preference is caution. We use a P/E of 100 as the outer limit of the comfort zone for all stocks that are not posting enormous (30 percent plus) growth. In early 1999, with a P/E of 36, ADP could nearly triple in price before it exceeded a P/E of 100. With ADP trading at $41, it could rise immediately to $112 before we would get even slightly nervous.

And remember that the PRP applies to ADP's *current* earnings of $1.12 per share and its dividend of 30 cents annually. As earnings and dividends rise, so should ADP's perfectly reasonable price.

THE CHAPTERS AHEAD

The remaining chapters will show you more than just how to find companies like ADP. In the next chapter, we focus on how to build a solid relationship with your stocks, so that you don't make the terrible mistakes that have cost the average investor three-quarters of the profits she could have made in the market in recent years.

In other words, we teach 36ers how to stop themselves from doing things like selling ADP because the financial pundits say its P/E is too high or its dividend yield is too low. Part of that process can involve finding a good broker (we tell you how) or doing it yourself (we tell you whether it makes sense).

In Chapter 11, we look at that great democratic invention: the mutual fund. What is a fund anyway? Why have so many performed so poorly? Should you forget about funds managed by human beings and instead buy index funds? How can you avoid the pitfalls, the high fees, and the surprising tax bills? And which funds, by name and manager, are the best?

In Chapter 12, we offer five good reasons to buy individual stocks instead of funds—and then explain the smartest ways to purchase them. In Chapter 13, we tell 36ers where to find the stocks that meet our strategy, listing the questions you should ask before you make your investment and discussing great companies to own.

The subject of Chapter 14 is asset allocation—the specifics on how to build a maximizing portfolio of stocks, bonds, and cash. And Chapter 15 sums up the theory and the practice and looks to the changes in politics and culture in a future when the bull and the bear are both dead and wealth explodes.

All the elements are here for successful investing.

CHAPTER 10

How to Build a Winning Relationship with Your Stocks

The problem seems to be that while economists have gotten increasingly sophisticated and clever, consumers have remained decidedly human.

—Richard H. Thaler, *The Winner's Curse*

UNLIKE OTHER ANIMALS, humans have the capacity to take the long view. But we don't always use it. The moment often rules our better judgment.

For example, the state of West Virginia recently passed a law that took away the driver's licenses of teenagers who dropped out of high school. In the first year, the drop-out rate declined by one-third. Interpretation: The immediate discomfort of not being able to drive kept kids in school while the long-run economic costs could not—even though they were enormous in comparison.

Not only teenagers have trouble with self-control. Dieters break their vows when colleagues bring chocolate chip cookies to work. Vacationers, bent on beating the beach-traffic crush, say they'll wake up extra early on a Saturday, but then roll over and go back to sleep after turning the alarm off.

Of course, if you want to make sure you get on the road early, you can put the alarm clock across the room. To turn it off, you have to get out of bed, and once you are out of bed, you are less likely to get back in and start snoozing again.

Investing is no different. Fear (like sloth) is always lurking below the surface, and surrendering to fear can cost you a fortune. The solution is to build a strong personal relationship with your stocks. That way, you will be more inclined to take the long view and behave profitably. Learning what stocks are really worth (which is the point of this book) is the best way to overcome your fear. But, for many investors, it's not enough. Stocks fluctuate in price; they can drop 10 percent or 20 percent a few days after you invest for the first time. If you are like most people, when your stocks head south, you are going to feel a strong urge to sell. In the end, building the right relationship with your stocks may require the financial equivalent of putting the alarm clock on the other side of the room.

In this chapter, we'll discuss the kind of behavior that leads to losses and begin to show you ways to reduce the chances that short-run weaknesses will lead to long-run costs.

HOW TO DEFEAT YOUR OWN WORST ENEMY

In *The Intelligent Investor,* first published in 1949 and still one of the best financial books around, Benjamin Graham wrote, "The investor's chief problem—and even his worst enemy—is likely to be himself."

In other words, you may make brilliant selections of stocks and still do poorly in the market because you can't rule your own emotions. None of us is immune, for example, from the impulse to dump shares when prices fall—frequently the worst time to sell.

Don't take our word for it. A Boston research firm, Dalbar, Inc., has studied the behavior of actual investors by using data from purchases and sales of mutual funds. From January 1, 1984, to December 31, 1997, the Standard & Poor's 500-stock index, a good proxy for the broad market, returned 820 percent, including reinvested dividends. In other words, an investor who put $10,000 into the stocks of the index in 1984 would have $92,000 by the end of 1997. But the return over the same period for the average investor who bought mutual funds was only 148 percent. An investment of $10,000 became just $24,800.

In other words, while the market rose by a factor of 9, the typical investor's holdings did not even triple. Why?

"The gap," concluded Dalbar's research, "is explained by the behavior of equity fund investors. In their attempt to cash in on the impressive stock market gains, investors jump on the bandwagon too late, and switch in and out of funds trying to time the market. By not remaining invested for the entire period, they do not benefit from the majority of the equity market appreciation."

A mutual fund is a company that owns a portfolio of assets—stocks (equities), in the case of the Dalbar study. An investor in a mutual fund owns a piece of all of those assets, a fraction of a share of this stock, a few shares of that. Investors did not go wrong because they chose the wrong mutual funds, which chose the wrong stocks. No, investors went wrong because they did not hold on to the funds they did choose.

The report summed up its findings this way: "Investment return is far more dependent on investor behavior than on fund performance."

Another way of looking at the results is by average annual return. Between 1984 and 1997, the return for the S&P was 17.2 percent, but the return the average stock-fund investor actually achieved was only 6.7 percent. That is barely higher than the 6 percent return on Treasury bills during this period!

Investors get carried away. They sell when pessimism reigns and prices drop, and they buy when optimism soars and prices rise. In the terms that we use in this book, when investors get scared, they bid up the risk premium. They say, in effect, "I am not going to buy this stock until its price gives me a huge margin of safety compared with other investments like bonds or Treasury bills." But, paradoxically, when prices fall, many investors want *more* reassurance. They become worried the decline will get worse, so they demand an even higher risk premium. They sell and wait for the bottom—when the risk premium reaches its maximum—but most of them time, when they buy back, they have missed the low point by a mile. They buy *after* prices have recovered.

This process may sound strange, but it is continually repeated. In fact, stocks are the only things people like to buy when they become expensive, rather than cheap. You wouldn't rush down to the local grocery if it advertised hamburger marked up from $2 a pound to $3 a pound. But stocks tend to bring out the irrational in people. And no wonder: Stocks fluctuate in price in dramatic ways. That volatility cannot fail to touch our emotions. As Graham wrote:

> The investor may as well resign himself in advance to the probability, rather than the mere possibility, that most of his holdings will advance, say, 50 percent or more from their low point and decline

the equivalent of one-third or more from their high point at various periods in the next five years.

Hold your own mental fire drill: If the Dow were to fall by one-third (that's 3,333 points from a level of 10,000), either in one sickening free fall or in a long, grinding bear market, how would you react?

Would you hang on to your shares? The honest answer—for the ad hoc investor or the speculator who thinks he can time the market—has to be no. You would probably sell, and sell at close to the bottom.

Knowing that it is your own human frailty that produces results such as those of the Dalbar survey, you are faced with a difficult problem. You can't have yourself tied to the mast like Ulysses in an effort to resist the song of the Sirens. What can you do?

First, bear in mind what you should not do . . .

DON'T EVER, EVER "TIME" THE MARKET

Market timing is buying and selling stocks in anticipation of the market's near-term moves. It is, in short, impossible—because in the near term (the next day or year) the market's movements are random and unknowable.

Yes, investors can put too low a value on individual stocks, or on the market as a whole—that, of course, is what we firmly believe is happening right now. But it is the long-run value of stocks that is being underestimated, not their prices tomorrow or a few months or even a year from now. We have no opinion on short-term prices, and people who claim to have an opinion are feeding you nonsense—either out of ignorance or for their own profit.

Market timing is always a temptation for investors because they think, erroneously, that making money in the market means being able to stare into a crystal ball and tell the future—to predict that, say, Compaq will develop a new computer that will drive IBM out of the PC business, or that war in the Middle East will boost oil prices and help Exxon, or that investors will suddenly wake up after an earnings disappointment from Microsoft and realize that high-tech stocks are wildly overpriced.

Investing actually has nothing to do with predicting events that no one can possibly predict. (Thank goodness.) Instead, it involves simply becoming a long-term partner in an excellent business, which will endure both good times and bad over the course of its lifetime but, if well-managed, should prosper.

In fact, as Buffett puts it, "the true investor welcomes volatility . . . because a wildly fluctuating market means that irrationally low prices will periodically be attached to solid businesses."

But this simple notion is nearly impossible for most people to grasp. In early 1999, for instance, a debate raged in the financial press over whether companies would increase their profits at double-digit rates that year or see them fall a bit. But earnings for the year ahead are meaningless unless they indicate long-term structural or competitive problems for a business. You certainly don't want to own a company whose profits will grow by just 2 percent annually for the next ten years, but you should delight in a firm with a transitory setback. Its stock will drop, and you can buy shares cheaply.

Unfortunately, much of the commentary in the press and on television focuses on what stock prices will do next—a fruitless obsession. Of market timing, John C. Bogle, the venerable chairman of the Vanguard Group, the Valley Forge, Pennsylvania, mutual fund house, has written:

> After nearly fifty years in this business, I do not know of anybody who has done it successfully and consistently. I do not even know anybody who *knows* anybody who has done it successfully and consistently.

In a series of books, David Dreman, a veteran money manager, cites dozens of examples of the inability of experts to divine the future, in fields as varied as horse racing and radiology. In one study, Dreman examined fifty-two surveys over fifty years in which experts in publications such as the *Financial Analysts Journal* picked their top stocks or industries for the coming twelve months. In 77 percent of the cases, Dreman found, the experts' selections actually underperformed the market as a whole.

"Overall," wrote William A. Sherden in his book on the limits of short-term professional forecasting of all sorts, "we have not made progress in predicting the market, but this has not stopped the investment business from continuing the quest, making $100 billion annually doing so."

Andrew Metrick of Harvard looked at the performance of twenty-nine financial newsletters—all of them employing some form of market timing—which had been in business between 1982 and 1997. These survivors themselves should have been a hardier, more successful breed than letters that folded during that period. His results, published by the prestigious National Bureau of Economic Research, found that of the twenty-nine letters only one—*The Chartist* of Seal Beach, California—managed to beat the Wilshire 5000, an index comprising all the stocks traded on the three major markets. And over the five years ending in 1997, only 2 of 105 newsletters outperformed the Wilshire. More than 98 percent couldn't beat the averages.

Even if you happen to stumble on the perfect day to pull out of the market, how do you know when to get back in? Philip A. Fisher, the legendary California investor, wrote in his 1958 book, *Common Stocks and Uncommon Profits*:

Never sell out of an outstanding situation because of the possibility that a bear market may be about to occur. If the company is really the right one, the next bull market may see the stock making a new peak well above those so far attained. How is the investor to know when to buy back? Theoretically, it should be after the decline. However, this presupposes that the investor will know when the decline will end. When a bear market has come, I have not seen one time in ten when the investor actually gets back into the same shares before they have gone up above his selling price.'

TRADING KILLS PROFITS

Another reason not to try to time the market is that moving in and out of stocks can be expensive. Research published in early 1998 by two economists, Brad M. Barber and Terrance Odean of the University of California at Davis, concluded, "Our central message is that trading is hazardous to your wealth."

The term "trading" means buying and selling stocks in anticipation of their prices rising or falling in the short term—in other words, market timing. Barber and Odean persuaded a large discount brokerage firm to provide them with records of actual stock trading by 64,715 customers between 1991 and 1996. They discovered that over this period the average investor earned a gross return of 17.7 percent, compared with 17.1 percent for the market as a whole: Excellent! But, unfortunately, the net return after transaction costs (mainly brokerage commissions, even at a discount house) was 15.3 percent.

More important, the 12,000 investors who did the most trading earned a return of only 10 percent while those who traded least frequently earned 17.5 percent. That's an enormous difference over time. Using the rate of return of the active traders in the study, we found that $1,000 would grow to $6,700 in twenty years; for the infrequent traders, $1,000 grows to $25,200.

In fact, most of the investors in the study traded far too much. The average household, Barber and Odean found, "turns over more than 80 percent of its common stock portfolio annually." In other words, investors at this discount firm held the typical stock for only fifteen months. The active traders registered a turnover of 300 percent a year. They held the average stock for just four months.

The main reason for poor performance, the authors emphasized, "is the cost of trading and the frequency of trading, not portfolio selection." That's the same conclusion as the Dalbar study.

The second direct cost of trading is taxes. We discuss tax consequences at length in Chapters 11 and 12, but in summary: One of the few benign aspects of our tax law is that you don't have to pay Uncle Sam for your gains until you sell a stock. By contrast, interest generated by U.S. Treasury or corporate bonds is taxable every year, even if you let the money sit in a brokerage account. Market timers pay a big price for their hunches—up to 39.6 percent of their profits in federal taxes alone.

If you learn one practical lesson from this book, it should be this: Trade as little as possible. You can't get the most from the Dow 36,000 strategy if you jump in and out of stocks. With the market so undervalued, the best approach is to buy a diversified portfolio and sit on it. "If you aren't willing to own a stock for ten years," writes Buffett, "don't even think about owning it for ten minutes."

FUN AND GAMES

Can't help yourself? Then, set up what we call a "fun and games account," or FGA, representing no more than 10 percent of your total financial assets. Do your trading in your FGA, a completely separate account from your serious long-term investments. Use the lowest-cost broker possible—preferably online. What you will certainly find is that over time you won't be able to keep up with the market averages, or with your long-term account.

It only stands to reason. A long-term investor has to make a single decision: which stock or mutual fund to buy. The market timer has to make three, even after she has decided on the stock or fund: when to buy, when to sell, and when to buy back. At the very least, traders will leave cash in their FGA accounts as they dither over when to buy back, or when to buy new shares. Stocks will outperform the cash, and transaction costs (however low) will devour profits.

Of course, there's always the possibility that you are a truly brilliant stock-picker. But if you're that smart, why fool around trading? Just find a single great company and buy it. All it takes is one.

THE 1987 CRASH AND ITS AFTERMATH

Some investors actually think that trading is *necessary* to achieving success in the market. The contrary is true.

Go back to October 19, 1987, when the Dow Jones industrial average plunged 508 points, or 22.6 percent, in a single day of trading. The close that day, at 1738, was a bottom. The Dow has never since finished a trading session lower. By July 1989, the Dow had returned to its pre-crash peak of 2722. No, the recovery did not occur overnight; it took twenty-three months. But investors who kept their cool and refused to sell, or market-time, ended up well ahead.

Assume that an investor put $10,000 into the stocks of the S&P 500 index on October 1, 1987, just before the crash, and left it there, reinvesting the dividends back into S&P stocks. Despite this horrific timing, his account would have been worth $41,050 in ten years (for simplicity, figure no tax bite). The average annual return over this period was 15.3 percent, despite the one-day disaster.

We looked at some well-known stocks over the ten years, again figuring that our fictional investor had the misfortune to buy shares on the precipice of the record 1987 one-day crash and didn't add a penny more. A stake in General Electric Co. rose from $10,000 to $58,696. The same amount in Boeing Co. became $59,489; in PepsiCo, Inc., $66,058; in Exxon Corp., $41,268; in Microsoft Corp., $359,491.

Talk about bad timing: Analysts at Capital Research and Management Co. invented a fellow called "Louie the Loser," who every year put $5,000 into Investment Company of America, an actual mutual fund managed by Capital Research that has consistently produced returns that closely track the market as a whole.

As his name implies, Louie the Loser had terrible timing. Each year, from 1974 to 1994, he chose the worst possible day to invest his $5,000 in ICA: the day the Dow hit its annual peak. Still, after twenty years, Louie's total investment produced an average annual return of 13 percent. By contrast, a perfect market timer, who invested $5,000 annually on the day the market hit its *low* each year, scored a return of 15 percent. Not far off.

So Louie is really a winner. Indeed, the sad fact is that the Loser outperformed the vast majority of Americans who invested in mutual funds. While he buys at the worst possible time, he leaves his money in the market no matter what. This strategy is the simplest and the best: Buy stocks and hold them.

FIND WAYS TO DISCIPLINE YOURSELF

For most investors, however, that strategy is easy to recite but hard to follow. Are there techniques that help enforce a regime of discipline in the face of either a sharply rising stock market, which tempts investors to sell and lock in profits, or a sharply falling one, which tempts investors to sell and avoid further losses?

Yes, there are, and over the next few chapters we will lay them out. But the fundamental principle is that you want to set things up so that you pay a high immediate psychic—or real—cost if you panic and sell your stocks.

For example, a good first step is to buy stocks and mutual funds through a third party—a broker or financial advisor you trust. The Dalbar study found that investors who buy from intermediaries get better real-life returns than those who buy directly. The main reason is that investors hold on to funds longer when they've been sold them by someone else. The broker provides a line of resistance—even if it is a weak one—when you try to sell. Simply telling a client, "Are you sure you want to do that?" can have a dramatically salutary effect. The broker can make you feel like a coward if you sell for the wrong reasons, and that shame can work to your advantage. Brokers also charge transaction fees, and the desire to avoid those can keep you from selling out when you start to panic.

Of course, many brokers *want* you to sell—so they will make another round of commissions. We will tell you how to spot and avoid such sharks in Chapter 12. And certainly, buying through a broker adds fees that a direct purchase can avoid. But reputable advisors, charging reasonable commissions or annual fees, provide a buffer between impulse and action.

A similar approach is to buy a mutual fund that charges you an upfront fee, or load. This is heresy to many investors, who insist on no-load funds, but it can be a cheap way to buy courage, and courage can save you far more than the load charges.

Consider a fund that carries a hefty front-end load of 5 percent. Say you invest $10,000, which means you'll pay a commission of $500. Is that fee worth it? Probably not, as far as the performance of the fund is concerned: the average load and no-load funds do about the same (not including the fees). But the load could enforce discipline. In the early years of your investment, the load will seem like such a big outlay that it will discourage you from selling too soon. Think about it: You certainly wouldn't want to sell a fund the next week if you have just paid $500 for the privilege of investing in it. But if the fund carried no load, you would feel little reluctance to sell.

A sensible investor still would feel like an idiot (we hope) selling the fund even after two or three years and flushing $500 down the drain. Over a longer period, the effect of the one-time fee dissipates, but by that time, the investor should be used to a buy-and-hold strategy. Also, remember that when you're a shareholder in a fund you're subject to the whims of other shareholders. If *they* panic and redeem their shares, the manager will have to sell stock he wanted to keep—and you get hit with the tax bill. A front-end load (or a back-end one) is a deterrent to selling for *all* shareholders.

Recognizing personal weaknesses can change the calculus of investing significantly. The least expensive way to invest may not always be the best, if it carries with it a high risk that you will behave in the wrong way.

SUMMING UP

The nature of discipline requires that it come from within. To stay in stocks for the long run, you need to be secure in believing that stocks are a wonderful investment. Here, in summary, is our catechism:

1. Over 190 years of history, the U.S. stock market has returned an average of 11 percent annually, or about 7 percent after inflation—including both price increases and reinvested dividends. That's twice as much as the alternatives. In the past, if you kept your money invested, your buying power would double in ten years, quadruple in twenty. And under the Dow 36,000 Theory, growth will even swifter and sharper.

2. Investors who try to time the market—that is, guess whether it will rise or fall in the near term—invariably fail.

3. Even if you figure out correctly when to exit the market, you are highly unlikely to figure out when to get back in.

4. Trading is expensive, in commission costs, in opportunity costs while you are out of the market, and in tax bills.

5. Research shows that over a recent fourteen-year period investors who stayed in the market did more than four times better than those who traded.

In the end, recognize that making money in the stock market is hard work. You earn your money when you ignore the desire to sell good businesses when times get tough.

Now that we're finished with the sermonette, it's time to move on to the fun part of investing—actually buying things. We'll begin by exploring the most fabulously democratic investment vehicle ever invented, the mutual fund.

CHAPTER 11

Making Sense of Mutual Funds

Wealth is not without its advantages, and the case to the contrary,
although it has often been made, has never proved persuasive.
—John Kenneth Galbraith, *The Affluent Society*

I N 1935, in the depths of the Great Depression, a group of Wall
Street investors decided to assemble a portfolio of stocks that would
thrive into the next century. The idea was to form a mutual fund and
hold on to all the stocks—just thirty of them—until the year 2015. The
rules were not to sell a company unless it was merged out of existence
or went bankrupt.

Some of the early records of the fund, which eventually became
known as Lexington Corporate Leaders, were lost, but we have data
going back to 1941. Assume back then that you put up $10,000. The
load, or up-front commission, at the time was a hefty 12 percent, so
only $8,800 of your money actually went into shares of the fund. As-
sume you automatically reinvested all dividends and capital gains in
new shares. By May 1999, your investment was worth $5.6 million.

The original thirty stocks did not include an airline or a computer
firm or a high-technology company of any sort. There were no pharmaceutical firms or restaurant chains or banks (this was the depression,
remember). The portfolio was top-heavy in the big, clumsy businesses
of the day—with one-fifth of the assets in industrial cyclical stocks,
such as auto companies; another one-fifth in energy; and one-seventh
in electric utilities.

The original investors were not especially prescient. They made
mediocre choices at best, including four railroads, two of which went
out of business, and only three consumer-products firms.

Still, their portfolio—which included General Electric; Procter & Gamble; Sears, Roebuck & Co.; AT&T; and other stalwarts—did well, trailing the Standard & Poor's 500-stock index, the most popular benchmark for fund managers, by only one percentage point over the past half-century—and with lower risk. Corporate Leaders, with twenty-six stocks now in its portfolio (twenty-three of the original twenty-six plus three spinoffs), ranks in the top 5 percent of all growth-and-income funds over the fifteen years ending in 1998. And it's still whipping its peers. In the first six months of 1999, the fund was returning more than the S&P.

The story of Lexington Corporate Leaders is a vivid reminder that the stocks you choose are less important than the way you behave after you choose them. And the best way to behave is to hold on. It's doubtful that today you would assemble a portfolio for the next century that includes Union Carbide and Consolidated Edison, yet the folks at Lexington have decided to extend the life of their fund through the year 2100. They've done so well so far, why change?

Two reasons for the fund's success are disarmingly simple: It charges low fees, and it changes its holdings only once every decade or so. Its twenty-six stocks may not be the best choices, but they are diversified enough to keep up with the market as a whole—and to outperform it in some years, especially when the going gets tough.

Its bull-headedness is admirable, and the stocks in its portfolio meet our Dow 36,000 criteria. They're big growth companies, with strong track records of earnings and dividend increases. The world will change in the next century, but companies like Procter & Gamble and Eastman Kodak, even if they suffer a few bad stretches, have the size and flexibility to adapt. In fact, we love Corporate Leaders. Sadly unique, it is a great mutual fund for 36ers. There are other good ones, as well. In this chapter we will tell you what to look for and offer specific funds to choose. But, first, why own mutual funds at all? Why not buy individual stocks?

DIVERSIFY BUT DON'T "DIWORSEIFY"

Mutual funds give investors something they have to have: diversification. Even if you are convinced that the market is ready to double, triple, or quadruple, you would be irredeemably foolish to put all your money into a single stock, or even two, three, or four.

A bull-market tide does not lift all boats. From 1989 to 1998, an investment of $1,000 in the thirty stocks of the Dow swelled to $5,700, but the prices of gold-mining shares fell by more than one-fourth, and firms like Mediavision, once a high-flying computer company, went out of business. While the riskiness of the market as a whole declines over time, an individual stock can do all sorts of alarming things—including disappear.

To dampen this risk, investors need diversification. How much? Not a great deal. Studies show that, if you own ten stocks in different industries, the risk in your portfolio—that is the severity of annual ups and downs—is nearly the same as if you owned one hundred stocks. Owning four stocks is about 40 percent less risky than owning one stock, but owning five hundred stocks is only 60 percent less risky. If you decide to own individual stocks, we suggest a mix of about twenty, with no more than three in one sector. But don't be in a rush. You can build to twenty slowly, starting with a half-dozen and adding one or two a year.

For a buyer of individual stocks, diversification can actually be dangerous since it is impossible for an amateur to know enough about a lot of companies to make good choices (and stick with them when the going gets tough). Even professionals prefer smaller portfolios. James Gipson, manager of the Clipper Fund, based in Beverly Hills, California, explains, "If you are intellectually honest with yourself, you'll admit that you don't have that many good ideas. So you serve your clients better by concentrating on your best ideas."

The famous British economist John Maynard Keynes, who was also a skilled investor, wrote in 1934:

As time goes on, I get more and more convinced that the right method in investment is to put fairly large sums into enterprises which one knows something about and in the management in which one thoroughly believes. It is a mistake to think that one limits one's risk by spreading too much between enterprises about which one knows little and has no reason for special confidence.

Warren Buffett is fond of quoting Mae West: "Too much of a good thing can be wonderful." And Peter Lynch likes to call spreading your money across too many stocks "diworseification." He adds, paraphrasing another Massachusetts savant, Ralph Waldo Emerson, "A foolish diversity is the hobgoblin of small investors."

Still, some diversification is a necessity to modulate risk. And for investors who don't have the time or the inclination to seek out individual stocks, the best way to achieve variety is through mutual funds.

WHAT'S A MUTUAL FUND?

A mutual fund is an investment company that exists solely to own financial assets and to pass virtually every dime of the earnings of those assets on to its own shareholders.

A fund is a pool. Shareholders put their money into the pool, and the manager of the fund uses the money to buy stocks, bonds, or what's called "cash"—usually certificates of deposit from banks or very short-term government securities, notably Treasury bills, which are IOUs that mature in less than one year.

At the start of 1999, a total of $3 trillion was invested in the 3,513 U.S. stock (or, as they are called, "equity") mutual funds. By contrast, in 1988, just $195 billion had been invested in only 1,011 equity funds.

The average stock fund owns shares in more than a hundred companies. A small investor could not get such broad diversification in any practical way. If, for example, you have $10,000 to invest, you could put an average of only $100 into each of 100 stocks; you might be able to afford one share of some stocks, nine shares of others and so on. The bookkeeping time and commission costs would be absurdly wasteful. Instead, a mutual fund itself, with $1 billion in assets, could invest $10 million in each stock. Your $10,000 would buy you a 1/100,000th share in the mutual fund, which also buys you a 1/100,000th share in each stock holding.

Consider the top holdings, on September 30, 1998, of the Clipper Fund:

• Philip Morris: 2.6 million shares at $46 per share = $119 million in market value, or 12.3 percent of the fund's total assets.

• Freddie Mac: 1.9 million shares at $49 per share = $94 million, or 9.8 percent of assets.

• Fannie Mae: 1.4 million shares at $64 per share = $89 million, or 9.2 percent of assets.

• Johnson & Johnson: 444,000 shares at $79 per share = $35 million, or 3.6 percent of assets.

• Nike, Inc.: 804,000 shares at $38 per share = $30 million, or 3.1 percent of assets.

On that one day, the market value of all nineteen stocks (plus cash) in Clipper's portfolio was $962 million. There were about 12.5 million shares outstanding, so the price per share of Clipper was $77. If you bought 125 shares at a total of $9,625, you would own 1/100,000th of all the assets.

Since the fund owned 2.6 million shares of Philip Morris, you would, in effect, own 26 of those shares, as well as 19 shares of Freddie Mac, 8 shares of Nike and so on.

But the fund's manager does not have to keep these five stocks in the portfolio all the time. He can buy and sell shares at will. He might dump all of his Philip Morris and purchase PepsiCo with the proceeds. Or sell 500,000 shares of Fannie Mae, the giant mortgage maker, keep the cash for a while, then use it a month later to buy 600,000 shares of Starbucks, the coffeehouse chain, at $50.

A mutual fund portfolio is continually changing. Turnover is typically 80 percent annually, which means that a manager holds the average stock for just fifteen months. Clipper's turnover averages about 50 percent. Check it out a year from now, and two or three of the top five stocks may be gone.

Also, the assets of a mutual fund rise and fall according to the purchases and sales of its own shareholders. When a fund becomes popular, money pours in from new investors and the fund issues new shares and buys more stock in the market with the proceeds. Between 1992 and 1998, for example, the total shares of Clipper quadrupled.

The manager of a popular fund has to put the additional money to work by buying more stock, either in companies he already owns or in new ones. But when investors sour on a fund, they can sell—or "redeem"—their shares at "net asset value," a figure determined each day (and reported in newspapers) by totaling up the market value of the stocks the fund owns and dividing that dollar amount by the number of shares the fund has outstanding.

Most equity funds keep a cushion of cash to cover possible redemptions, but investors have sometimes stampeded out of funds, forcing managers to dump their stock holdings in order to raise money to pay the departing hordes. In 1993, American Heritage Fund had 100 million shares outstanding, but, after losing 35 percent of its value the next year, it began losing shareholders too. By 1998, the fund had barely 16 million shares. To meet redemptions, the manager was forced to sell stocks on the way down. That is rarely a profitable pursuit, especially if the stocks are those of small companies with little "liquidity"—not much activity in a typical day. When managers need to sell illiquid stocks to meet redemptions, they have to take whatever price they can get from a buyer. Imagine if you had to sell your house tomorrow to raise cash—and buyers knew you were pressed.

One of the serious drawbacks of mutual funds is that, in a brief but severe market downturn, managers will be required—by panicky shareholders—to sell at the worst time. And they're selling *your* stocks! Smart investors hold on during corrections or bear markets, but if you own a fund, you may not have a choice.

DIFFERENT STYLES FOR DIFFERENT FOLKS

Equity funds have different objectives and styles. For example, growth funds seek capital appreciation—or an increase in the prices of the stocks they hold, without much regard for dividends. Aggressive-growth funds search for fast-growing, riskier stocks. Growth-and-income funds want growth plus moderate dividends, lately between 1 and 2 percent. Equity-income funds lean more toward companies that pay higher dividends and tend to own a high proportion of utility stocks and real estate investment trusts (REITs) with higher yields.

Other funds specialize in industry sectors. There are technology funds, REIT funds, utility funds, funds that own health care, Internet, or regional bank stocks.

Some funds own only small-company stocks—or, as they are called, small-cap (for "capitalization") stocks. Capitalization is a measure of a company's market value, or what investors believe it is worth. The figure is derived by multiplying the market price of a firm's stock by the number of shares outstanding. There is no standard definition, but these days, small-caps generally have caps under $1 billion and mid-caps have caps between $1 billion and $5 billion.

Other equity funds own only foreign stocks (the term of art here is "international funds") while others own both foreign and U.S. stocks (global funds). Mutual funds can specialize in regions, such as Latin America, or even large individual countries, such as Japan.

Managers have distinct styles, the main division being between those, like Robert Olstein of the Olstein Financial Alert Fund, who prefer "value" (stocks that carry low P/E ratios and other indicators that they may be overlooked bargains) and those, like Scott Schoelzel of Janus Twenty, who favor "growth" (stocks that may be expensive but have been roaring ahead, both in earnings and in price).

Morningstar, Inc., the excellent Chicago-based research firm with a subscription service that tracks mutual funds, invented a "style box" that gives nine separate designations, such as small-cap value or large-cap blend (between value and growth). Unfortunately, fund managers don't necessarily stick to the style with which they started. For instance, Legg Mason Value Trust, a fund that has been brilliantly successful in the 1990s under manager William Miller, has gradually migrated from value to growth. Its top five holdings at the beginning of 1999 included America Online, Dell Computer, and Compaq Computer—all go-go stocks. His shareholders aren't complaining about Miller's move; from the start of 1994 to the end of 1998, he quadrupled their money. But if their objective was to own some value stocks, Miller's fund no longer met the test.

Investors make money off mutual funds in two ways—from the increase in the fund's share price and from periodic distributions, usually in December, of capital gains and dividend income. Under the tax laws, mutual funds get special treatment: responsibility for taxes on gains and income is passed through to the shareholders. The fund doesn't pay the taxes, you do, and the consequences can be unsettling (as we'll explain below).

Other than this quirk, a mutual fund is a simple, useful device: a portfolio of stocks picked for you by an expert.

HOW FUNDS ARE MANAGED

But the experts have been turning in disappointing performances.

In eleven of the fifteen years from 1984 to 1998, a majority of fund managers failed to beat the S&P 500, the target for most equity funds.

For the year that ended on March 31, 1999, the average equity fund returned just 4 percent (in both price appreciation and dividends), according to Lipper, Inc., while the S&P returned 18 percent and the Dow returned 13 percent. For the past ten years, the average stock fund trailed both the S&P and the Dow by four full percentage points.

Why do managers have such a hard time beating the averages? One reason is that funds charge high fees and indexes don't have fees at all. When a mutual fund reports an annual return of 15 percent, expenses have already been subtracted out.

On average, according to the *Value Line Mutual Fund Survey,* diversified stock funds charge expenses that amount to 1.4 percent of their total assets. International stock funds charge even more—an average of 2 percent. If such a fund grosses 12 percent in a year, then one-sixth of those profits will go to pay its expenses.

Funds hit you with a management fee, which goes to the advisor who makes the stock picks; an administrative fee, to pay for the day-to-day operations of the fund; and a 12(b)-1 fee, named for a clause in securities law, which defrays marketing and distribution costs. (Yes, you are being charged for the cost the fund incurs to entice new investors—even though a bigger fund might not be in your best interest. The manager may find it harder to invest new money profitably.) In 1997, for example, the Kaufmann Fund listed such expenses as $9 million for ads in print, broadcast, and Internet outlets. That same year, the S&P outperformed the fund by twenty-two percentage points.

In addition, there are smaller expenses, mainly brokerage costs that are incurred when a fund buys and sells stocks. All of these costs get passed through to investors, reducing total returns. Think of it this way: A mutual fund with $2 billion in assets, charging 1.4 percent in expenses, is grossing $28 million for the benefit of the people who run it, plus another $4 million or so for the fund's brokerage firm.

Many funds also charge "loads," which are up-front (or, sometimes, back-end) commissions that often go to brokers. Loads have been declining in recent years, but they can still be steep. Pioneer Growth A, for example, charges a front-end load of 5.75 percent for typical accounts (very large accounts are charged less). Traditionally, loads are not subtracted when returns are computed. So, if you buy $10,000 worth of Pioneer shares, an expense of $575 is immediately deducted from your investment. If the fund rises 20 percent, your $10,000 becomes $11,310 instead of $12,000.

Often a fund with a big load will charge lower expenses. Thus, Investment Co. of America, a large fund rated "1" (best) for timeliness by Value Line, a service similar to Morningstar, has a load of 5.75 percent, but an expense ratio of just 0.6 percent—or less than half the average. Some funds, however, give their shareholders a double whammy. Federated Capital Appreciation, for instance, carries a load of 5.5 percent and expenses of 1.3 percent. The Securities & Exchange Commission offers an online calculator to figure the precise costs of these expenses to you: www.sec.gov/mfcc/mfcc-int.htm. The SEC says that the calculator answers such questions as "Which is better, a no-load fund with yearly expenses of 1.75 percent or a fund with a front-end sales charge of 3.5 percent?"

It would be logical to assume that funds that charge high expenses justify those costs by producing high returns. Not so.

We asked researchers at CDA/Wiesenberger, Inc., a Rockville, Maryland, firm that tracks mutual funds, to compare fees and performance. They found that a sample of 704 general-equity funds that charged expenses between 0.5 percent and 0.99 percent had average annual returns over a recent three-year period of 21.1 percent. But the 749 funds that charged between 1.5 percent and 1.99 percent had returns averaging just 18.7 percent.

Notice that the difference in returns—2.4 percentage points—is much larger than the difference in expenses alone, which averaged just one percentage point. So, on the whole, low-expense funds are not only cheaper, they are also better managed.

In another study, Financial Research Corp. looked at the performance of the best equity mutual funds—those rated four or five stars (tops) by Morningstar. The study found that "stock funds that charge the lowest fees normally generate the highest returns over time."

For example, in the large-cap blend category (portfolios that have both growth and value stocks, in roughly equal measure), the average return for funds in the quartile with the lowest expenses was 27.4 percent a year while the return for funds in the quartile with the highest expenses was 24 percent.

With small-cap funds, the discrepancy was even broader. The low-expense group averaged total returns of 151 percent over five years, but the high-expense group had returns of just 119 percent. "The results of our analysis," reported Financial Research Corp., "support the general theory that fund expenses erode performance. The extent to which that erosion occurs, however, is striking."

For followers of the Dow 36,000 Theory, expenses are especially important. The longer you hold stocks (and 36ers are long-term holders), the more returns between high-fee and low-fee funds diverge. Consider two funds. Each produces a gross average annual return of 12 percent, but one has an expense ratio of 2 percent of assets; the other, 1 percent. So, in one case, your returns are 10 percent of your initial investment per year while, in the other case, 11 percent.

In other words, it appears that the low-fee fund generates returns that are one-tenth higher than the high-fee fund. But, if you reinvest your dividends and gains in the fund (as most people do automatically and as all 36ers should), then, thanks to the miracle of compounding, over thirty years a one-time investment of $10,000 in the high-expense fund becomes $174,000 while the same $10,000 in the low-expense fund becomes $229,000—or about one-third more.

Still, the poor performance of mutual funds versus the stock indexes can't be explained entirely by expenses. For the past ten years, the S&P has beaten the typical equity fund by three percentage points, but expenses (including brokerage commissions) come to no more than two percentage points.

Again, don't scoff at that one-point difference. Over time, it means a great deal.

But where does it come from? One place is cash. To an alarming degree, fund managers try to time the market. When they think stocks are too high, they will build up cash reserves of 10 percent or more. At the end of 1998, Wallace Weitz, manager of Weitz Value Fund, held cash amounting to 19 percent of the total assets of his fund. He's a good stock picker, and as a result, his fund returned a hefty 29 percent that year, but he would have done better allocating all of his cash hoard to the stocks he owned.

When he managed Fidelity Magellan, the largest equity fund in the country, Jeff Vinik let his cash and bond holdings rise to more than one-third of his assets. He was anticipating a drop in the stock market. His timing was poor, but that's not the point. If stocks return 11 percent historically and cash returns less than 4 percent, then, on average, a fund manager will sacrifice 7 percentage points of returns when he moves into cash. Even if 90 percent of his portfolio remains in stocks, the sacrifice amounts to 0.7 percent—again, a significant number in the 36ers' world.

But even after accounting for fees and cash, we find that fund managers have been trailing the market over the past decade—largely because they make precisely the mistakes that 36ers should avoid:

• **They trade too much.** They try to time the market, jumping in and out of stocks. It is human nature to buy and sell when you shouldn't—purchasing shares when they have soared and dumping them when they have plummeted. While "buy low, sell high" sounds like a good credo, it is nearly impossible for anyone—including professional fund managers—to follow. Emotions get in the way. For that reason, a better credo is "buy anywhere, hold forever." Mutual fund managers have incentives to buy and sell that go beyond greed and fear. They believe it is their job. They are well paid to "manage" a portfolio. Their employers (not to mention shareholders in their funds) tend to define managing as buying and selling. They might look with displeasure on a manager who simply sits on his holdings for years.

• **They practice "diworsesification."** Fund managers own too many stocks. One reason is misguided Securities and Exchange Commission rules, which, with rare exceptions, require portfolios of at least two dozen companies. Another is the same impulse we just cited: Managers have to look as though they're managing. The result is funds like Kaufmann, with 217 holdings—impossible for most managers, or even teams of managers, to follow.

• **They just aren't good stock pickers.** Shocking, but true. Many fund managers are not adept at their chosen profession. Like sheep huddled on a hillside for warmth, they tend to do what their colleagues are doing. They don't want to stand out. In 1998, if a fund manager had returns of 15 percent, he could tell his boss, "Well, I trailed the S&P by double digits, but so did the majority of my peers." There's a strong tendency among managers to buy and sell the same stocks—to be "momentum players," following the direction of prices.

• **They are victims of a changing market.** While the S&P is the benchmark for most funds, it does not truly reflect the entire stock market. The index is composed, with some minor exceptions, of the five hundred largest stocks on U.S. exchanges. And it is cap-weighted, meaning that the companies with the highest market values have the most effect on its movements. For instance, the top ten companies— just 2 percent of all stocks on the index—represent 20 percent of the index's total assets. The top fifty companies represent a majority of the index's assets. In the mid- to late-1990s, larger companies outperformed smaller by a wide margin—an average of six percentage points annually between 1994 and 1998. Is this an aberration or a fundamental shift in the market? We think it is a little of both. So, to the extent that a fund owns smaller companies, it will trail the S&P 500.

UNIT INVESTMENT TRUSTS

One alternative to equity mutual funds that avoids some of the pitfalls is the unit investment trust (UIT) or defined portfolio. Like conventional funds, these are pools that use investors' money to buy stocks. But the roster of companies is meant to be fixed for a set duration. UITs, then, are buy-and-hold portfolios, usually with a theme. For example, in May 1999, the John Nuveen Co., based in Chicago, was offering a new "e-Commerce" UIT, consisting of 35 companies benefiting from the rise of the Internet and electronic business, including Amazon, AOL and Priceline. The portfolio terminates in two or five years (your choice), and, until that time, it is not intended to change in composition. Nuveen also sells a UIT based on the Dow 10 (Dogs of the Dow), a UIT comprising the 10 "most admired companies" in *Fortune's* annual survey (GE, Coke, Microsoft, etc.), and many others. Merrill Lynch's UITs include fixed portfolios chosen by quantitative methods plus funds that concentrate on sectors like health care, technology, and real estate.

The drawback of UITs, assembled by many large investment firms, is that they can be expensive. It's not unusual to pay 1 percent up-front and another 1.5 percent to 2 percent each year. But we would much rather pay higher fees for a sensibly run UIT than lower fees for a mutual fund run by a manic manager who can't stop trading.

CLOSED-END FUNDS

Another portfolio choice is the closed-end fund. While conventional mutual funds simply issue new shares as money pours in from new investors—or reduce their shares when investors cash in, or redeem—closed-ends function the way that individual stocks do. When they're launched, a certain fixed number of shares is issued. After that, the fund company steps aside and lets buyers and sellers find each other in an open market, usually the New York Stock Exchange.

While the price of a mutual fund share is determined by its "net asset value"—that is, the total value of all the shares of stock it owns—the price of a closed-end share is determined by the market's assessment of that share itself. Strangely enough, many closed-ends trade at big discounts to their net asset value. For example, the price of a share of Adams Express at the end of 1998 was 16 percent lower than the value of that share if Adams were to have liquidated all of the stocks it held and paid off its shareholders. Another closed-end that we admire, General American Investors Co., traded at a 12 percent discount.

One big advantage of a closed-end is that if disaster strikes, shareholders can't redeem their shares, forcing managers to sell good companies at bargain basement prices. (For that reason, closed-end funds are especially good vehicles for the stocks of a single country, such as Brazil or Taiwan, whose markets might be especially illiquid in a crisis.) Another plus is that expenses tend to be low—about 0.3 percent for Adams, 0.7 percent for General American, and 0.6 percent for another strong large-cap closed-end, Tri-Continental.

Since you buy closed-ends the way you buy stocks, you'll need to pay brokerage commissions. But even if you pay a broker 1 percent of the purchase price, you will pay less in fees and expenses over time than with conventional mutual funds. One drawback: While it would seem logical for discounts to narrow toward the true net asset value, they could do the opposite—widen. That has been the trend in recent years—for no discernible reason. Also, closed-ends suffer from the same management ills as their open-end counterparts. Of the twenty-three closed-ends that own diversified portfolios of U.S. stocks, twenty-two failed to beat the S&P over the three years from 1996 to 1998.

AVOIDING MANAGERS ENTIRELY

A simple solution to the problem of bad funds is to avoid managers entirely. Instead of buying funds managed by actual human beings, you can buy funds that are run by computers that have as their objective reflecting the market averages.

An index fund that is based on the S&P 500 won't beat the S&P 500, but it is guaranteed to trail it by no more than a few tenths of a percentage point—that is, by the expenses that the fund charges.

Founded in 1975, the Vanguard Index 500 Fund, the largest of its kind (and, after Fidelity Magellan, the largest fund, period), beat 88 percent of all mutual funds in 1998 and at least half of all funds in each of the years from 1992 to 1997. For the five years ending in June 1999, Index 500 beat all but one of the twenty-five largest funds. And for the ten years ending in 1998, it scored an average annual return 3.6 percentage points higher than the average stock fund. That's a huge difference. If you had invested $10,000 in the average fund in 1988, you would have accumulated $40,456 by 1998. But if you had invested the same amount in Index 500, you would have had $54,888—or 32 percent more.

In 1978, writing the third annual report for Vanugard Index 500, John C. Bogle, the firm's founder, twisted a famous quotation of Dr. Samuel Johnson, the eighteenth-century wit and lexicographer. Johnson called a second marriage "the triumph of hope over experience." But Bogle called his index fund "the triumph of experience over hope." While investors wish fervently that they can find a fund that can beat the averages, they rarely achieve this goal. Only 7 percent of all funds outperformed Index 500 for the twenty years ending in 1998.

Vanguard is a firm that emphasizes both index funds and low fees. For Index 500, it charges just 0.2 percent—or, in the language of Wall Street, 20 basis points (a basis point being one one-hundredth of a percentage point)—in expenses each year, mainly because Vanguard does not have to pay a fund manager. (Don't feel sorry for Bogle. With $80 billion in assets, Index 500 is grossing about $160 million a year.) Fidelity, in an attempt to crash Vanguard's market, was recently charging 19 basis points in expenses for its Spartan Market Index Fund. Both these funds—and other S&P funds like them—simply buy all the stocks in the S&P index, according to their weightings.

But the S&P 500, as we said, is *not* the market. Its 500 stocks in 1999 represented about three-quarters of the capitalization of all U.S. stocks, but that figure can rise or fall depending on the popularity of large-caps. The index has only a few mid-caps and even a stray small-cap. It is heavily tilted toward the New York Stock Exchange, the old-line market for stocks. Only 40 of the 500 companies are traded on the Nasdaq Stock Market, which was founded in 1971 and is still seen as a breeding ground for stocks that will "graduate" to the New York (though this is an outmoded concept today, since the Nasdaq is home to Microsoft, which in 1999 became the U.S. stock with the largest market cap) and only 2 on the American Stock Exchange, a market that now features energy stocks and some interesting specialty portfolios we'll get to later. The S&P 500 index has just one biotech firm (Amgen) and just 13 companies that it lumps in a category called "computers," which includes both hardware and software and even America Online. Meanwhile, the index is top-heavy with retailers (37 of them) and electric utilities (27).

For that reason, when we asked Bogle which index fund he would choose for himself if he had to pick just one, he rejected Index 500 for another of his firm's offerings, Total Stock Market Index. That fund is based on the Wilshire 5000 index, a concoction of a Beverly Hills firm called Wilshire Associates, that tries to capture the performance of every single stock on the three large U.S. exchanges. The title has become a misnomer as the markets have grown, and in early 1999 the Wilshire tracked 7,200 stocks—or more than 14 times as many as the S&P. Still, the 6,700 smallest stocks together accounted for only about one-fourth of the index's assets.

While the Wilshire has trailed the S&P, it has still beaten most mutual funds. An analysis by the firm found that the index outperformed two-thirds of all equity funds between 1984 and 1998. For the five years ending in 1998, Vanguard Total Stock Market fund returned 165 percent while Vanguard Index 500 returned 193 percent and the average fund returned 122 percent.

Like the S&P 500, the Wilshire is cap-weighted, so big companies have the most effect on the index's ups and downs. The top ten stocks on the S&P, remember, account for 20 percent of that index's capitalization; the top ten stocks on the Wilshire (the same stocks, of course) account for 15 percent. The Wilshire is simply more diversified, but not by much. But if small- and mid-cap stocks make a comeback after languishing in the late 1990s, then the Wilshire should rise more than the S&P. So, the Wilshire could be seen as a play on "reversion to the mean"—a bet on small-caps rising to their historic relationship with large-caps: Over the past seventy years, small stocks have beaten large, but at greater risk, or volatility.

But the Wilshire can also be seen as a "market-neutral" investment. If you believe in the random walk, you don't play favorites since the price of a stock today reflects all possible information. You can't predict a stock's next move, so it makes little sense choosing particular sectors of the markets. You want to expose yourself to the whole market, and the Wilshire, more than any other index, equals the whole market. It's the way to be a partaker, rather than an outsmarter.

Another popular index fund, which falls between the S & P 500 and the Wilshire in its intensity of large-caps stocks is Schwab 1000, composed of the 1,000 largest companies by market cap. It returned 175 percent for the five years ending in 1998.

Why buy the market? By "investing in an index fund," wrote Warren Buffett in the 1993 Berkshire Hathaway annual report, "the know-nothing investor can actually outperform most investment professionals. Paradoxically, when 'dumb' money acknowledges its limitations, it ceases to be dumb."

In other words, if you lack the time or the inclination to build your own portfolio of stocks, you can buy managed mutual funds—only a small proportion of which have outperformed the market since the mid-1980s—or, as Buffett suggests, you can buy the market itself, either through Vanguard Total or through a new fund that Wilshire itself mounted in 1999, Wilshire 5000 Index Fund.

It may be surprising, but neither the Vanguard nor the Wilshire fund owns every stock in the Wilshire index. There are just too many, and the smallest ones are so tiny they have little effect. Vanguard, at last count, owned 3,118 stocks, or about 30 times as many as the average equity fund. Wilshire owned about 2,000—the 1,000 largest, plus another 1,000 that attempt to mimic the characteristics of smaller stocks.

Another way to buy the market—or a big chunk of it—is through SPDRs (pronounced "spiders"), or Standard & Poor's Depositary Receipts, which trade on the American Stock Exchange under the symbol *SPY.* Similar to an open-end mutual fund like Vanguard Index 500, the SPDR is actually a long-term unit investment trust—in other words, a package of stocks intended to reflect the S&P 500 and changing only when the composition of the index changes.

SPDRs charge roughly the same expenses as the Vanguard index funds (18.5 basis points, or 0.185 percent), but of course, you have to pay a brokerage commission when you buy and sell them. They are more popular with traders than with long-term investors, but there's no reason you can't buy them online or through a deep-discount broker at a cost only slightly higher than that of open-end funds.

Another index portfolio that trades on the Amex, charges low expenses and resembles an SPDR is called the Diamonds Series Trust (symbol: *DIA*) which tracks the thirty stocks of the Dow Jones industrial average. Or you can buy an open-end fund such as Strong Dow 30 Value, which owns all the Dow stocks, but not in the same proportion as the index. Instead, a human manager, Charles Carlson, plays favorites and tries to beat the Dow as a whole.

Dow stocks have the characteristics 36ers should seek: long records of growing profits, decent dividends, and strong brand names. Over the ten years ending in 1998, the Dow stocks returned 19.8 percent, only a whisker behind the S&P. Given a choice, we would pick the Dow, which is a highly concentrated portfolio of just the kind of stocks we like, over the S&P.

THE MATTER OF TAXES

Another advantage of index funds—and SPDRs—is that they are tax-efficient. Since their portfolios are stable, changing only when the S&P does (the index normally adds or subtracts about twenty-five companies a year), the funds don't incur capital gains liabilities that are passed on to shareholders.

Capital gains are profits on the increased value of stocks, bonds, real estate, or other assets. One of the advantages of the law on gains is that you pay taxes only when you sell. If you buy individual stocks, you can let your capital gains build up—untaxed—until you decide on your own when to unload the shares. That decision can be based on personal considerations. For example, do you have any losses to offset the profits?

But if you buy mutual funds, you are letting someone else determine your annual tax liability—someone who, frankly, doesn't care whether you get clobbered on taxes. Most mutual fund managers (and the bosses who hand out their bonuses) are transfixed by only one number—total return—and that number is unaffected by matters of taxes. As John Rekenthaler, former editor of *Morningstar Mutual Funds,* put it, "Fund companies consider investor taxes unworthy of the attention of their investment managers."

Funds are required to distribute their net gains—profits minus losses—each year to shareholders in the form of dividends (also called "distributions"). Most shareholders ask the fund automatically to invest those dividends back into the fund—a good idea since it takes advantage of the miracle of compounding. But, unfortunately, even though the gains stay within the fund (that is, you never get a check), you still owe taxes.

Capital gains can be crushing—and they often have little to do with a fund's performance. Believe it or not, shareholders sometimes have to pay capital gains taxes on funds whose values have dropped during the year. For example, in 1998, the Oakmark Small-Cap Fund produced a loss of 13.2 percent. In other words, if you had bought $10,000 worth of shares of the fund at the start of the year, you could have sold them for just $8,680 at the end of the year. Yet—surprise!—investors in the fund were notified that they were responsible for capital gains of $2.11 for every share they owned. At a rate of 20 percent, that's 42 cents on a share that was trading at year-end at just $14.77. In other words, on that $10,000 investment, you found yourself with a tax bill for $284.

This was no fluke. In 1997, Invesco Asian Growth fell 39 percent, but it distributed capital gains that represented 21 percent of its assets, according to Morningstar. One Merrill Lynch fund dropped 41 percent that year but had taxable gains of 18 percent.

Talk about adding insult to injury! When a fund has a particularly bad year, its manager tends to dump old stocks in order to buy new ones. In fact, if the year is truly terrible, investors flee, demanding cash for their shares. The manager then has to sell stocks—even if she would rather not—to raise the money. If the fund has done well in the past, then many of the stocks in the portfolio have built up huge gains over the years. Selling them means incurring big tax liabilities.

Nearly all funds currently have large "unrealized appreciation" or gains—in other words, increases in the overall value of their portfolios. For example, at the start of 1999, Idex Growth Portfolio had unrealized gains amounting to 41 percent of its total assets. It doesn't matter when an investor buys a fund, he's still responsible for paying taxes on any gains that are realized—or cashed in—during a year in which he owns the fund.

A fund may have bought Coca-Cola stock in 1994 at $20 a share. If the fund sells all its Coke in 1999 at $70, then all shareholders in the fund—whether they owned the fund in 1994 or just bought it a few weeks ago—are responsible for paying taxes on the gains. That may sound unfair, but it's the way the law works.

Shareholders get credit for paying those taxes, lowering their tax bills when they eventually sell their shares. But a good rule is that you always want to pay taxes later rather than sooner. If you have to pay $1,000 to Uncle Sam today, then that money won't be earning profits for you.

The worst surprises greet investors who buy a fund toward the end of the year. Most funds make their distributions in late November or December, but don't announce them far in advance. So be wary of those months. You could invest $2,000 on Monday and find yourself with taxes on a $400 profit that is declared on Thursday.

There is no sure way to avoid being hit with a big tax bill from a fund, but the best protection is to stay away from managers who are addicted to high turnover. Funds that rarely sell shares rarely incur lofty gains. That is the advantage of index funds. In 1998, Vanguard's S&P 500 fund had turnover of only 4 percent while its Wilshire fund had turnover of 2 percent. By contrast, Fidelity Capital Appreciation fund had turnover of 199 percent, indicating that it kept the average stock just six months. (The fund owns shares in 217 different companies.)

Not all low-turnover funds are based on an index. Lexington Corporate Leaders has an average annual turnover of less than 1 percent.

Franklin Growth I, managed by Jerry Palmieri since 1965, never exceeds 10 percent in annual turnover. Mairs & Power Growth, a superb fund that specializes in companies headquartered in Minnesota, stays below 5 percent. And Burton D. Morgan, who runs a closed-end fund called Morgan Funshares, which was called "Sin Shares" before he took it public in 1994, sums up his philosophy this way: "Buy low and never sell." Fun (or Sin) stocks in the portfolio include companies involved in such pursuits as smoking (Philip Morris), drinking (Seagram), gambling (Harrah's Entertainment), and fornicating (Carter-Wallace, condom maker).

Of course, even a fund with low turnover can whack you with taxes if it sells a few stocks with huge gains. And that's a potential problem with a fund like Index 500. We can assume that the fund owns shares of General Electric purchased at $10 (adjusted for splits) and Coke at $5. (We can't know for sure because funds do not have to report this information.) It's unlikely that GE or Coke would be taken off the S&P index, but it's certainly possible that the fund will have to sell them in a market correction to meet redemptions.

Josh Charlson of Morningstar (which has an excellent website at www.morningstar.net) also warns that when a new manager takes over a fund, he frequently revamps the portfolio, tossing out stocks his predecessor bought—and incurring gains in the process. For example, in 1996, when Jeff Vinik left Fidelity Magellan, the new manager, Bob Stansky, made distributions of $12.85 a share (or about one-sixth of the stock price), the result of gains on stocks he wanted to purge that had been bought by Vinik.

Mutual funds also pass through dividends paid by their stock holdings—even though most shareholders direct that the dividends be used to buy new shares. Dividends are taxed at each shareholder's individual income tax rate, which can reach 39.6 percent in federal taxes alone. Short-term capital gains—for holdings of less than one year—are taxed at the income rate as well.

Of course, the easiest way to avoid the tax traps of mutual funds is to hold them in the tax-deferred part of your portfolio—in your IRA or 401(k) plan. But that's not always possible. In the meantime, just be careful. Paying taxes is bad enough, but paying taxes on gains in which you don't share is much worse.

FUNDS WITH MANAGERS

We agree with Buffett. The best mutual fund for many "know-nothing" investors who want to practice the Dow 36,000 Theory is a Wilshire index fund, an S&P 500 fund, or Amex Diamonds (the Dow package)—your choice. But we have not given up on funds managed by real human beings. Perhaps, contrary to Bogle's warning, we are letting hope rule experience, but we believe there are good funds out there for 36ers.

At the very least, you should become familiar with the best that's available. Even if you don't want to own funds, you should check the stocks that managers have in their portfolios. That's where we get some of our best ideas. (Funds have to report their holdings every six months.) Also, it is difficult for small investors to select stocks in certain sectors—especially small-caps and international stocks. If you want this kind of diversification (and you should), it is hard to avoid mutual funds.

But the managed funds to consider first are the ones that will form the foundation of your portfolio. Here are the attributes we look for in such a "core" mutual fund, one that could comprise your only long-term equity holding or, better yet, would be the main holding in a portfolio of three to six funds and ten to twenty stocks:

• **Solid performance over the past three to ten years.** We search for funds that have come within one percentage point of the returns of the S&P 500 at risk levels that aren't too high (both Morningstar and Value Line offer ratings that measure a fund's risk, or the volatility of its returns from year to year). Also, we generally disregard last year's record entirely and consider only the longer term. A good trick is to look at what the fund has done over the past three years and the past ten. That way, you can be sure the manager has fresh ideas but also has a substantial track record. We also look for funds with expense ratios under 1 percent. Some large fund houses, including Fidelity, have been cutting their expense ratios lately. Fidelity Blue Chip Growth fund, for instance, with an average annual return between 1989 and 1998 of 23 percent (compared with 19 percent for the S&P), charges just 0.7 percent in fees. Safeco Equity, whose twenty-year return trails the S&P by only half a point, has an expense ratio of 0.7 percent.

• **A concentrated portfolio.** While the average mutual fund holds 134 stocks, we prefer funds that own fewer than 40. A good example is Janus Twenty, with just 28 holdings (slightly more than the eponymous 20), which produced average annual returns of 30 percent, compared with 24 percent for the S&P, for the five years ending in 1998. Other excellent concentrated funds: Enterprise Growth, with returns of 26 percent; Clipper, at 21 percent (and low risk levels); and Marsico Focus, a newcomer that is managed by Tom Marsico, who used to run Janus Twenty (in 1998, Marsico's new fund returned 51 percent). The concentrated fund with the best long-term track record, managed by Bill Ruane, is Sequoia, which has been closed to new investors since 1982. (Funds close when their managers believe they can't put new money to work without hurting overall performance.) Ruane, at last count, owned only thirteen stocks, a list headed by Buffett's Berkshire Hathaway, which itself is a holding company that owns big chunks of businesses like Coca-Cola, Gillette, and the Washington Post Co.

• **Low turnover.** Even if you hold your mutual fund in a tax-free account, you should search for funds with low turnover. We agree with Philip A. Fisher, who wrote in *Common Stocks and Uncommon Profits* in 1958 that "it is only occasionally that there is any reason for selling at all." We're more confident in a manager who is confident in his own choices. A 36er certainly should not sell a stock with fast-growing earnings simply because it is considered "overpriced" in terms of its P/E ratio or its low dividend yield. As Fisher wrote, "If the growth rate is so good that in another 10 years the company might well have quadrupled, is it really of such great concern whether at the moment the stock might or might not be 35 percent overpriced?" Turnover at Tweedy Browne American Value, one of our favorite funds, has averaged a mere 9 percent since inception. Another excellent fund for 36ers is Kemper-Dreman High Return—which, using David Dreman's contrarian principles, has averaged 10 percent turnover since 1992.

• **A great manager.** Most mutual funds are the work of a single person or a small team. Find a great manager, and you'll find a great fund. Unfortunately, there aren't many—and the best of them seem to concentrate on value stocks, or what appear to be underpriced bargains. While we always look for good prices, value is less important than growth in the Dow 36,000 Theory. A stock that trades at a P/E ratio of just 8—and thus would be a value picker's dream—does not excite us if its profits aren't growing powerfully and consistently. We prefer a company whose earnings are zipping along at double digits, even it trades at a P/E of 40 or 50, because, over time, the fast grower will put more cash in your pockets. Of course, the ideal stock is one that is both cheap and red-hot. Still, we are fans of such value mavens as Bob Torray of the Torray Fund, Ron Yacktman of the Yacktman Fund, Marty Whitman of Third Avenue Value, and John Spears of Tweedy Browne. Other managers with strong track records: Mario Gabelli, who runs his own fund family; Mark Mobius, who specializes in Asian emerging markets for Franklin Templeton; and Marsico, one of the best growth-stock managers around.

A 36ER MUTUAL FUND PORTFOLIO

It's time to put principles into practice by looking at some of the best mutual funds. This is not meant to be a definitive list but a way to show you what is on offer and why index funds do not have to have a monopoly on your portfolio.

CORE FUNDS

The first step is to select a core fund (or even two or three). The fund should come from one of two categories—growth-and-income or growth.

Growth-and-income funds seek both capital appreciation (that is, rising prices) and a decent dividend payout—which, in 1999, would be in the area of 1.5 percent to 2 percent. Most such funds own large-cap stocks (since small-caps are less likely to pay dividends) and are less volatile than growth or aggressive-growth funds. Both of the big Vanguard index funds—*Index 500* and *Total Stock Market*—fall under the growth-and-income rubric, as does *Lexington Corporate Leaders.*

Another excellent choice for 36ers among managed funds is *T. Rowe Price Dividend Growth.* Its manager, William Stromberg, follows a simple, profitable strategy: investing in large-cap stocks that have a good track record of increasing their dividends at a rate above the market average—and good prospects for continuing that record. Stromberg especially likes companies with strong balance sheets (not much debt) and lots of free-cash flow (that is, no pressing need to invest a big portion of earnings back in the business). He wants firms that are free to reward their shareholders directly.

His portfolio in 1998 had few technology stocks (since they rarely pay dividends), stressing instead financial firms like Banc One Corp. and drug companies like Bristol Myers Squibb. The fund has a turnover of only about 30 percent a year and an expense ratio of just 80 basis points. It receives a top rating from both Value Line ("1") and Morningstar (five stars). Between 1994 and 1998, the fund returned an annual average of 21 percent, compared to 24 percent for the S&P. But its level of risk is one-third to one-half lower than the S&Ps. During the brief bear market of 1998, the fund lost 7 percent, compared with 12 percent for its peers. So it has another 36er virtue: With low volatility, it is less likely to scare investors into bailing out in rough times. T. Rowe Price, by the way, is an excellent fund house, with low fees and conservative growth-oriented management, in the tradition of its late namesake.

Fidelity, the largest fund firm, also offers a growth-and-income fund, called *Fidelity Dividend Growth,* which has a superb track record, whipping the S&P with a 27 percent average return for the five years ending in 1998. But manager Charles Mangum is not such a stickler for the "dividend" part of his fund's title. Many of his holdings, including number-one Microsoft, pay no dividends at all, and the fund's yield in 1998 was only 0.4 percent, compared with 2.2 percent for the T. Rowe Price fund. But Mangum justifies these picks with 36er reasoning. His strategy is to own stocks that have the potential for either dividend growth or dividend *commencement.* The expense ratio is only 0.7 percent, but turnover is high for our taste at 110 percent.

Another fine Fidelity choice is called, simply, *Fidelity Fund,* started in 1930 and still going strong. Over the past twenty years, it has trailed the S&P by only 0.4 percent. Manager Beth Terrana, who has run the fund since 1993, owns stocks that she believes combine both growth and value qualities: firms whose earnings are rising but whose possibilities are underappreciated by the market. Her portfolio, with turnover averaging about 100 percent, recently includes large doses of General Electric, Time Warner, Inc., and CVS Corp., the drugstore chain. The expense ratio is a mere 60 basis points, and both ratings services give the fund their highest scores.

While we shy away from new funds, *TIAA/CREF Growth & Income,* is an exception. The world's largest private pension system, which provides for the retirement of 2 million employees of universities and similar nonprofits, opened its funds to the public in 1997, and results have been dazzling. The CREF style is to invest partly in the S&P index (at least 20 percent of assets) and partly in stocks that help beat it. The fund emphasizes large-caps that pay modest dividends but have fast-growing earnings. Two attractions are a low initial investment requirement—just $250, or one-tenth the minimum for Fidelity funds—and rock-bottom expenses of 43 basis points. The Growth & Income fund returned 31 percent in 1998, its first full year.

Growth funds can also be core holdings but, first, some nomenclature. The term "growth" is often used in opposition to "value." A growth stock is one whose earnings are moving up smartly, but whose price—as measured by P/E, for example—seems high. Value stocks, on the other hand, have low P/Es and usually less earnings growth as well. They are overlooked bargains, languishing now but (investors hope) soaring soon—and probably becoming growth stocks themselves. But the term "growth fund" does not refer to the characteristics of the stocks in a manger's portfolio. Instead, it simply means a fund which, like a growth-and-income fund, mainly owns U.S. large-cap stocks, but which concentrates on capital appreciation and pays little or no attention to dividends. At the start of 1999, growth funds held $890 billion in assets; growth-and-income funds, $1 trillion. Together, the two categories accounted for nearly two-thirds of all the money invested in stock funds.

As we have shown, for most good companies, P/E ratios can triple or quadruple without causing concern, so our own bias is for growth funds that lean toward growth stocks. A good core package could include both a growth-and-income fund (which, since its dividend yields are higher, will probably lean more toward value) and a growth fund.

For years, our favorite growth fund has been *Fidelity Contrafund,* which, despite its name (the implication is that it is "contrarian," or value-oriented), mainly owns growth stocks. For the ten years ending in 1998, it beat the S&P by four percentage points annually and its peers by seven points—and at risk levels lower than average. But there's a catch: The fund is closed to new investors. The good news is that Fidelity has launched a *Contrafund II,* run by Jason Weiner, a disciple of the original fund's legendary manager, Will Danoff. Contra II comes highly recommended by Eric Kobren, who runs *Fidelity Insight,* an independent newsletter that keeps an eye on Fidelity funds. The drawback, however, is a 1.2 percent expense ratio, coupled with a 3 percent front-end load.

Another growth fund, *Dreyfus Appreciation,* may turn out to be a better performer for 36ers than Contrafund itself. It has several advantages to start: an expense ratio of 0.9 percent (with no load), incredibly low turnover of under 5 percent annually and a relatively small portfolio of seventy stocks, the top eighteen of which account for more than half the fund's assets. For the ten years ending in 1998, the fund almost precisely matched the S&P, but with lower volatility. The managers, Christopher Sarofim and Russell Hawkins, who took over in 1990, have a simple philosophy: Buy great companies with fast-growing profits and hold them forever: Pfizer, Coca-Cola, Intel, Johnson & Johnson. . . . Like most growth funds, the dividend yield is minimal—only 0.6 percent recently—but we would rather have companies like these reinvest our money in the business, so we can take our dividends later. By the way, Hawkins also directs *Dreyfus Premier Worldwide Growth,* a superb global fund that owns both U.S. and foreign stocks. It, too, has had turnover in the single digits, and for the five years ending in 1998 it has ranked in the top 1 percent of its category. Hawkins once told us that high P/E ratios don't bother him: "If you've got good visibility of earnings, there aren't many stocks that are too expensive." By "visibility," he means likelihood or predictability. With great companies, growth, in other words, trumps price—a good credo for 36ers.

The number-one growth fund over the past ten years has been *Janus Twenty,* with a highly concentrated portfolio (the top ten stocks represent 57 percent of assets) of brand-name growth stocks. In 1997, Scott Schoelzel succeeded Tom Marsico, who had managed the fund for a glorious decade. Schoelzel did even better, and for the three years ending May 1999 Janus Twenty had scored average annual returns of 42 percent vs. 28 percent for the S&P. The new manager has focused on technology stocks and pharmaceuticals, including Dell Computer, Microsoft, America Online, Pfizer, and Warner-Lambert. At the end of 1998, his average company had a P/E ratio of 51. Does a "high" P/E like this mean high volatility? Not necessarily. In the third quarter of 1998, while the S&P was tumbling 10 percent and nearly every fund was down double digits, Janus Twenty lost a mere 1.5 percent. Again, 36ers take note: Growth and risk are not always companions. Despite this amazing success, the fund has an expense ratio under 1 percent.

A rival for Janus Twenty in the future may be the *Guinness Flight Wired Index Fund.* This is a new fund, launched in late 1998, so there's not much of a track record. In addition, it charges 1.4 percent in expenses, about average for all funds but too high for a passively managed index fund. (Fees should come down as the fund grows and fixed costs get spread over more shareholders.) The attraction of the fund is that it offers a list of forty stocks, brilliantly chosen by the editors of *Wired* magazine, the hip high-tech monthly, to serve as a bellwether for the new economy. Think of the list as a sort of Lexington Corporation Leaders for the next millennium. The emphasis is on technology with such selections as Yahoo! Inc., the search-engine portal, and Microsoft, but the list also includes more traditional but still innovative firms, including AMR Corp., parent of American Airlines and principal owner of the Sabre computerized reservation system; Nucor Corp., the mini-mill steel producer; Wal-Mart, whose use of information technology has allowed it to cut inventories but still keep shelves full; and Walt Disney Co., the diversified media firm that owns ABC Television.

A more traditional growth fund with a spectacular track record is *Merrill Lynch Fundamental Growth,* with returns of more than 30 percent in three of its first four years of existence, 1995 to 1998. The fund, in its no-load "B" version, has whipped the S&P despite an expense ratio of 1.9 percent annually. (An "A" version carries a load and lower yearly expenses.) The manager, Lawrence Fuller, shifted in early 1999 from technology and retail to telecommunications and financial stocks because he thinks the last two groups are better bargains. Still, his turnover in 1998 was a relatively low 40 percent, and his style is strictly large-cap growth, with such holdings as Pfizer, AT&T, and Disney. The fund is top-rated by both Morningstar and Value Line.

If you are looking for a single value fund among the growth funds, our top pick is *Babson Value,* whose manager, Nick Whitridge, says he "is not sailing in the part of the ocean where the fair winds are blowing." That can mean having a year like 1998, when the fund returned only 6 percent, or less than half the average of its peers and less than one-quarter the S&P's gains. Top holdings at the end of that year included SLM Holding Corp., which provides student loans; Chase Manhattan Corp.; and E.I. du Pont de Nemours, the chemical company. All were out of favor, compared with tech stocks and hot consumer companies, but that's the point, and for the first five months of 1999, the fund easily outstripped the S&P. Babson has posted excellent numbers since 1984; expenses are under 1 percent; and turnover averages less than 10 percent.

Finally, there is Bill Miller of *Legg Mason Value Trust,* whom some consider the next Peter Lynch, a fund manager with the golden touch. Miller in 1998 achieved the incredible feat of beating the S&P eight years in a row. He has slowly moved the fund from value stocks to growth, but he contends that the companies he owns, including Dell and America Online, combine both qualities—which is just as a 36er would want. Turnover is only 15 percent annually. Expenses are a stiff 1.8 percent, but Value Trust returned 635 percent between 1989 and 1998, more than twice the rate of the average fund.

AGGRESSIVE-GROWTH AND SMALL-CAP FUNDS

After picking one to three core funds, 36ers can move on to diversify into specific sectors or styles. For example, if you pick a conservative core fund like T. Rowe Price Dividend Growth or Babson Value, you'll need to spice up your portfolio with a fund in a category called "aggressive growth"–an ill-defined group that tends to have lower dividend yields (if any dividends at all) and particularly high valuations.

One of the best such funds is *Transamerica Premier Aggressive Growth,* started in 1997 by the San Francisco insurance and asset management company. Although the fund is new, its manager, Philip Trieck, has been running portfolios for more than a decade, with great success. This concentrated fund (his top eight holdings represent half the assets) typically owns a delightful mix of stocks, which recently ranged from Amazon.com to Berkshire Hathaway to a small-cap health care firm called Alternative Living Services, Inc. Since the selections are so quirky, investors simply have to have faith in Trieck, which is not difficult considering the 84 percent return the fund scored in 1998, its first full year. Trieck's specialty is understanding Internet stocks—a subject in which most fund managers are not well-versed. Turnover is low, but expenses are on the high side at 1.4 percent.

Another aggressive-growth fund to consider is *Spectra,* which, for the twenty years ending in 1998, had beaten the S&P by nearly four percentage points annually, on average. Managed for the past thirteen years by David Alger, the fund, with a five-star rating from Morningstar, has produced hefty but highly volatile returns, mainly with large-cap growth stocks. One drawback is Alger's penchant for high turnover (he holds the average stock for eight months) and the fund's lofty expense ratio (over 2 percent). But in this case, as with the Merrill and Legg Mason funds, you get what you pay for. Through the five years ending in March 1999, Spectra returned an annual average of 31 percent, compared with 26 percent for the S&P 500. Alger seems to have at least some of the 36er spirit. After the Dow first broke 10,000 in March 1999, he wrote investors, predicting that the index would break 20,000 within five years. Our own timetable is swifter.

Up to now, all of our funds have specialized in large-cap stocks. But investors also need to diversify into small-caps, despite their poor performance in the late 1990s. From the start of 1994 to the end of 1998, the Russell 2000 small-cap index returned an annual average of 13 percent while the S&P returned 24 percent. But from 1991 to 1995, the figures were almost exactly reversed: Small-caps returned 25 percent; large-caps, 17 percent. And those weren't the widest discrepancies. From 1974 to 1978, according to Ibbotson, small-caps returned an annual average of 24 percent while large-caps returned just 4 percent. Then, from 1986 to 1990, large-caps ruled, 13 percent to 1 percent.

The point is that small-caps and large-caps move in cycles. Just when investors are about to give up on a sector, it rebounds. And it's important to recognize that, again according to Ibbotson, small-caps have outperformed large-caps over the past three-quarters of a century, 13 percent to 11 percent—though at higher risk.

Skyline Special Equities is among the best of the small-caps, with ten-year returns (through 1998) only one percentage point behind the S&P. Bill Dutton is a value manager who owns fairly boring companies like New England Business Service, Inc., a direct marketer of business forms, checks, and envelopes. A more aggressive small-cap fund with an excellent track record is *Ivy U.S. Emerging Growth,* which in the third quarter of 1998 lost 18 percent and then in the fourth quarter gained 31 percent—for an overall return of 18 percent in a year the Russell 2000 was losing money. In early 1999, the top holding for manager James Broadfoot was Seriologicals Corp., which sells specialty human antibodies to health care companies. In early 1999, it was trading at a P/E of 17, despite an annual earnings growth rate of 30 percent—that's value plus growth. A third small-cap fund we favor is *CGCM Small-Cap Equity,* which is managed by a consortium of three firms. With a "2" rating from Value Line (highest for a small-cap), it carries an expense ratio below 1 percent and turnover in the 50 percent range. About half the assets in the fund attempt to repeat the performance of the Russell 2000; the rest try to beat it, which has been done impressively.

SECTOR FUNDS

Funds that concentrate on individual sectors abound, with *Fidelity* offering the most in its "Select" series. Three such funds topped Lipper's charts for the highest returns over the ten years ending in June 1999: *Select Electronic* (which rose by a factor of 16), *Select Computer* (by 14), and *Select Technology* (by 12). It's hard to go wrong with these, but another good way to buy technology is through a spider-style trust called *Nasdaq 100 Shares,* which trades on the American Stock Exchange under the symbol *QQQ.* It owns a portfolio made up of the stocks of the Nasdaq 100 index, which is heavily weighted toward high-tech companies. Microsoft, Intel, Cisco Systems, Dell, and MCI World-Com alone make up more than 40 percent of the assets.

Sector funds work best for industries you want to own but have a tough time analyzing. One example is real estate. It is difficult for the average investor to understand the portfolio of a real estate investment trust (REIT), a company that owns properties or mortgages. Instead, rely on managers like Martin Cohen and Robert Steers, who began running *Cohen & Steers Realty Shares,* the largest REIT fund, in 1991. *Fidelity* also has a REIT fund called *Real Estate Investment Portfolio,* with no load and an expense ratio of less than 1 percent. (The Select funds usually carry a load of 3 percent plus high expenses; Select Computers charges 1.3 percent, for example.) Another well-run REIT is *Longleaf Partners Realty,* with expenses of 90 basis points and low levels of risk.

REITs fell sharply out of favor in 1997 and 1998, and while they seem to be sluggish value-style funds, we think 36ers should consider them. In fact, REITs do something magical. They pass on 95 percent of their earnings to their shareholders each year, through dividends and capital gains, so they retain only a tiny bit of their reported profits. Still, they have managed to increase their earnings nearly every year—often by double digits. For example, at the start of 1999, REITs were expected to yield an average of 7 percent while boosting their earnings by 10 percent. Like small-cap stocks, REITs should come back into favor, but they should comprise no more than 5 percent of your portfolio.

Another sensible category for sector funds is health—especially biotech, a field that amateurs can't really fathom. The best of the funds is *Fidelity Select Biotechnology,* which began operations in 1985. Rajiv Kaul, the manager, has heavy weightings in the obvious suspects— Amgen, Biogen, and Genentech—but also invests in large pharmaceutical houses such as Merck & Co. and small-cap research firms. Returns for the ten years ending in 1998 easily beat the S&P, but volatility has been wild. Like most sector funds, this one is to have and to hold. *Vanguard* offers a broader fund called *Specialized Health Care,* with no load and a minuscule expense ratio of 40 basis points. Between 1989 and 1998, it returned an annual average of 24 percent, compared with 19 percent for the S&P. Or consider the pharmaceutical UIT offered by Nuveen and health care UITs from Merrill Lynch and other firms.

One sector we avoid is natural resources. These stocks rise and fall with the prices of commodities—energy, precious metals, and the like. While we are not averse to owning strong integrated oil companies like Exxon, betting on the rising prices of *things* is less productive than investing in the minds of smart people. If you own a single such fund, it should be *T. Rowe Price New Era,* which, in mid-1999, was making a strong comeback with its broad holdings in depressed energy and oil service stocks. The fund was started in 1969 and has achieved creditable returns (though still four points below the S&P over the past twenty years) at an expense ratio of less than 0.8 percent.

FOREIGN-STOCK FUNDS

With foreign stocks, there are four choices: (1) global funds, which own a mix of U.S. stocks and those of other countries, (2) international funds, which own strictly foreign stocks, (3) regional funds, which own the stocks of individual companies or areas, and (4) emerging-markets funds, which own shares of companies in less developed countries.

Among global funds, it's hard to beat *Dreyfus Premier Worldwide Growth,* which we mentioned above. We are also impressed with *Mutual Discovery,* a value-oriented fund managed by David Marcus and Rob Friedman. Its focus is European conglomerates like Suez Lyonnaise des Eaux in France and Montedison in Italy, whose managers are beginning to sharpen their focus and run companies for the benefit of shareholders—aiming for earnings rather than market share, a new concept for much of Europe and Japan. The best returns in recent years have been achieved by *Idex Global Portfolio,* which, like Mutual Discovery, has about one-third of its money in U.S. stocks and nearly all the rest in Europe. The fund, managed by Helen Young Hayes, has consistently outperformed its peers. Hayes also co-manages *Janus Overseas,* a no-load fund with expenses under 1 percent annually and sparkling returns. A lower-risk fund is *Tweedy Browne Global Value,* run by a venerable Wall Street firm with ties to the great Benjamin Graham. The fund looks for value stocks around the world, without regard to country. Top holdings range from Compagnie Financiere Richemont, a Swiss firm with broad interests, to Singapore Press Holdings. Our final choice is *Templeton Growth,* founded in 1954 by the brilliant stock picker Sir John Templeton, who is now retired. His successor, John Holowesko, follows the master's bottom-up (that is, stock- rather than country-oriented) strategy of looking for fast-growing companies that are being ignored by the market. He keeps both risk and turnover low.

A drawback of global funds is that managers have complete discretion over where to put your money. Some have half their funds in U.S. stocks; others just 10 percent. As a result, getting true geographic diversification is difficult. Another drawback of all funds that own foreign stocks is exposure to currency fluctuations. A few funds, including Tweedy Browne's, are fully hedged (that is, protected) against a drop in the value of foreign currencies (but don't gain if the currencies rise).

One of the best international (that is, all-foreign) funds is *Artisan International,* whose chief stock picker, Mark Yockey, was named "manager of the year" in 1998 by Morningstar. Founded only in 1995, the fund is in the top 1 percent of its peer group, according to Value Line. Yockey shifts his money around among countries (turnover is 100 percent), but he has recently focused on Europe. Average annual returns for the three years ending in early 1999 beat the Morgan Stanley foreign-stock index by a whopping fifteen percentage points. *Montgomery International Growth,* managed by John Boich and Oscar Castro, has a track record that nearly matches Artisan's, but with a portfolio that has more diversification across regions. Both the funds, however, have expense ratios over 1.5 percent and turnover over 100 percent. We are also impressed with *Goldman Sachs International Equity,* with lower turnover. And *Vanguard International Growth,* which has soundly whipped the foreign indexes over the past ten years and carries expenses of only 0.6 percent; manager Richard Foulkes keeps his average stock for three to four years. Top holdings run from Japan's Fuji Photo Film to France's Vivendi, which operates water utilities around the world.

All of the Asian funds have suffered in the past decade. The top performer, *Merrill Lynch Pacific,* has returned an annual average of only 6 percent for the ten years ending in February 1999. The fund, founded in 1976, has nearly three-quarters of its assets in Japan, which, like Europe, appears on the brink of a managerial revolution similar to the one in the United States in the 1980s. The result will almost certainly be a lower risk premium and higher stock prices. *GAM Pacific Basin* fund, managed by Michael Bunker, has beaten the Morgan Stanley Asian index by nine percentage points on average over the past ten years, but returns have still been under 5 percent annually. Still, it is a good place to be when Asia roars back.

T. Rowe Price European is probably the best managed fund specializing in the continent, with returns averaging 24 percent annually between 1994 and 1998 and an expense ratio of just 1 percent—about half the level of its peers' charges. *Vanguard International Equity Index European* takes a passive approach, with expenses of 28 basis points and turnover of 4 percent. Its returns have closely matched those of the Price fund.

You can buy emerging markets by country, mainly with closed-ends like the *Singapore Fund* and the *Mexico Fund;* by region, with funds such as *Scudder Latin America* or *Matthews Pacific Tiger* (Korea, Hong

Kong, etc.); or by category, with funds that own stocks of smaller economies around the world, such as *Templeton Developing Markets* and *AIM Developing Markets.*

Exactly how to divide up your assets among these fund categories is the subject of Chapter 14. But here's a preview: The bulk of a 36er's holdings should be in large-cap growth and growth-and-income funds—or in large-cap growth stocks themselves. Which ones? We'll tell you in the next two chapters.

CHAPTER 12

Getting Started in Stocks

As one goes through life, it is extremely important to conserve funds, and one should never spend money on anything foolish, like pear nectar or a solid-gold-hat. . . . Finally, let us bear in mind that it is easier to spend two dollars than to save one. And, for God's sake don't invest money with any brokerage firm in which one of the partners is named Frenchy.

          —Woody Allen, *Without Feathers*

Buying individual stocks means taking a lot more initiative, time, and trouble than buying a mutual fund. Why do it? We'll give you five good reasons. Then we'll tell you all you need to get started. And, in the next chapter, we'll tell you which stocks to buy.

So, why stocks?

REASON 1. WHEN YOU BUY STOCKS YOU ALWAYS KNOW WHERE YOUR MONEY IS

When you buy a mutual fund, you are putting your trust in a manager. You can look at the manager's history and get a sense of how he will behave under fire, and you can read the fund's prospectus and note its limitations—but they are rarely narrow. Funds allow themselves enormous flexibility in where they can invest your money. Even if you choose a fund with a good track record and a consistent style (for instance, a propensity to buy large-cap value stocks), the manager, like any other investor, may change his approach at just the wrong time or, worse, dump stocks in favor of bonds or cash.

Look what happened in 1997 to an excellent manager named Foster Friess. From 1988 to 1996, Friess compiled an amazing record with his

Brandywine Fund, beating the S&P in seven of nine years, often by a wide margin. He was a terrific stock picker with an eye for high-tech growth companies. Every portfolio needs an aggressive-growth fund, and Brandywine, for many years, filled the bill.

But shortly after the frightening downdraft on October 27, 1997, Friess, apparently fearing that stocks were entering a bear market, shifted out of high-tech—and out of equities. At the start of 1997, Brandywine had 99 percent of its $8 billion in assets in stock and 1 percent in cash, but by the end of the year, the fund had just 46 percent in stock and an incredible 54 percent in cash and commercial paper (short-term loans to corporations). Mainly as a result, Brandywine investors were treated to a total gain of just 12 percent in 1997, a year in which the S&P returned 33 percent despite that 554-point one-day loss. In 1998, Friess persisted in cash, then switched to stocks just before the market declined sharply in the summer. It was an adventure in terrible market timing. Brandywine ended up with a loss of 0.7 percent in a year in which the S&P returned 29 percent. Redemptions in 1998 cost Brandywine nearly half its total assets.

Earlier, we mentioned Jeff Vinik, who became Peter Lynch's successor at the helm of Fidelity's flagship fund, Magellan. Vinik had a strong track record as a picker of large-cap stocks when he ran Fidelity's Contrafund and Growth & Income fund. When he moved to Magellan, he started off beating the market. But in 1996, he switched almost one-third of the fund's assets into bonds. It was a bad call: Bonds fell while stocks boomed. Since Vinik, like Friess, made a market timer's bet against stocks at just the wrong time, Magellan became one of the worst-performing large funds in America. Many shareholders were enraged. They had given Vinik their money because they thought he was investing in stocks. They had already allocated portions of their portfolios to bonds. (Since Vinik's departure, the fund has gotten back on track, returning 34 percent in 1998.)

Other mutual funds simply switch focus. For example, Arthur Moretti, manager of Merrill Lynch Growth Fund, which once had $5 billion in assets, moved heavily into oil and gas stocks, thinking they were bargains. By the end of 1998, 37 percent of his assets were in energy companies like Tidewater, Inc., the petroleum services firm, and Apache Corp., which explores for natural gas. By comparison, only 7 percent of the value of the S&P 500 index was in energy stocks. A fund with "Growth" in its name became an extreme hunter of value, betting that the earnings of depressed energy companies would improve as oil prices rose. The result: devastation. The fund fell 24 percent in 1998, trailing the S&P by more than 50 percentage points after trailing it by 16 points the year before. As with Brandywine, shareholders voted with their feet, and in little over a year, the fund's assets fell to $1.5 billion and a new manager was installed.

The simple fact is that mutual funds have very few constraints. Managers and strategies change, and there is no guarantee that the fund will continue to do what you thought it would do when you gave it your money. If you invest in individual stocks yourself, you can be sure you are fully invested at all times. You can be sure, as well, that if you want half your money in growth stocks and half in value, no one will ignore your decision. Ambrose Bierce, the great American aphorist, in 1906 defined finance as "the art or science of managing revenues and resources for the best advantage of the manager." Buying individual stocks allows you to be your own manager, keeping your own interests first.

REASON 2. YOU CAN PUT THE DOW 36,000 THEORY TO WORK

Of the more than three thousand equity mutual funds, none bases its strategy on the Dow 36,000 Theory—not yet, anyway. There are good choices, as we noted in the last chapter: index funds and managed funds such as T. Rowe Price Dividend Growth and Transamerica Aggressive Growth. But none is a true 36er fund. If you buy individual stocks, however, you can make your own selections using the principles laid out in this book.

For instance, we have shown that a sensible price-to-earnings ratio for a mature, income-generating stock that has posted healthy dividend or earnings growth is around 100. Even in the "overvalued" late 1990s, the P/E for the market as a whole was less than 30. But many managers remained reluctant to invest in high-P/E stocks.

If we were building a mutual fund, one of the first stocks on our list would be Johnson & Johnson, the health products company, which in May 1999 was trading at a P/E ratio of 31 (based on projections of its earnings for the full year). That is well below what we consider the fair price of a mature, income-generating stock. The company is a very steady grower, with a portfolio—including Johnson's Baby Shampoo, Tylenol, the contraceptive Ortho-Novum, and the anti-wrinkler Retin-A—that is nearly guaranteed to stand the test of decades and provide healthy earnings growth for many years. Johnson & Johnson in recent years has been increasing its profits at a rate of 13 percent annually, but even if the growth rate falls by half, the stock deserves a P/E of well over 100.

J&J's dividend has also been a marvel. It has grown from 25 cents to $1.12 in ten years—a rate of increase of 16 percent annually. The yield in mid-1999 was 1.2 percent, but, if you had bought J&J shares a decade ago, the yield in 1999 on your original investment would be more than 10 percent.

Johnson & Johnson is underpriced by a significant margin. If you buy an index fund—or a fund run by a good manager—you will certainly get some stocks like J&J. But if you invest in individual stocks, you can weight your portfolio heavily toward such 36er stocks—with strong, consistent growth and great brand names.

REASON 3. STOCKS INSTILL DISCIPLINE

Deciding which stocks to purchase is less important than making your relationship with the stocks you own as profitable as possible. And for many investors, stocks help cement that relationship better than mutual funds.

Here's what we mean: The market will always have ups and downs. When it drops suddenly, you may feel a strong urge to sell some of your shares. If you act on that urge, you will lock in losses forever. If you sell in order to wait until things look better, you are likely to re-enter the market after a big surge, buying long after the best gains are behind you.

Such behavior explains the findings of the Dalbar survey that found that actual-investor returns were less than one-fourth of market returns—because investors sell and buy at the wrong time, instead of just holding.

But why do individual stocks encourage long-term holding?

Suppose you put all of your money in a single index fund. A few years after you enter the market, a crash like the one in the fall of 1987 knocks the market down 30 percent, wiping out almost all of your gains. The newspapers are filled with stories that the end is near. Articles remind readers that back in 1929 small investors thought that the damage was over after the market had dropped 30 percent, but in fact severe declines continued. It wasn't until 1931, more than a year after the great crash, that stocks fell the most: 43 percent. Is today different? (In September 1988, after stocks had fallen 18 percent in the preceding twelve months, *Time* magazine ran a cover story titled, "Buy Stocks? No Way." The article told readers that "the market has become a crap-shoot" and that "the small investor has become an endangered species.")

Frightened investors will decide that they can't bear the thought of losing any more money, that the risks of stocks just aren't worth the rewards. Selling is easy. Pick up the phone. It's a free call, and most mutual funds don't even charge you a redemption fee. Also, selling an index fund means abandoning an abstract concept, not a flesh-and-blood, brand-named corporation. That makes bailing out even easier. Of course, the investor who is fleeing is probably figuring she will get back in—when stocks are safe again. But, as Fisher says, this strategy rarely works. (By the way, immediately after the scary *Time* cover was published in 1988, the market bounced back, returning 46 percent in the next twelve months.)

Suppose that instead of investing in an index fund, you decided to buy a diversified portfolio of twenty stocks that you picked yourself. You also asked your stockbroker to reinvest your dividends each quarter. Now, when the panic hits the market, you have a much more difficult decision to make. Getting out requires twenty transactions—the sale of each stock. Even if you manage your funds using a discount broker that charges $10 a transaction, you will have to pay $200 to liquidate your position. There's another reason to pause: If you sell, your tax return will be a nightmare to compile.

If you sell 100 shares of a stock that has gone up a dollar a share since you bought it, you have a capital gain of $100. When you file your Form 1040, the Internal Revenue Service will want to know how long you held the stock and will charge you a capital gains tax accordingly. Rates are lower for stocks that are held longer. If you sell twenty different companies, each transaction may have its own tax rate, and getting the information and figuring out what you owe could take hours or days. If you reinvested your dividends, then the situation is even more complicated. Some of the shares of, say, Exxon, were held for three years, some for only a month. The vintage matters to tax collectors—and the gains for each clump of only a few shares will be different.

This complexity can be used to your advantage. By reinvesting dividends steadily, and investing in stocks instead of mutual funds, you have built a structure that will be difficult to dismantle if you get the urge to sell. You will have to pay large transaction fees and condemn yourself to a weekend shuffling tax forms—and if you have a full-service broker, you'll have to place the sell order with a real-live person.

Your broker, if she is a good one, will say, "Now, hold on. Are you sure you want to sell now? Why?" Also, you will have to dump stocks with which you have developed a personal relationship. It's easier to love Johnson & Johnson than it is to love an index fund. Yes, you might sell, but the odds of your finding the strength to ride out the bad times will improve dramatically.

In other words, by investing in individual stocks, you set yourself up to succeed. By investing in mutual funds—especially funds you buy directly, without an adviser as intermediary—you make failure easier.

REASON 4. STOCKS ARE FUN

One of the miracles of the stock market is that anyone with a few hundred bucks can become a partner in a great business. You might not be able to join an exclusive country club without the right social credentials, but the only barrier to joining (and that's the word) General Electric is the price of one share of stock. J.P. Morgan & Co., America's most prestigious large bank, may not accept you as a client, but it can't stop you from becoming a partner. Amazon.com is one of the most fascinating businesses the world has ever seen—an electronic retailer, operating in cyberspace with a nearly infinite inventory. You can still get in on the ground floor—or at least the mezzanine—by buying a few shares.

Not only are stocks democratic, they can be fun. Back in the early 1980s, the most popular television show in America was *Dallas*. J. R. Ewing, as played by Larry Hagman, ruthlessly pursued profit in the oil patch. Viewers tuned in each week to see how J. R. could sucker his hapless competitors into selling him land that was oil-rich, or convince them to buy worthless property from him. Business and personal crises were around every corner. Cheap imports threatened to put the Texans out of business, and they responded by shoveling cash at politicians. A big multinational was continually plotting a hostile takeover. Each week, you wondered if Ewing Oil would survive.

When you buy stocks, you become a partner in a business. If you are like most people, you won't be buying a big share—more likely, a small slice, like those of the long-lost Ewing cousins who occasionally showed up with claims on little pieces of the firm. But your small stake will involve you in a soap opera that is every bit as exciting as the one on *Dallas*—and profitable too.

It is a drama that is easy to follow since main events will be covered in *The Wall Street Journal* and financial magazines, in the business section of your local newspaper, in annual reports, which will be mailed to you as a shareholder, and in filings by your firm with the Securities and Exchange Commission—which are now easily available on the Internet through the SEC's wide-open system, called Edgar (www.sec.gov).

Let twenty stocks into your life, and you are taking on twenty new storylines. Buy stock in Minimed, Inc., and become an owner of a company that makes insulin pumps that help diabetes patients get just the right dose. In early 1999, Minimed had a 75 percent share of its market and was increasing its earnings by 40 percent a year. Will competitors try to copy Minimed's success and sell profitable insulin pumps? Or is the market too small? Will a big health care firm like J&J buy Minimed out? And what about the company's new product, a glucose sensor? Will it succeed?

Buy stock in MCI Worldcom, Inc., a telecommunications company that is trying to get around the telephone regulators, bust the local telephone monopolies, and deliver cheap and reliable service to consumers. Will it succeed? Will political contributions by adversaries induce regulators to change rules to your disadvantage?

Buy stock in Intuit, Inc., maker of Quicken, the popular accounting software, with over 15 million users. Can the company expand beyond its base? Will an attempt to establish an Internet-based payroll business succeed against the likes of Automatic Data Processing and Paychex?

Or will the firm be swallowed up—or put out of business—by Microsoft or another software giant, as so many other single-product computer companies have?

In short, when you buy stocks, you are establishing a personal link with a thriving business that is navigating the world marketplace. That's far more exciting and entertaining than owning an anonymous index fund.

REASON 5. BUYING STOCKS CAN BE CHEAP

The average mutual fund reduces your returns by 1.4 percent annually to pay its management fees and expenses, plus another few tenths of a point for transaction costs—the commissions it pays to brokers when it buys and sells stocks. If that sounds like a good deal, remember that the expenses come out of your gains *every* year. Also, when charges are deducted, you suffer an "opportunity cost": You can't invest the money that goes to the fund manager.

Consider a fund whose yearly expenses, including brokerage costs, are 1.4 percent. With an investment of $10,000, you are charged $140 to start. But let's assume that your account grows in value to $40,000 in ten years (any good Dow 36,000 account should do even better). That's an average annual return of about 14 percent—or about four percentage points below the S&P's performance over the past twenty years. Since your account grows each year (even though you don't put in any new dollars), so do your fees. In year 10, expenses will be $560, and the total charges over the life of the fund will be an incredible $3,546—or more than one-third the value of your original investment. Imagine a mutual fund that charged you a 35 percent up-front load but nothing during the life of your investment!

But the true cost is even higher than $3,546 since the money you paid in expenses could itself have been invested. If you had simply put the money to work in a money market fund at 5 percent, it could have earned another $600; in a mutual fund at 14 percent, it could have earned another $2,000. In other words, the mutual fund will deprive you, over ten years, of costs that amount to 56 percent of your original investment.

Even with a passively managed fund, like Vanguard Index 500, the fees, at just 0.2 percent a year, can mount up. Growing at 14 percent annually, a $10,000 stake generates expenses of $388—and $572, after adjusting for lost investment opportunities—in ten years.

When you invest in individual stocks, you pay your broker a transaction fee when you purchase the stock—a fee, which, with a full-service firm, could be as high as 2 percent. But you pay no more fees until you sell, and, for a buy-and-hold investor, that may be never. If you set up an account with a discount brokerage firm, costs could be as little as $7 for each transaction. Datek, one of the larger online discounters, was charging a flat $9.99 for the purchase or sale of an unlimited number of shares. At that price you can set up a diversified $100,000 portfolio with twenty stocks for $200—or the same amount you would have paid Vanguard in just the first year for its Index 500 fund.

But consider an investor paying hefty full-service commissions of 2 percent and holding a $10,000 stock portfolio for ten years. In the first year, the purchases cost $200. In the tenth year, assuming the portfolio has quadrupled, the sales cost $800. Total fees: $1,000, compared with $3,546 for the mutual fund with 1.4 percent annual expenses. Including lost investment earnings, the expenses on individual stocks are $2,800—or one-half the freight on mutual funds.

In addition, many brokerage firms allow you automatically to reinvest dividends your stocks throw off in more shares of the company—at no commission. Those dividends could eventually accumulate more shares than you originally bought.

Finally, there is the tax advantage we noted in the last chapter. With individual stocks, investors themselves—not fund managers—decide when they will take capital gains.

There is a more subtle tax bonus for stocks as well. If you buy shares in a company like Microsoft, which has copious earnings but pays no dividends, then the price of the firm should go up each year when earnings are retained. That increase in price is just like income to you—indeed, you could sell a small percentage of your holdings and turn the gain into real income whenever you want. If you do sell a little stock, then the profits that you earn (the difference between the sale price and the price you originally paid for the stock) will be taxed—but only at the capital gains rate, which in 1999 was 20 percent, a good deal lower than the 28 percent the average American family confronts on an extra dollar of income, either from salary or dividends—and about half the rate that the highest earners must pay.

But even better, if you don't sell your Microsoft stock, the IRS doesn't think that the stock has given you any income. From 1993 to 1998, an investment of $5,000 rose to $70,000, but that $65,000 gain is not taxable until the stock is sold. By contrast, bonds provide a steady stream of *taxable* interest payments, even if you never see the money, instead reinvesting it in new bonds. By contrast as well, equity mutual funds pass through tax liabilities to their shareholders, whenever managers get the whim to take gains.

Mutual funds hit shareholders with these nasty tax surprises all the time, but if you own individual stocks, you can manage your own destiny. You never, ever, pay taxes on phantom gains.

There is one more tax angle. Many investors like to anchor their individual stock holdings with a mutual fund or two or three. If you choose to do that (and it makes sense), then each year, as your funds hit you with capital gains, you can reduce your total tax bill by selling stocks in your portfolio that are trading below the price at which you bought them. As a steady investor in stocks, you will probably own some winners and some losers at any point. So balance your fund gains with stock losses. (If you want to continue investing in the stock, then sell it and buy it back after a decent interval.) You may be able to keep the tax bill from the equity portion of your portfolio very close to zero.

THE FOUR WAYS TO BUY INDIVIDUAL STOCKS

Convinced that you should buy stocks?

Begin by setting up an account at a brokerage firm. It's much like a bank account, except that your funds aren't insured by the federal government (though they are usually backed by private insurance). Brokerage accounts pay a competitive interest rate on cash you aren't investing, and many even allow check writing.

A broker buys and sells stocks—on your order. (Don't set up a discretionary account that gives the broker control over such decisions; you might as well own a mutual fund.) The broker makes money by charging you a transaction fee every time you buy or sell something. There are three different kinds of brokerage firms—each with its advantages. The fourth way you can start investing is to buy stock directly through a company. Here are the details.

FULL-SERVICE BROKERS

These firms, which range from behemoths like Merrill Lynch & Co. to smaller firms like Baltimore-based Legg Mason, Inc., typically assign a specific broker—sometimes called an investment or financial advisor— to each client. He keeps in frequent touch, suggesting stocks, offering free research on companies and industries, providing tax tips. The cost of this personal attention is defrayed through commissions, which usually run between 1 and 2 percent of the cost of the stock when it's purchased and sold. Brokerage firms are trying to move toward a system that compensates them with annual management fees (again, in the 1-to-2-percent range) instead of trading fees. The transition has not been easy, but it should soon be upon us—and it will be a change for the better.

Many financial writers denigrate full-service brokers. We don't. Since your relationship with your portfolio is more important than the stocks you pick, you will almost certainly need help in making that relationship a profitable one. That's where a good broker comes in. Even 2 percent is a small price to pay for counsel that stops you from selling at the wrong time or that encourages you to buy the sort of companies that meet the Dow 36,000 criteria. Also, you should know that most brokers have wide leeway in setting commissions. With so much competition, you can usually get a break by saying, "Gee, one and a half percent is awfully high. I could do this online for seven bucks."

But a warning: A bad broker is worse than no broker. Since most brokers still make their money off commissions, some have a propensity to pester you about selling your stock. "It looks like Gillette has broken through its support level" is a typical line. Still, it's not hard to tell good brokers from bad, and you can ask to be reassigned—or simply pull your account and go somewhere else. A good broker or financial advisor will return your calls promptly, know you by name, and offer advice on asset allocation and on how to react to market volatility. If you come up with an idea on your own, he can often send you a careful analysis of the stock from in-house experts. Most important, a good broker will know that the best thing you can possibly do is buy and hold. The cost of all that attention is higher transaction fees than the alternatives.

Here is a checklist of questions you should ask brokers, to separate the good from the questionable:

1. What do you do you for your clients? (What the broker says first is usually what she sees as her most useful function. "Keep you from getting into trouble" is a reassuring response. "Help you set your objectives and keep you on track" is another. If she answers "Pick stocks for you," then move on to another firm.)

2. Do you have a program or a questionnaire that will help me decide how to allocate, or divide up, my assets among stocks, bonds, and cash? (This should be the very first step the broker takes with you.)

3. What are your commissions on trades? Would there be an advantage for me if I paid you a set percentage of my holdings each year?

4. If I ask for a full analysis of a company from your research department, how quickly can I get it? Do you provide special research services for large clients that you won't provide for me?

5. I am especially concerned about two figures when I analyze a stock using the 36er strategy: earnings growth and dividend growth. Can I get these statistics for any stock going back five years, plus projections from your analysts going forward five years?

6. What are your own views on the market? (This is another open-ended question, like the first one. The correct answer for 36ers is something like this: "In general, stocks are very much undervalued, but, of course, I cannot predict what the market will do next week. Short-term forecasts are for tarot cards.")

7. When is the right time to sell a stock? (This is a vital question. You don't want a broker who is trigger-happy. There are reasons to sell—for example, when there's a management change for the worse or when a product fails. But selling should be a rare event.)

8. If the market falls sharply and I call you to put in a sell order on a good company, what will you tell me? (Correct answer: "I'll ask you if you have made a considered judgment.")

9. Since you make your money off commissions, how can I be sure you won't want to churn my stocks? (The purpose of this question is simply to put the broker on notice that you're no dummy.)

10. Will you sell me any mutual fund I want to buy? What do you get paid on a no-load fund I could buy myself without paying commission? (Your broker or advisor should sell you practically anything. He'll get a share of the fund fees, which is fair.)

11. Can I reinvest my dividends in more shares of stock without paying a commission? (Using cash payouts to buy new shares is a key element in the 36er strategy.)

12. What are the special services your firm provides? (The most important will be recordkeeping. Ask to look at a sample statement. Make sure it is easy to understand. Find out if it is issued monthly, as it should be, rather than quarterly.)

DISCOUNT BROKERS

Between 1989 and 1998, the fourth-best-performing stock in the market was the Charles Schwab Corp., which rose by a factor of 10. Schwab is a discount broker, and like many successful businesses, it found a niche others had missed: offering investors a cheaper way to buy stocks. Of course, for a lower cost, you don't get as much service as with a full-service broker like Smith Barney or PaineWebber, but then, many investors don't need as much.

The main function of discount brokers is to execute trades by investors who know what they want to buy and sell. You rarely develop the sort of long-term personal relationship you can with a full-service broker. Schwab, for example, suggests that clients visit a branch office, establish a rapport with a broker, and ask for her each time they want to make a trade. But she will not actively manage the account or suggest stocks—though Schwab, like many other discounters, offers such services at an additional cost. In early 1999, Schwab was charging $110, or about 1 percent, for a $10,000 trade and $210, or less than one-half of 1 percent, for a $50,000 trade. For trades that you handle online yourself through www.schwab.com, there's a flat fee of $29.95 for up to 1,000 shares, or 3 cents per share for trades over 1,000. So, buying 2,000 shares of a $25 stock will cost only $60, compared with $210 over the phone. (These fees continually change, but you get the idea. Schwab, Fidelity, and other discounters also offer hundreds of mutual funds at no commission charge.) With its rock-bottom minimum account, Schwab also charges a $29 per year maintenance fee, but this is waived if you keep at least $10,000 in assets with the firm. Other features: access to margin loans (so you can buy stock by borrowing money—a practice we discourage as very risky), unlimited check writing, and a bill-paying service.

If you sign on with one of the discount brokerages today, you will be able to buy and sell stocks and bonds just as effectively as you would with a full-service broker and the price of each transaction will be significantly lower. You lose, however, the personal attention and some of the extensive research services that come with having your own broker. Schwab, for example, allows all clients access to research on a special website but charges you if you want something more expensive, or if you want it faxed.

Discount brokers will help you allocate your assets, but they are essentially order takers and bookkeepers. Don't expect them to discourage you from selling at the wrong time. That's not their job. Most of the questions above for full-service brokers are irrelevant here. But you should pin down four things from the start:

1. Exactly how much will trades cost under different circumstances?
2. How much research will I get for free?
3. What does your statement look like, and how often will I get one?
4. How accessible are you? Can I have my own broker?

ONLINE TRADING

Aggressive firms like Ameritrade, DLJ Direct, and Datek responded to the success of the discounters and the growth of the Internet by offering stock trades at rates undercutting Schwab and the others by 50 percent and more. The only condition is that you enter your orders yourself by computer. In turn, by early 1999, a little more than half of the 107 national discount brokerage firms were offering inexpensive online trading themselves. Some of the deals are spectacular, and commission rates have plummeted. In 1996, E-Trade had the lowest fees, at $14.95 per trade. But three years later, Suretrade was charging just $8 for up to 5,000 shares, with no minimum to start an account.

Most of these firms are just as sound as full-service brokers (that is, they are not about to walk off with your money), but the relationship and service components are set fairly close to zero. Still, all brokerage firms—from full-service to online—provide statements of your holdings and transactions.

Online trading is spreading with amazing speed. By the end of 1998, the Internet was the site of 15 percent of all U.S. stock trading. That figure was up from 7 percent the year before and heading for 30 percent by 2002, according to International Data Corp. No wonder. To buy 5,000 shares of Coca-Cola at $60 each, Datek recently charged just $9.99. Period. A full-service broker with a 1 percent commission would charge $3,000, and Schwab was charging $1,650 for a phone order. Datek also promises to execute your order within sixty seconds, or there is no commission charge at all.

But buying stocks by computer presents dangers. The biggest is that, with no intermediary at all, it's just you and the screen—like a video game. While, in theory, you can save thousands of dollars in commissions by using a firm like Datek or Waterhouse WebBroker, the question is whether you will have the self-discipline to remain a buy-and-hold investor or whether you will start day-trading—jumping in and out of stocks—if it costs only 20 or 30 bucks for a round-trip.

Another problem with online trading is that many firms charge extra for "limit orders"—that is, for having the broker follow the direction of an investor to sell only above a certain price (rather than "at the market") or to buy only below a certain price. With highly volatile Internet stocks, for instance, investors who place market orders can find themselves buying 1,000 shares at $50 when the stock was trading at $30 as they entered their orders on the computer.

The scary part is that you are completely on your own. Can you handle it?

DIRECT INVESTMENT

For many investors, an even cheaper way to buy stocks is to get them directly from companies themselves. More than five hundred companies offer these direct purchase plans, or DPPs. They are the logical extension of an older idea, the dividend reinvestment plan (or DRIP), available for more than sixteen hundred stocks. With DRIPs, instead of receiving cash for your dividends, you automatically receive more shares of stock.

Say you own 500 shares of Exxon Corp. Rather than getting a check for $205 next month (or a credit of cash on your brokerage account) as your quarterly dividend, you can ask Exxon to pay you in stock. If Exxon is trading at $82, as it was in May 1999, you will get 2.5 shares; then, the next quarter, you will earn dividends on 502.5 shares—and your holdings will mount quickly through the miracle of compounding. (Yes, DRIPs can credit your account with fractions of shares.) As DRIPs have grown in popularity, brokerage firms have responded by offering their clients the same kind of deal.

But DPPs are even better. They let you bypass brokers completely. To make the process easier, several websites, including www.netstockdirect.com and www.stockpower.com, can speed the way, serving as clearinghouses for enrolling in DPPs online, letting you monitor your stock accounts, and providing research. The best source of information about DPPs is the *Drip Investor* newsletter (also on the Web at www.dripinvestor.com), edited by Charles Carlson, author of a book on the subject, *No-Load Stocks.* You can even buy some stocks directly from individual companies online, including Home Depot, Inc. (www.HomeDepot.com).

But direct-purchase plans aren't free. For example, the most popular stock offering at Net Stock Direct is Campbell Soup Co., which charges $15 as an initial fee and 3 cents a share for purchases. So, if you buy 100 shares, the cost is $18—or more than most online discounters charge and not much less expensive even than a full-service broker with a commission of 1.5 percent ($60). But if you buy 10 shares a year for ten years, the cost is still only $18, while, even with the cheapest discounter, you will pay about five times as much. Campbell, like many other companies offering DPPs, charges more to sell than to buy (12 cents a share plus a $12 sale fee)—a good disincentive for the trigger-happy. Campbell is a wonderful stock for 36ers, with a recent yield of 2.2 percent, a dividend that has been growing at better than 10 percent annually, a P/E ratio of 24, and a great brand name.

Some companies charge far less than Campbell for their DPPs. Exxon, for instance, has no fees or commissions at all for purchases.

Can't beat that. Sales are $5 plus 10 cents per share. Home Depot has a $5 initial fee and a $10 fee when you sell, but no commissions. Walt Disney Co. charges $10 to begin, $10 for sales, and a commission of 4 cents per share.

Direct investing is designed for people who want to make small purchases over a long period. Wal-Mart Stores, for example, allows initial investments as low as $250. Campbell's minimum is $500, but after that, you can buy as little as $50 worth of stock a month. Nearly all the plans offer automatic debiting from your checking account to buy shares regularly.

Other popular DPP stocks that 36ers should consider: Fannie Mae, General Electric, IBM, Lucent Technologies, Compaq Computer Corp., and Walgreen, the exceptionally well managed drugstore chain.

Some companies even sell stock at a discount price to direct buyers. Advanta Corp., a credit card firm, and Chase Manhattan Corp., the New York–based bank, take 5 percent off if you buy stock regularly through a purchase plan. Other firms give perks: Colgate-Palmolive, discount coupons worth $15; Sears, Roebuck & Co., a 10 percent store discount; Starbucks, free coffee; and William Wrigley, Jr., Co. (another great 36er stock), twenty packs of gum. Details are on the StockPower website.

If you already own shares of a particular company and want to begin a DRIP, your stock has to be transferred out of your brokerage firm's name and into yours—a simple process. But most brokers will, in effect, allow you to set up your own DRIP with the firm, adding shares instead of cash. By automatically buying more stock for you, DRIPs are a superb investment discipline.

BUT WHICH TO CHOOSE?

Which route to choose depends on who you are, so take a critical personal inventory. For instance, are you going to run for the exits at the first sign of trouble, or will you calmly ignore fluctuations and stay invested for the long run?

Most investors are more weak-willed than they think—which is why we believe that full-service brokers, or independent financial advisors who place trades through broker, are well worth the cost. We recommend you start your foray into stocks with one. If you hire a good broker, you will acquire a friend who will keep you calm when stocks become frightening and whose fees will also serve as a deterrent to acting rashly or trying to time the market.

If you are confident in your self-control, then the online brokerages, including Schwab's, which has an easy-to-use interface, offer an attractive and inexpensive alternative. But remember that day-trading is a sure ticket to underperforming the market—or losing money. With these risks, the best strategy for such a self-starter is to buy stocks through direct-investment plans. The transaction costs are about the same as with superdiscounters, but the discipline of steady investment and reinvestment contrasts sharply with the day-trading enticements supplied by the online firms. The limitation, of course, is that not every company sells its shares directly, but the list of choices keeps growing.

WHAT ABOUT DIVERSIFICATION?

As much as we love buying individual stocks, there is no denying that the great advantage of mutual funds is diversification. The average fund owns more than one hundred stocks. Few small investors could handle portfolios of that size. The bookkeeping alone would be a nightmare.

But if you are careful, you can construct a portfolio that gives you almost the same high return-low risk package provided by index funds and the best managed funds. Careful research shows that all you need to dampen the risk of concentration is about twenty stocks—but even as few as eight or ten may be enough. If your hot biotech stock, EntreMed, Inc., plummets, then your stable consumer stock, Coca-Cola, might boom. In a typical year, in a typical portfolio of ten stocks spread over different industries, two will fall in price, three will rise sharply, and five will move up modestly. But imagine a portfolio that includes just the two that fall.

The key for most investors is diversification across industries. Inflation will hurt banking stocks, but it will help gold shares. A portfolio that has most of its assets in banks—or Internet stocks or gold stocks—will bounce around like crazy. Pick your favorites, but pick from many different industries.

When you decide to dedicate your stock purchases to individual stocks, you have two choices. You can pick a few stocks that you feel have an unusually high chance of success, or you can buy twenty diverse stocks in a portfolio that looks like a mini Vanguard 500 Index. The best arguments for choosing just a few stocks have been made by Warren Buffett and by Tom and David Gardner, founders of the excellent Motley Fool website (www.fool.com). Their idea is that you should concentrate on truly magnificent companies, in whatever industries, and forget the rest. The Fool's "Rule Breaker" portfolio, for example, which recently included thirteen stocks—weighted toward high-tech (with companies like Excite@Home and Amazon)—has been wildly successful. On the other hand, the narrow focus exposes their holdings to more risk than index funds.

We prefer a broad portfolio. Since we believe the market is on the verge of quadrupling, we are happy just to keep up with it as partakers rather than outsmarters.

So a portfolio that is just as safe as an index fund is relatively easy to construct. How can you tell if you are diversified enough? Just calculate the value of your holdings every day for two months or so, and then compare the swings in your portfolio to those of the market as a whole. Do your holdings fall 5 percent on a week the market falls 2 percent? If they do, you need to add a few more stocks.

But which stocks to add? Which stocks to start with? We'll answer those questions in the next chapter.

CHAPTER 13

Which Stocks Should You Buy?

October. This is one of the peculiarly dangerous months to specu-
late in stocks. The others are July, January, September, April,
November, May, March, June, December, August, and February.
—Mark Twain, *The Tragedy of Puddn' head Wilson*

Like the partnership in the dry cleaning store we discussed in the first half of this book, a company's stock will be a good buy if it puts more cash into your pockets over time than alternative investments that carry similar risks.

Fine, you say, but there are more than seven thousand stocks listed on the New York, American, and Nasdaq exchanges. Some will soar, some will glide along, some will fall to earth. How can I decide which will do which?

In this chapter, we will tell you. First, we will introduce you to a professional stock picker who has never heard of the Dow 36,000 Theory yet uses its criteria to select winners. Next, we will look closely at some of our own favorite stocks and explain why they are attractive. Then, we will give you the five most important questions to ask before you buy a stock. Finally, we will examine Internet stocks, to see if their sky-high valuations make sense.

THE GENIUS OF CLEVELAND

Most Americans recognize a Tootsie Roll even if they haven't eaten one in thirty years. It's a log-shaped slab of chewy, gooey chocolate produced by a Chicago-based company called Tootsie Roll Industries, Inc., whose stock is a lot more delicious than its candy.

Tootsie Roll, in fact, is the archetypal Dow 36,000 stock. It is a reliable cash machine whose profits and payouts have been growing since it was started in 1896. Through 1998, it had paid cash dividends for fifty-five consecutive years. Every year since 1977, Tootsie Roll has posted record sales; and every year since 1982, record profits.

Tootsie Roll has a great brand name, which forms a "moat" around the company. Other firms can make chocolate candy, but no one else can make a Tootsie Roll. Or a Tootsie Pop, for that matter—the lollipop with the chocolate center which made its debut more than sixty years ago and to which we were especially partial in our youth.

As for growth: Between 1993 and 1998, Tootsie Roll increased its earnings per share at an average rate of 15 percent annually and its dividends at 21 percent. That provides quite a margin of error for investors. Since the assumptions on which the Dow 36,000 Theory is based require earnings growth of just 5 percent, Tootsie Roll's rate could fall by two-thirds and still justify a price-to-earnings ratio of 100. In fact, in April 1999, Tootsie Roll's P/E ratio was just 30. No wonder the stock returned 22 percent annually during the 1990s, beating every other major food company except two, which have similar characteristics: William Wrigley Jr. Co., the chewing gum king, and Campbell Soup Co., one of the great brand names in the world.

We'll get back to Tootsie Roll a little later, but, first, here is the man who introduced us to the stock.

His name is Elliott L. Schlang, and we'll bet you have never heard of him. He lives in Cleveland and runs a research service called LJR Great Lakes Review, which is owned by Lynch, Jones & Ryan, Inc., a regional investment firm. Schlang publishes a quarterly newsletter and more extensive reports, none of which you can get. His clients are large mutual funds, pension funds, and university endowments, which pay him well to call good stocks to their attention.

Schlang's own stock-picking philosophy meshes almost perfectly with 36er strategy. Companies that meet our criteria are those that can be expected to survive a long time and to post steady, positive earnings growth that at least keeps up with the increases each year in gross domestic product—or the nation's output of goods and services. Companies that meet Schlang's standards look the same.

He searches for firms with the following six characteristics: (1) earnings that consistently increase year after year, (2) high growth rates, (3) above-average profit margins, (4) minimal debt, (5) managers who own lots of stock in the firm, and (6) headquarters in Ohio, Michigan, Indiana, or western Pennsylvania.

Let's examine Schlang's requirements and see how they fit the theory we presented in the first half of this book.

At the time that the Dow Jones industrial average was about 9,000, we calculated that its reasonable level should be 36,000. In other words, the average stock should quadruple. Our arithmetic assumed that the company behind the stock would grow at a modest but steady rate for many years. This, in the aggregate, is what the companies in the market had done for at least 120 years. But, for an individual firm, consistent growth is not easy. Recall that an entrepreneur who made big profits by investing in vending machines would soon be faced with stiff competition from others who bought their own machines in an attempt to copy his success. How can you tell if a firm can avoid the vending-machine trap and grow profitability for a long, long time?

1. CONSISTENT INCREASES IN EARNINGS

One way is to think carefully about the company's economics. Firms can remain consistently profitable if they offer something that consumers want and that is very difficult for someone else to make. Anyone can go out and buy a vending machine, but only one company can make a little log of chocolate with a wrapper that says Tootsie Roll and always tastes like one. Drug companies have patents on their pharmaceuticals, making it illegal for others to manufacture them. So do software firms. (And with both drugs and software, the cost of getting the first product out the door can be huge, but the cost of each subsequent product can be pennies.) Coca-Cola has a secret formula for a soft drink that others have been unable to duplicate, a distribution infrastructure that delivers its products throughout the world, and a presence in the global consciousness that has been carefully nurtured with billions of dollars' worth of advertising over a century. "Coke" is the world's second most-recognized phrase, next to "OK." Could a start-up company challenge Coke or Tootsie Roll? Of course not.

Strong brand names, or, as Warren Buffett calls them, "franchises," provide the protection against competition that keeps sales strong and allows prices to be raised without too much resistance. So, by looking for goods and services that are difficult to duplicate, you can identify individual companies that will provide the steady, long-term growth necessary that justifies a P/E of 100 of more.

But Schlang uses a simpler route to the same destination: He looks for firms that have posted steady growth for a long time. History is not a perfect guide to the future, but in this case, it's a big help.

Go back twenty years and look at the firms that existed then. Many of them had something special—some edge. But it may have been ephemeral. Tastes could change, or competitors could make something just as good. But over the same two decades, other companies found profits that would keep rolling in either because they had an explicit patent, or because the know-how or scale of their operation provided them with an advantage against would-be interlopers. A good example is one of our very favorite companies, Gillette, which controls three-quarters of the market for manual razors.

The winning companies are the ones that successfully defended their turf. How did they do it? You don't really need to know. The fact that they posted healthy profit growth for the past ten or twenty years is an excellent indicator that they have something special, something that should last another few decades—or much longer. What's "healthy"? Well, Gillette's earnings grew annually at 19 percent during the 1990s; dividends, at 16 percent. But let's go back even farther.

One of Schlang's favorite companies is RPM, Inc., of Medina, Ohio, maker of specialty coatings and chemicals for waterproofing and rust control, as well as stains and finishes used in woodworking. Like most of Schlang's selections, this is hardly a sexy business, but the firm has notched fifty-one consecutive years of record sales, net profits, and earnings per share. RPM has also increased its dividends every year since 1974. Earnings growth for the five years ending in 1998 averaged 10 percent annually, and analysts predict the same increases for the next five years.

In May 1999, RPM was trading at $14 a share and paying a dividend of 47 cents, for a yield of 3.4 percent. If the dividend increases at a 10 percent annual rate, then in twenty years, it will be $3.15—for a return, in that year's dividends alone, of 23 percent on the $14 investment made in 1999.

Has the market rewarded RPM for its consistent growth? Not

nearly enough. Over the ten years ending in 1998, the company's returns, in dividends and price appreciation, averaged 15 percent annually—good, but still well behind the 19 percent average for the thirty companies on the Dow. RPM, with a market capitalization of about $1.5 billion, has regularly traded at a P/E between 15 and 20, but by our analysis, the company's growth rate could fall by half and the stock would still merit a price at least five times as high—immediately.

Why has RPM boosted its earnings every year for more than half a century? One reason may be management, but more vital is a reputation for making high-quality coatings. That reputation is especially important with a relatively low-cost component in an expensive finished product. For instance, anyone making a piece of furniture goes to enormous trouble and cost to develop a pleasing design; buy the right wood; and cut, glue, and sand the pieces. If an extra dollar buys a reliable stain like RPM's, then spending the money makes sense. Why risk another stain, even if it's cheaper?

But the truth is, we would never have noticed RPM's potential as a 36er stock if we had not followed Schlang's simple screening process: A company that makes record profits fifty-one years in a row must have an unbeatable edge—one that should offer the consistency that the Dow 36,000 Theory requires.

2. HIGH GROWTH IN EARNINGS

Schlang's second criterion is that a firm have a high rate of earnings growth. Actually, high growth is not necessary to 36er theory, but it gives us what Benjamin Graham says is the most important feature in a stock: a large "margin of safety."

When we calculated that a P/E of 100 would be about right for the average stock, we assumed that earnings growth would actually be about two percentage points lower than the 7.3 percent that has prevailed since 1946. But suppose you are considering one hundred stocks for purchase. Some of them have grown at an average rate of 5 percent for the past ten years, others have grown at an average rate of 20 percent. (For the Dow as a whole, earnings growth for the five years starting 1999 is estimated by analysts' consensus to be 15 percent. For the preceding five years, it was 13 percent.)

The point is that the faster growers offer a bigger comfort zone between the firm's experience and our assumptions. They're the safer picks.

Schlang loves another boring company called Cintas Corp., which rents uniforms to 2 million blue-collar American workers in such sectors as security, food and lodging, health care, and auto service. Sales and net income have increased every year since 1969, and earnings per share grew at an average annual rate of 19 percent from 1989 to 1998. Value Line's analysts project that incredible rate to continue through 2004, with dividends increasing at 17.5 percent.

So Cintas is another company whose growth rate could fall by more than half and still justify a P/E of 100. It is, however, a stock that hasn't been overlooked. An investor who put $1,000 into Cintas shares at the start of 1989 saw his holdings rise to more than $12,000 by the end of 1998. In May 1999, Cintas was trading at a P/E of 43—cheap by 36er standards for a company whose earnings are growing even at 10 percent, let alone 19 percent, a year.

The single most important factor in a company's value to its owners is the rate of increase of the cash they can put in their pockets—that is, dividend growth and earnings growth. When that rate is high, the starting point—stock price, dividend yield—doesn't matter very much over long periods of time. Look for companies that have grown a lot in the past and should grow a lot in the future, and you'll profit immensely from the 36er strategy.

3. HIGH PROFIT MARGINS

The third requirement is that companies can sell their products for much more than they spend to make them. "Profit margin" is actually a vague term that can refer to profits at various stages as a percentage of total revenues. For example, in 1998, the gross profit margin (before selling and administrative costs, interest expenses, and taxes) for another of Schlang's favorite companies, DeVry, Inc., which operates two hundred post-secondary schools that offer degrees in business and technology, was 42 percent; the after-tax profit margin after all of those expenses was 9 percent. Both of these figures are impressive. In the average business, bottom-line margins of 5 percent or more are an indication of high profitability, but the figures aren't meaningful unless they are compared to other companies in the same industry. A mass-market retailer might have margins of 2 percent; a software company, 20 percent. Cintas had an after-tax margin in 1998 of 11 percent while Tootsie Roll's was an incredible 17 percent—and rising.

High margins are important because they measure a firm's ability to protect its markets against price-cutting competitors. If competition is fierce, then firms have to sell their products very close to cost. Firms that can maintain big markups for a long time have clearly found a line of business with a broad moat.

The most famous moat in America is the one that surrounds Coca-Cola. It was built with Coke's brand name, secret formula, and distribution system. Mainly as a result, Coke's after-tax margins are an amazing 20 percent. By comparison, Cott Corp., which makes soft drinks that sell under the private labels of grocery retailers, has barely a puddle to protect it, with a margin of just 2 percent.

4. LOW DEBT

The fourth criterion, that firms have very little debt, provides assurance that the company will be around for a long time. Firms that have borrowed lots of money are riskier than firms that have not. If the economy goes into recession and income drops, then the steady drain of interest payments can force a firm to skimp on capital investment and reduce the quality of its products—or, worse, push the company into bankruptcy. Firms without much debt can weather storms.

Such companies exist. One of those cited by Schlang is Landauer, Inc., which dominates the market for equipment that measures exposure to radiation in such places as doctors' offices, hospitals, airports, and nuclear plants. In 1998, the company had no long- or short-term debt but $15 million in cash and securities. Meanwhile, after-tax profits were $13 million, or nearly three times the firm's annual requirements for new capital investments. Partly as a result, Landauer pays a hefty dividend, which grew during the 1990s from 40 cents to $1.40 a year, bringing the yield in 1999 to 5.5 percent. As a small-cap stock, Landauer was out of favor in the late 1990s. It returned an average of just 12 percent annually from 1996 to 1999—or half the gains of the S&P.

DeVry also has a gorgeous balance sheet. In the first quarter of fiscal 1999, it paid off all its debt—although, to be safe, it maintains an arrangement with banks to borrow up to $85 million. Meanwhile, cash totaled nearly $49 million, or more than one-third of the company's capital. This sort of strength is reassuring in a company that is growing at a 20 percent annual clip. Typically, fast growers have to borrow heavily to finance the investment in new buildings and machines that help them bloom. But DeVry has been paying for its investment out of its own cash flow. Shareholders don't earn dividends; instead, their profits are reinvested in the company, which is producing a net return on their equity after taxes of 24 percent. You can't get that at a bank.

Nearly all companies have *some* debt, and a little isn't bad at all. For example, Johnson & Johnson, the health-products company, had $1.3 billion in borrowings at the end of 1998. If that sounds substantial, it represents only 7 percent of the company's capital. Interest expenses comprised just 1 percent of J&J's total costs and about 3 percent of its earnings before taxes.

5. MANAGERS WHO OWN STOCK

Schlang wants to own companies whose managers own their own stock. Ownership aligns the interests of managers with those of shareholders. They will think twice before handing themselves huge bonuses and buying corporate jets, and they will be more receptive to a lucrative buyout that could put them out of their jobs—but make all shareholders a good deal richer. Also, they will feel the pain if the stock declines. When managers hold stock, you can be fairly certain that they will spend your money (and their own) cautiously.

How do manager-owners reinforce the Dow 36,000 Theory? They are more likely to concentrate on consistent earnings growth (which lifts a stock's price) than on market share (or bigness for its own sake—and the sake of impressing other CEOs). Under our strategy, size makes no difference; growth does. Also, manager-owners will be more conscious of using profits well—which means paying them out to shareholders when the company itself cannot use them to generate high returns.

The chairman and the president of Tootsie Roll, Melvin and Ellen Gordon (husband and wife), own nearly half the shares. The chairman of Cintas owns 27 percent while the CEO holds 3 percent. Any ownership of 10 percent or greater by managers is reassuring. Landauer's chairman, for instance, owns 7 percent of the company; its president, 3 percent. It is rare, however, for managers to own large chunks of venerable large-cap firms. After all, 10 percent of Johnson & Johnson was worth $13 billion in April 1999.

6. NEARBY COMPANIES

Schlang's final criterion is that the company be headquartered near his office: Cintas in Cincinnati; DeVry in Oakbrook Terrace, Illinois; etc. Schlang, like many money managers, wants to meet the people who manage the companies in which he invests. What is he looking for? Brains, broad understanding of the business, integrity.

When we recently asked the chairman of Allied Capital Corp., a company that makes loans to small businesses, what he valued most in a CEO, he said without hesitation, "Honesty."

Of course, most small investors have a hard time making such assessments. They aren't ushered into the chairman's office for a chat. Still, Schlang's emphasis on proximity is a reminder to invest in companies in which you are familiar. In your hometown, is there a company whose CEO you hold in high regard? Did you just research refrigerators for your kitchen remodeling and find that one was much better than all of the others? If so, then you might be able to add value to your portfolio. Maytag Corp., for instance, had a dividend yield in 1999 of 1 percent and a dividend growth rate, projected by Value Line for the five years ahead, of 8.5 percent. Those figures totaled 9.5 percent at a time when Treasury bond rates were 5.5 percent. And Maytag's P/E ratio was a mere 17. It easily fits our criteria, undervalued by a factor of 5 or 6.

One of Peter Lynch's top finds when he was running Fidelity Magellan fund came after his wife pointed out that a company called Hanes was selling pantyhose in grocery stores in lovely egg-shaped containers. Lynch writes that many of his best stock finds came from what he calls "common knowledge":

> Taco Bell, I was impressed with the burritos on a trip to California; La Quinta Motor Inns, somebody at a rival Holiday Inn told me about it; Volvo, my family and friends drive this car; Apple Computer, my kids had one at home and then the systems manager bought several for the office; Service Corporation International, a Fidelity electronics analyst (who had nothing to do with funeral

homes, so this wasn't his field) found on a trip to Texas; Dunkin'
Donuts, I loved the coffee . . . .

Remarkably, investors overlook what's at hand. Dentists seem to
prefer investing in oil stocks to investing in the stock of the maker of
the fabulous new drill they just bought.

Trust your own judgment. Stay away from tips that you have not
checked out yourself. And when in doubt, stay away, period. You need
only twenty good stocks in a lifetime, and there are quite a few RPMs
and Tootsie Rolls out there.

WHAT OUR OWN FAVORITES HAVE IN COMMON

Great buys come in all forms. Some are high-tech companies with a
foot in the door of a rapidly expanding industry. Some are household
names that have been around for generations. The firms are different,
but their key characteristics are the same. Here are three that illustrate
the Dow 36,000 Theory in practice: General Electric, Microsoft, and
Tootsie Roll.

GENERAL ELECTRIC CO.

In 1999, once again, General Electric finished number one on *Fortune*
magazine's list of America's most-admired companies. No wonder. The
firm has increased its profits and dividends at a spectacular rate year
after year. It has precisely what our strategy requires—consistency and
growth.

After adjustments for stock splits, the price of a share of GE in 1977
was about $3 per share. By early 1999, it was $100 per share. Dramatic
price increases like this are always accompanied by dramatic growth in
earnings and dividends. A stock may jump in the short-term on good
news, but in the long-term the rise can only be maintained if real profits show up. As Benjamin Graham said, "In the short run, the stock
market is a voting machine, but in the long run, it is a weighing machine."

In twelve of the years between 1977 and 1997, GE increased dividends per share by at least 10 percent. In the worst of the years, it
boosted dividends 6 percent; in the best, by almost 20 percent. On average, GE's dividend grew 11 percent annually for two decades.

While GE is a respected company with the second-largest capitalization (or market value) of all U.S. stocks, few investors understand the true meaning of double-digit dividend growth. Remember that dividends are the lower-bound, or minimum, estimate of the cash flow from holding stock and that cash flow is what should determine a stock's price. "A stock," wrote John Burr Williams in a groundbreaking book, *The Theory of Investment Value,* published by Harvard University Press in 1938, "is worth the present value of its future dividends, with future dividends dependent on future earnings."

The dividend per share of GE in May 1999 was $1.40 a year, and the stock was trading at $105 for a yield of 1.3 percent. That seems low compared to interest rates on bonds of 5.5 percent. But over time, the dividend will grow. How much is the growth worth? Suppose that GE can achieve the same dividend increases over the next one hundred years that it has achieved over the past twenty years, but then it goes bankrupt, with your shares becoming worthless. We calculate that, under those circumstances, the present value of the stream of dividends that you buy when you pay $105 for a share today is $4,075. That price—$4,075 a share—is reasonably justified by history.

But can GE's growth continue at such a torrid pace?

The company began its long tenure more than a century ago with the merger of The Edison General Electric Light Co. and the Thomson-Houston Co. It was founded on the premise that research—into ways to improve both technology and management—is the key to profits. GE is now the leader in such businesses as lightbulbs, home appliances, jet engines, electric-power generators, plastics, and sophisticated medical equipment. It is also one of the world's largest lenders and owns NBC, one of the three top American TV broadcasters.

From Thomas Edison to Jack Welch, GE has had impeccable leadership for decades. Welch's management strategy has emphasized "speed, stretch, and boundaryless behavior" and a requirement that the company be number-one or number-two player in all its businesses. Among other things, leaders have pricing power. Subsidiaries that don't meet this standard are "fixed, sold, or closed." This strategy required GE to shut down or sell many plants, keep the most profitable, and maintain only a few of the stragglers that could be salvaged quickly. Like many other U.S. companies, GE restructured its operations two decades ago, firing more than seventy thousand employees and selling off more than a hundred businesses from 1981 to 1983.

Above all, GE is flexible. In 1990, after the Berlin Wall fell and the company's managers concluded that Eastern Europe was going to open up to the world, the company bought a majority share of the Hungarian firm Tungsram, which owned the international rights to valuable lighting technologies. Tungsram has helped boost the efficiency of capital invested in the lighting division of GE by 15 percent annually.

As the 1993 annual report put it, "We run this company on a simple premise: the only way to win, in the brutally competitive global environment in which we operate, is to get more output from less input in all 12 of our businesses and, by doing so, become the lowest-cost producer of high-quality goods and services in the world. We believe the only way to gain more output from less input—to grow and win—is to engage every mind within our businesses—exciting, energizing, involving and rewarding everyone."

But judge GE's deeds, not its words. At a growth rate of just 5 percent, we would be comfortable with a P/E of 100 for a company like General Electric. But GE is increasing its dividends at twice that pace, and its P/E in mid-1999 was only 36 (a significant number). It was, by our conservative standards, trading two-thirds below its perfectly reasonable price.

MICROSOFT CORP.

Microsoft has been the most notable beneficiary of the computer revolution and the biggest financial success story of our time. A tiny company quickly became the supplier of the operating system for almost every personal computer on earth. The profits have been staggering, and in July 1999, the company, started in 1975 by a Harvard dropout, Bill Gates, and his young friend, Paul Allen, was worth $463 billion. Since Gates owns 20 percent of the stock, his shares were worth about $90 billion, making him the richest man on earth.

In 1980, Microsoft signed a contract with IBM to install its operating system, MS-DOS, on all the giant company's personal computers. Gates sold the same system to companies making IBM clones, and he allowed makers of applications software (for word processing, spreadsheets, and so on) access to the MS-DOS code. Apple, which had a better operating system, made the mistake of keeping its architecture closed. Microsoft quickly became the industry standard.

In 1983, with fewer than five hundred employees, Microsoft released its first Windows program, a user-friendly system that was nearly as easy to operate as Apple's, but cheaper. In 1986, Microsoft went public, and profits began to fly, rising at an average of 48 percent annually. As Microsoft has grown in size, the pace of earnings increases has barely slowed. Between 1994 and 1998, they grew 34 percent a year.

We have cited Microsoft many times in this book as an example of a great company. It has a virtual monopoly on operating systems (even though they represent less than half the firm's sales) and has expanded its reach into every corner of the computer industry. Chances are, if you are playing a game, writing a letter, or balancing your checkbook on you computer, then you are using a Microsoft product. Even though we are writing this book on an Apple and a PC computer, we both use a Microsoft word-processing program, Word.

Microsoft meets the Schlang criteria with ease. No large company matches its consistency and growth. Its profit margins are astronomical—30 percent after taxes. It has no debt, and cash and securities total more than a year's revenues—and its top managers and directors own 40 percent of the company's stock.

Microsoft's patents comprise a vast moat that keeps out competitors. In fact, the company's only serious threat has come, not from the private sector, but from the government, which accused the company in 1997 of antitrust violations.

While the Internet and the PC industry have grown tremendously, the diffusion of computers in the U.S. market—much less the world—is far from complete. Of course, there are no guarantees that a programmer in Bangladesh won't come up with an operating system that is faster and cheaper and can be distributed to millions of users via the Web—or that someone won't come up with a computer that doesn't need an operating system at all. But with such a strong franchise, Microsoft will be difficult to dislodge.

Hardly anyone doubts that Microsoft is a great company. The question that investors ask themselves is whether it is too late. In other words, is Microsoft stock too expensive? Have high-growth assumptions already been built into its stock?

Of course, investors have been worried about Microsoft being too high since at least 1994, when it was trading at one-twelfth of its 1999 price. But simply scoffing at past errors by others isn't a method of analysis.

This is where the Dow 36,000 Theory comes in. You can look quickly at Microsoft's numbers and determine if its current price falls within a comfort zone.

Microsoft pays no dividend—yet—so we have to look at earnings. But first, let's check to see what the company does with those earnings. We want to be sure that Microsoft is not the kind of company that devours its profits in capital investments just to keep those profits coming. But no, statistics published in the annual report and in the *Value Line Investment Survey* show that Microsoft spends very little on capital investment each year—only $700 million in 1998, which is about equal to its depreciation. In other words, nearly every dollar of earnings could be passed on to shareholders. No wonder Microsoft has built up such an enormous pile of cash.

Now, back to earnings: Value Line analysts project that they will rise at 30.5 percent annually for the next five years. Even if we cut that rate by one-third and then assume that only half the earnings will eventually flow to shareholders' pockets—both assumptions being ridiculously conservative—Microsoft's growth rate for cash would be over 10 percent, or nearly twice the Treasury bond rate. Microsoft's P/E in May 1999 was 62, so its price would have to rise by one-half before exceeding a P/E of 100. The company is easily within our comfort zone.

TOOTSIE ROLL INDUSTRIES

Microsoft is the number-one stock, in terms of market value in America, but we're still dazzled by Tootsie Roll. With a capitalization of just $2 billion, the company has been growing both by selling its traditional products and by acquiring candy lines from other companies and making them more profitable through low-cost production, shared distribution, and marketing know-how.

In 1972, Tootsie Roll bought Mason Candy Co., which makes Dots and Crows. In 1993, it bought the candy business of health products firm Warner-Lambert Co., with such brands as Junior Mints (of *Sein-*

feld fame), Charleston Chew, Sugar Daddy, Sugar Babies, and Pom Poms.

Americans consume more than twenty-six pounds of candy each year, up more than 60 percent since 1980. Sales by manufacturers total $10 billion annually, and Tootsie Roll has less than 1 percent of the market. So there's room to grow.

You can glean detailed information about Tootsie Roll—and any other publicly traded company—from the Edgar database, which you can access through the SEC's Internet website (www.sec.gov). For example, we checked Tootsie Roll's 10-K, an annual report filed on March 30, 1998. We learned, among other things, whether the Gordons, who head the company, had worked out any sweetheart deals that give the couple inordinate perks or other benefits (they hadn't) and whether Tootsie Roll's computer systems were ready for the year 2000 (they were—or, at least, so the company claimed in its official representation to the government). But mostly, we wanted to check the financials.

Net earnings had slowed their torrid pace a bit, but they were still rising smartly—up 12 percent in 1998 after rising 27 percent in 1996. Then we checked the Consolidated Statement of Cash Flows to find out what Tootsie Roll did with its $67 million in earnings. The key figures were capital expenditures (that is, new investments in plant and equipment) of $15 million and depreciation (that is, write-offs of old investments in plant and equipment) of $13 million. In other words, as with most mature companies, Tootsie Roll's capital outlays each year are roughly the same as its depreciation (which is already taken out as an expense before the earnings figure of $67 million is arrived at). So nearly all the company's officially reported earnings could be distributed to shareholders in 1998. How much did they actually get in cash dividends? About $9 million, up from $6 million just two years before.

So, like Microsoft, Tootsie Roll is building up its cash. Let's check the balance sheet to be sure. Yes, there's $81 million in cash and $83 million in "investments" and no debt (other than a $7.5 million industrial revenue bond that costs the company $500,000 a year in interest). But what does this word "investments" mean? Again, Tootsie Roll and Edgar provide the answer, in the notes: "various marketable securities with maturities generally of less than one year." In other words, very short-term bonds—probably municipals.

So the company looks very, very sound. The other key figures we can get from Value Line: Earnings and dividends are each expected to grow at 12 percent annually, while, under our theory, a growth rate of just 5 percent would justify a P/E of 100. So Tootsie Roll, with a P/E of around 30, could triple before bursting out of our comfort zone.

FIVE QUESTIONS TO ASK BEFORE YOU BUY

A manufacturing leader, a software firm, and a candy maker: What they have in common is an affirmative answer to the following five questions, which a 36er should ask herself before she buys any stock.

1. DOES THE FIRM MAKE MONEY?

Don't laugh. Lots of high-fliers don't. It is easy to become enamored of start-up Internet companies or biotech firms that have very promising products and no earnings. The problem is, great products don't always make profits; great companies do. Apple had by far the best computer, but the company nearly went bankrupt in the late 1990s and the stock returned precisely zero from April 1989 to April 1999. Or consider the airline industry. In 1949, Benjamin Graham warned speculators who were wildly buying airline stocks to be wary since the fact that airline traffic was going to increase did not mean that airline profits were going to increase. As usual, Graham was right. Airlines have suffered for two reasons: first, their earnings get consumed in buying newer and better planes, and second, flying has become a commodity business, meaning that consumers rarely differentiate among brands. So the business goes to the company that offers the flight at the lowest cost. There's no moat around an airline company. As Buffett said in North Carolina in 1995, "If you go back to the time—and we're in the right state for that—from Kitty Hawk, net, the airline business in the United States has made no money."

Earnings and dividends are the only measurement of a company's price. If a company hasn't made any profits yet, you are just taking a wild guess about what a stock is worth. Pass up start-ups in favor of companies that have shown they can deliver. Yes, you may miss some winners, but you'll lower your risk of failure.

Think back to our dry cleaning example. The woman at the cocktail party asked you to invest in a new store and held up her highly profitable old store as an example of what might happen. Wouldn't you feel better buying a share of the store that was already proven to be profitable—even if that share costs a little more?

2. DOES THE FIRM HAVE SOMETHING SPECIAL?

If the firm has a patent, special know-how, or a great brand identity, like Coca-Cola or Tootsie Roll, then it will be able to harvest profits year after year with little fear of competition. If it does not, then its profitability could disappear quickly.

The best stocks to buy are those of companies that have a franchise that others can't duplicate or a moat that others can't cross without massive investments. And it's important that the franchise not require constant nurturing with vast amounts of capital each year. Most companies that make semiconductors, for instance, have to devote huge sums to building new plants to turn out products that must continually get better—unlike, say, a Coke or a Tootsie Roll. For instance, in 1995, a typical year, Advanced Micro Devices spent $600 million on new capital investment, with depreciation of just $300 million. Meanwhile, total earnings were $290 million. So more cash went out the door than came in. How can a company operate that way? Well, it can borrow: Advanced Micro's total debt is $1.5 billion. It's not surprising, then, that the stock averaged returns of just 9 percent during the decade ending in 1999.

It may be a very fine company, but it lacks "something special"—a product that doesn't devour earnings.

3. DOES THE FIRM HAVE A LONG-TERM RECORD OF EARNINGS GROWTH OF AT LEAST 7.2 PERCENT?

High P/Es are justified only if a company can be counted on to keep growing. What increases the odds that it will? Having something special is a great start, but a long history of steady growth is even more reassuring. We can't tell what Hewlett-Packard's leading business will be in twenty years, but the firm's track record indicates that whatever it is, the company will thrive.

How much growth do we want to see? Our calculations of the PRP assumed only that the earnings per share grow at about 5 percent annually, the same as the economy as a whole. Perhaps the strongest sign that stocks are still very cheap is the fact that so many companies have regularly grown much faster than that for many years. It would be relatively easy to construct a portfolio of stocks selling for current P/Es of 25 or less, with dividends of at least 1 percent and expected long-run earnings growth rates in excess of 10 percent.

In fact, here are some from among the thirty stocks of the Dow Jones industrial average: AlliedSignal, Alcoa, American Express, Hewlett-Packard, IBM, J.P. Morgan & Co., Minnesota Mining & Manufacturing (3M), Philip Morris Cos., Sears, Roebuck & Co., Citigroup, and United Technologies.

But we find a margin of safety in stocks with a growth rate as low as 7.2 percent—still, half-again as much as our assumptions for the market as a whole. We chose this figure because it makes quick-and-dirty calculations simple. Go back to the Rule of 72: When something (in this case earnings) grows at a rate of 7.2 percent, in ten years, it doubles. So look back a decade at any firm's earnings per share. Have they doubled? Can you expect them to double in the *next* 10 years? The best indicator you have is the past—plus your own analysis of the company's products and management, and the work of research firms like Value Line or brokerage houses.

4. WILL THE FIRM STILL EXIST FIFTY YEARS FROM NOW?

Growth produces huge returns only if it continues for decades. Of course, there is no way to tell for sure whether a company will survive for another fifty years, but you can make an educated guess. A firm with a single video game as its product or a restaurant chain capitalizing on a trend for Roumanian food is less likely to last than a company like GE, with a broad line of businesses and a long history. We would stay away from young firms built on one software program or firms built on a commodity (a metal or even petroleum) that could be replaced or driven down in price by synthetic competitors.

Still, the experience of Lexington Corporate Leaders Fund (see Chapter 11) shows clearly that companies with good balance sheets and brand-name products tend to weather the worst storms. Make sure you can answer yes to this fourth question, but don't obsess over it. No one knows whether a particular company will last for decades, but a stock on the Dow, for instance, is almost certainly built to last.

5. IS THE P/E WELL BELOW 100?

If a stock meets these criteria and is selling for a P/E below 100, then it is a good buy. We hesitate to establish a cut-off for P/E rates, even at 100, but there are so many great firms in double digits that you can ignore those trading higher.

Why 100? If a firm is currently growing 20 percent per year, we can be sure that at some point in the future that growth will slow. But when? It's difficult to say. Making such determinations may be very important when the Dow gets to 36,000. But today, with prices so low, it is a distraction to worry about whether a P/E of 150 or 400 is correct for Microsoft.

Still, for now, a P/E of 100 can be seen as an outer limit. A stock that trades at a P/E of 25 and meets all of our other criteria should quadruple. For the market as a whole, all we require for Dow 36,000 is that earnings and dividends grow at least as fast as the rest of the economy—or roughly 5 percent, including moderate inflation. For both an individual stock and for the market, if growth is much faster, then there is a significant comfort zone for the buyer.

HOW TO FIND GREAT STOCKS

We have looked at a few companies you should think about owning, but you will certainly want to buy more. How can you find them?

The first step is to build a list of promising stocks. The second is to analyze them to see if they meet the Dow 36,000 criteria.

Read the business section of your local paper and *The Wall Street Journal* or *Investor's Business Daily* each day. *USA Today* also has good business coverages. You will find breaking news stories that identify promising companies—a new drug discovery, a remarkable spike in profits, or a high-tech breakthrough. At this point, don't worry about price—or about whether you are too late to participate in a big run-up. Just look for good businesses.

Read *Barron's,* the Dow Jones weekly. Read business publications such as *Forbes, Fortune,* and *Business Week* and monthly investment magazines like *Money, Kiplinger's Personal Finance, SmartMoney,* and *Worth.* Concentrate on the coverage of companies.

As your list grows, check to see whether a company meets the requirements of our five questions.

Only a few years back, it was difficult for an individual investor to gather up-to-date information about stocks. The newspaper was a source for yesterday's closing price and perhaps a company's P/E ratio. Today, the Internet has dozens of websites dedicated to providing information about stocks—most of it free and unrestricted. In addition, most public companies have their own sites, where they post their own financial reports and press releases along with information about their products. And, then, there's the SEC's Edgar on the Internet. It would be impossible for any book to stay current with the Internet, but here are some starting points.

Consider quote.yahoo.com (notice, no *www.*), which allows you to create a personal portfolio with the stocks you own or may want to buy. The site also provides information about a stock's current and historic prices, P/E ratio, earnings estimates, market capitalization, dividend yield, and much more. After you type in the ticker symbol of a stock, Yahoo gives a menu, including "Research." Click on that, and you will have access to the kind of earnings and dividend growth information you need to evaluate whether a company has 36er characteristics. You can learn how long a company has been growing and what market analysts are saying about its future. For example, the consensus of analysts pegs the long-run earning growth projections for GE at 13 percent and Microsoft at 24 percent (Tootsie Roll is not followed by enough analysts for an estimate.) Another attractive stock for 36ers, Harley-Davidson, Inc., the motorcycle maker, had annual earnings growth of 22 percent from 1993 to 1998, compared to 10 percent for the average S&P stock. Projected earnings growth, say the analysts, is 19 percent a year through 2004, compared with 7 percent for the S&P. The site also lists more detailed research abstracts that you can purchase.

Another valuable Internet address is www.dailystocks.com, which claims to be the "biggest stock research site." It provides a constantly updated list of links to free online information. Find out about a company's competitors, compare the performance of different industries, and read earnings announcements and other news. You can get an annual report by going to a company's own website, or to www.icbinc.com/cgi-bin/wsj.pl, a free service of *The Wall Street Journal* that directs companies to e-mail you their reports. The websites of brokers such as Schwab and mutual fund houses such as Fidelity also offer research on individual stocks and funds, and sites like www.marketplace.com (free) and www.thestreet.com (by paid subscription) provide current market coverage.

A third type of website offers original content and commentary on individual stocks. The best right now is the Motley Fool, available through America Online or directly on the Web at www.fool.com. Founded in 1993 by two brothers, David and Tom Gardner, the site follows a simple principle—that small individual investors can outsmart the pros—especially when they share information and advice among themselves. The articles on this site are its real attraction, but as on quote.yahoo.com and others, you may create your own portfolio or check the latest stock prices.

IS THERE AN INTERNET BUBBLE?

Many investors are interested not merely in using the Internet but also in owning it. The prices of companies with little or no earnings, such as Yahoo! and Amazon, have risen 50-fold in two years. In May 1999, Ebay, Inc., the online auction service, had a P/E ratio of 907. Amazon had a larger market capitalization than Sears; Priceline's stock value was three times greater than that of Dow Jones, owner of *The Wall Street Journal,* and Sotheby's Holdings, Inc., the classy auction house, combined.

As we have shown, a little bit of growth can go a long way. Still, we advise caution when it comes to Internet companies.

A company can generate a consistent and growing stream of cash for many years only if it has protection against copycat competitors. The Internet makes entry extraordinarily easy. While an online retailer does not need an investment in bricks and mortar to sell books or computer equipment, neither does the next online retailer. And since shopping is easy on the Net (you don't have to walk down the street, or even pick up the phone, to compare prices), margins are probably going to be squeezed lower and lower. It will be hard to make profits that grow and last.

That, anyway, is one theory. Another is that the Internet will reward service, rather than price—since consumers will be wary of ordering goods from a store they cannot see. So a company that makes a huge investment in building a strong brand name and in rapid turnaround and user-friendliness (and, here, Amazon springs to mind) may be able to create a kind of "cyber moat." At this point, we just can't tell.

We don't believe there is an Internet bubble in the sense that investors have puffed up prices out of all contact with reality, the way tulip-bulb prices were inflated in the 17th century (see Chapter 2). The Internet will definitely make many investors very rich; it already has. But picking winners and losers is difficult with companies that have little or no track record in profits.

Of course, some Internet companies do. The best is Microsoft, which will be selling a new operating system to each new Internet customer. Cisco Systems and Lucent Technologies, both highly profitable, sell the infrastructure—the hardware and software that allow the Web's networks to operate. And AT&T and Time Warner, Inc., are just two of the many firms that have invested heavily in linking consumers to the Internet with new technologies. In 1998, America Online earned $134 million on $2.6 billion in sales, and that may just be for starters. (By checking www.dailyquotes.com, we found that analysts expect earnings of $500 million for the year ending in June 2000.)

Still, the lesson of this book is that the best buys today are the boring, cash-generating firms that are all around us—the Tootsie Rolls and the GEs. With all that low-hanging fruit around, why take a risky reach for Internet stocks? Wait until they become more ripe.

We also recognize, however, that investors are enthusiastic about Internet stocks—and with good reason. There is an excellent chance that the Net will become the greatest revenue-generating machine in history. Merrill Lynch analyst Henry Blodgett may have been understating the case when he said, "It is possible in ten or twenty years, we'll look back on this period in the way we now look back at the Industrial Revolution."

If you want to participate in that revolution as an investing partner, here are some suggestions:

• Decide what proportion of your total stock portfolio you want to devote to Internet companies and stick to it (the science of dividing up your assets is discussed in the next chapter). A good number is somewhere between zero and 15 percent.

• Buy only companies you understand and believe in—those whose businesses make sense. An example is DoubleClick, Inc., which measures website visits and places advertising. Its revenue jumped from $31 million in 1997 to $80 million in 1998, but profits remain elusive.

• Don't worry too much about price. You can't set a proper valuation for must Internet stocks, so you shouldn't sweat it. If you believe the company has a cool idea—perhaps Priceline, with its name-your-own-price system for selling plane tickets and everything else; RealNetworks, Inc., with its Net-based audio and video software; or VeriSign, Inc., with its secure digital IDs—then seriously consider purchasing the stock. For better or worse, deep analysis won't help. These are stocks you have to buy more for love than for reason.

• Own either a portfolio of a dozen Internet stocks or a mutual fund. Since there will be a few winners and lots of losers among these companies (and since you can't tell now which will be which), diversification is essential. Internet mutual funds don't have long track records, of course, but some of the better ones are Monument Internet, WWW Internet, the Internet Fund, and Munder Net Net. Also consider Internet UITs.

• Buy shares in the few Internet companies that actually have earnings. Almost certainly, those will be the stocks that managers of conventional growth-stock funds will be bidding up in the years ahead. For example, a favorite of Alexander Cheung, who runs Monument Internet, is Aware, Inc., developer of digital subscriber line (DSL) technology, which speeds up Net access over existing phone lines. Aware broke into the black in the fourth quarter of 1998.

While it is impossible to value a company with no earnings, you can make some educated guesses about firms whose prices vastly exceed their profits. Take America Online. In the first quarter of 1999, the company earned $117 million on revenues of $1.3 billion. The stock's P/E in May 1999 was 419.

Make some assumptions. For the fiscal year ending in June 2000, it is not hard to imagine AOL earning $500 million to $800 million on $8 billion in revenues. After that? Well, analysts have a wide range of forecasts for annual earnings growth over the next five years, generally ranging from 50 percent to 100 percent.

With growth near the lower end of that range, earnings will hit $6 billion, or roughly $6.50 per share, by 2005. AOL was trading in May 1999 at $125. Let's say the stock triples by 2005 to $375. The P/E that year would be 58, which is not outrageously high.

This exercise, however, may be futile since the key assumption—the earnings growth rate—could be far off. If AOL grows at 20 percent instead of 50 percent, then its earnings in 2005 will be $2 billion instead of $6 billion, and the P/E (if the stock triples) will be 173. Still, you can see that compound earnings growth is a powerful force, and ridiculing Internet prices may be an act of hubris and closed-mindedness.

Our own bias, however, remains with companies whose earnings we can count—and count on.

So far, we have talked only about stocks. But even with the Dow racing toward 36,000, stocks should not comprise the entire portfolio of most investors. How to determine how large a part? And how to allocate your money among different kinds of stocks? Those are some of the subjects for the next chapter.

CHAPTER 14

Stocks, Bonds, or Cash? How to Allocate Your Assets

There's husbandry in heaven.

—William Shakespeare, *Macbeth*

Wɪᴛʜ ᴛʜᴇ ᴅᴏᴡ headed for 36,000 and beyond, it would seem logical that *all* investors should put *all* of their investment cash into stocks.

But that would be a mistake. While the argument for the market going up sharply is powerful, it often makes sense to keep a cushion of bonds and cash. How much? For some investors, very little; for others, a lot. You first need to examine your own situation—your age, your financial requirements, your willingness to accept risk.

Dividing up your money into different financial categories is called "asset allocation." The process is even more important—though less fun—than picking specific stocks. There are three broad groups: stocks, bonds, and cash. Within each group, there are different subgroups—for instance, small-cap stocks, corporate bonds, and certificates of deposit.

But before you start allocating, you need to know the characteristics of each asset. In this chapter, we discuss the different places you can invest your money and how to decide what proportion of your portfolio you should put in each.

STOCKS

Stocks are the main subject of this book, but to refresh your memory . . .

When you buy a share of stock, you become a part-owner of a company. You have the right to vote on key corporate policies and elect the board of directors, but more important, you share in the firm's profits, which either are distributed to you directly each quarter in the form of dividends or are reinvested in the company and flow to you later.

Over the past two decades stocks have returned about twice as much as bonds annually, but over the short term, stocks have been far more risky. In the long term—especially periods of fifteen years or more—stocks still returned much more than bonds, but the riskiness of the two kinds of investments has been about the same.

Risk, remember, means volatility—the extremes of an asset's ups and downs. For instance, if stocks returned 11 percent every single year without fail, they would carry no risk at all. But in fact, between 1926 and 1998 (a period that has been studied thoroughly), stocks have bounced around wildly—a riskiness measured by a calculation called "standard deviation." Large-company stocks, the kind that dominate the S&P 500, have a standard deviation of about 20 percent, which means that in two-thirds of the years, their returns will range from twenty percentage points higher to twenty percentage points lower than the average—in this case, from a high of 31 percent to a low of minus-9 percent. But returns are even more extreme in the outlying years.

If you have saved $20,000 and intend to use it for a down payment on a house in the next twelve months, it would be foolish to invest that money in the stock market. While in an average year, your stock account will grow to $22,200 (before taxes), there is a chance that it will fall sharply. In 1931, the stock market lost 43 percent of its value; in 1974, it fell 26 percent. Since 1926, the market has fallen, on average, in one out of every four years.

Short-term investing in the stock market (also called "trading") is nothing more than gambling—which can certainly be fine as entertainment, but not as a way to accumulate a nest egg for retirement. Unless you enjoy the thrill of the market version of roulette and can afford to lose lots of money in a short time, stocks are an asset that must be held for the long term.

But what do we mean by "long term" when it comes to the Dow 36,000 Theory? If stocks are drastically undervalued—if they should rise immediately by a factor of 4 to get to their perfectly rational price—then why should we be concerned about the long run at all?

The answer is that we really can't be sure *when* stocks will hit the PRP. Our guess is the year 2005 or so, but there's no certainty. Before we developed our theory, we believed that no one whose horizon was shorter than ten years should have substantial funds in stocks. Now, we have shortened our view of the long term to five years. Still, even with Dow 36,000 imminent, stock investors should be long-term investors.

Now, let's turn to bonds, which require more explanation.

BONDS

A bond is an IOU—a piece of paper you get in return for lending money. When a borrower—let's use the U.S. Treasury as an example—sells a bond, it goes into debt. The Treasury receives, say, $1,000 from an investor and promises to pay that money back at the end of a set period, with the final date called "maturity."

In the meantime, the investor (the lender) gets interest from the Treasury. The essential nature of bonds is that the money that flows into your pockets is unchanging—which is why bonds are also called "fixed-income" assets. (There are a few exceptions to this rule, and we'll get to them.)

The rate of interest is determined by the prevailing market conditions at the time the bonds are sold by the Treasury. Bonds carry a "coupon"—or specific rate—throughout their life. The Treasury sells debt with different maturities, from three months to thirty years. Debt securities issued to mature less than twelve months are called "bills"; those maturing in one year to seven years are called "notes"; those maturing in more than seven years, "bonds." But we'll use the term "bonds" to mean anything that's not a bill.

Federal government agencies, such as the Tennessee Valley Authority and the Farm Credit Financial Assistance Corporation, also issue bonds. So do institutions like Fannie Mae, which is a private company with an "implicit"—but not an iron-clad legal—guarantee from the Treasury to back up the debt in case of disaster. Corporations issue bonds as well, and so do state and local government agencies.

Interest on Treasury bonds is exempt from state and local taxes, and interest on state and local bonds (called "municipals" or "munis") is exempt from federal taxes—and often from state and local taxes too.

Bonds sound straightforward: Buy a new $10,000 T-bond that carries a 5 percent coupon and matures in ten years, and you will receive two checks annually totaling $500 each year for a decade, then get your $10,000 back.

What makes bonds tricky is that most investors don't buy them when they are issued and sell them when they mature. Instead, they make their purchases and sales on the open market (there is a market for bonds, just as for stocks). During its life, the bond's price will fluctuate since our old friend, risk, is present here as well.

When a bond is issued, it will be priced at about 100, or 100 percent of its face value—say, $10,000. But, then, a few months later, the price might drop to 95 (or $9,500 for a $10,000 bond); a year later, it could be 103 (or $10,300). What's going on?

The market is constantly assessing the bond's riskiness. It is looking at two things: credit risk and interest-rate risk. In both cases, the more years the bond has to go before it matures, the greater the risk. That stands to reason. If someone owes you money and has promised to pay you back tomorrow, it's more likely you will get your cash (and more likely that the cash will have the same buying power as it does today) than if the borrower doesn't have to pay you for another twenty years.

Credit risk refers to the possibility that a lender won't be able to pay its debts—the interest or the principal (your original $10,000). The U.S. Treasury is probably the most stable financial institution in the world. You don't have to worry about credit risk with T-bonds or the bonds of federal agencies. But for corporations, risk varies widely, and the riskier the credit, the higher the interest rate investors will demand.

For example, in early 1999, a bond issued by IBM that matures in the year 2025 was yielding 6.5 percent while a bond issued by Ugly Duckling Corp., a real-life car-rental firm based in Phoenix, that matures in 2003 was yielding 13.3 percent. Obviously, IBM is a more stable company than Ugly Duckling (the name doesn't help much either), so investors won't lend to the rental firm—even for the short term—unless they receive much more interest to compensate them for the chances they are taking.

Credit risk can change during the life of a bond. For instance, when TWA first issued bonds maturing in 2004, the company had to pay a coupon of 11.5 percent. But as the firm's finances deteriorated, the price of the bond fell. In early 1999, it was trading at just 77. In other words, if you sold a bond with a face value (that is, the price TWA promises to pay at maturity) of $10,000, you would get just $7,700. But someone who *bought* the bond for $7,700 would be getting an annual return of 14.9 percent. The bond still pays that coupon of 11.5 percent, or $1,150 a year ($1,150/$7,700 = 0.149).

Corporate bonds like Ugly Duckling's and TWA's, which are particularly risky according to credit-rating agencies like Moody's and Standard & Poor's, are called "junk bonds" or "high-yield" bonds.

The second kind of risk is that interest rates will rise while you own your bond, making it less valuable. Let's say you buy a thirty-year Treasury bond when it's issued, with a coupon of 5.5 percent. So each year you will receive $550 in interest payments for an investment of $10,000.

Now, assume that twelve months later interest rates rise sharply, and investors can buy newly issued thirty-year T-bonds that pay 7 percent interest, or $700 for every $10,000. Naturally, your 5.5 percent bond has become less valuable. No one would pay you $10,000 for your old bond with its $550 in interest when new bonds are available for $10,000 that pay $700 in interest. In order to sell your bond, you will have to take a discount, determined by the market. Perhaps you will only get $8,000 for your bond. Its price, as listed in the bond tables, would have gone from 100 to 80.

Of course, the same process works in reverse. If rates fall, your bond becomes worth more. Your old bond at 5.5 percent interest might jump to 120 if rates fall to 4.5 percent.

This inverse relationship between bond prices and bond yields confuses many investors. So get it straight: When interest rates rise, bond prices fall; when interest rates fall, bond prices rise.

The reason rates rise is usually that investors fear inflation, a general increase in the price level. If you lend a friend $10,000 for ten years, you ask for interest (even from a friend) because the $10,000 he pays you ten years from now will not have the same buying power as $10,000 today. It will be eroded by inflation. You might be able to buy a bottom-of-the-line Honda today for $10,000, but in ten years, the same kind of new car would cost $14,000. So you have to be compensated.

Even at an inflation rate of 2 percent annually, over ten years, the buying power of $10,000 falls to just $7,800 in today's money. At an inflation rate of 4 percent, it falls to $5,200.

There is another risk investors take with many kinds of bonds (though not Treasuries): Certain issues are "callable," which means that the borrower can pay off the loan before maturity, just the way you can pay off your old mortgage and take out a new one. Most callable bonds provide protection for a while, but to have your bond called because interest rates have dropped from 7 percent to 5 percent can be a frustrating experience.

Two other kinds of bonds you should know about:

• **Zero-coupon bonds.** These are bonds that pay no interest but instead are sold at a deep discount to the price that the borrower promises to pay the lender at maturity. For example, in March 1999, a Treasury zero that matures in 2017 was trading at 33. In other words, for $3,300, you could buy a bond that would pay $10,000 in eighteen years. But, in the meantime, you get no interest payments; thus, the coupon is *zero*. In effect, your investment would be yielding 6.1 percent annually during the life of the bond. Still, you have the advantage of being able to lock in the rate of 6.1 percent. If you buy a conventional bond, you have to reinvest the dividends yourself, and interest rates could drop so your re-investment wouldn't be worth as much. (Of course, rates could also rise.)

For that reason, we like zeroes a great deal—but there's a drawback. The government taxes you on that "phantom interest" you don't receive, so you have to dip into your pocket to pay. As a result, zeroes work best in a tax-deferred account.

• **Inflation-protection bonds** In 1996, the Treasury came up with one of the best financial ideas of the century: bonds that protect investors against the risk of inflation (and thus most of the risk of rising interest rates). Since Treasuries carry no credit risk, these new bonds, which go by various names but are generally called "inflation-protection securities," are as close to riskless as any asset can be.

The Treasury guarantees that when the cost of living rises, the value of your bond will rise to keep up with it. The bonds carry a coupon that reflects the "real" rate of interest when they are issued—which has fluctuated in a narrow band between 3.4 percent and 3.9 percent. (That, in fact, is the only risk; investors are not completely settled about what the real rate should be.) Then, each year, the principal on the bond is increased by the consumer price index. This is a little complicated: The bond works like a cross between a zero and a regular bond. The more inflation rises, the more money you get when the bond matures. But the effect is simple: When inflation goes up 2 percent, your bond, which has a coupon of, say, 3.8 percent is really yielding 5.8 percent.

Unfortunately, these inflation-linked bonds have the same tax disadvantage as zeroes. You get hit for taxes each year on the inflation interest even though you don't actually get it until the bond matures (or until you sell it in the open market).

What's surprising is how high the real rates are on these bonds. They present an excellent buying opportunity—similar to the stock market. Investors don't seem to understand inflation-linked bonds yet, but as they learn, yields will decline (to 3 percent or lower) and prices will rise—the same process we expect with stocks.

The prices of zeroes and conventional bonds—long-term ones, especially—can bounce around in a disturbing fashion as interest rates rise. And trying to predict the course of rates is a fool's errand. As a result, we recommend bonds, not for speculation, but for one of these three uses:

• To generate reliable income for paying living expenses.

• To provide a modest, safe return for a relatively short period. For instance, if you have a child beginning college in two years, then the dollars you intend to use should go solely into bonds, not into stocks.

• To serve as ballast in a diversified portfolio. Short- and intermediate-term bonds (up to seven years' duration) will reduce the volatility of your retirement account while also, of course, reducing the returns.

We have two hard-and-fast rules with bonds:

1. *Stay away from corporates.* The safest ones carry interest rates that are too close to those of Treasuries: Why lend to IBM at 6.5 percent interest for thirty years when you can lend to the U.S. government at 5.5 percent interest and avoid state tax as well? And the riskiest bonds usually don't give you a big enough reward: You're better off buying the stock.

2. *Hold the bonds until maturity.* The reason to own bonds is that you know you'll get your initial investment back in full when they mature. You can't say that for stocks. Don't play the speculative game of trying to make money off interest rate movements.

Now, a few words about municipal bonds. First, invest in them only if they are top-rated (AAA or Aaa, depending on the agency) or guaranteed by one of the large private insurers, such as MBIA, Inc. Second, watch out for calls! A muni yielding 6 percent with a maturity in 2020 sounds good, but if the issuer can snatch it away from you in a few years and refinance it at 5 percent, it's worth a lot less. Third, buy munis as an alternative to Treasuries if they make sense in your tax bracket. For example, in early 1999, a California general obligation bond, maturing in 2028 was yielding 5.1 percent. (A general obligation, or "G.O.," bond is one that requires the state to use its taxing power to meet interest and principal payments; a "revenue" bond is less safe since the debt service is funded from a specific stream of revenue, such as turnpike tolls or airport fees.)

Now, is 5.1 percent a good deal?

To find the answer, we need to compare the return on the ultrasafe muni to the return on a comparable investment: a Treasury bond also maturing in 2028. At the time, the T-bond rate was 5.7 percent. But what about the tax advantage of munis?

There's a simple formula to derive what is called the "tax-equivalent" yield of a muni, so you can compare it to a Treasury. Just divide the muni rate by 1 minus your marginal federal tax rate (that is, the rate you encounter when you earn an extra dollar of income). If your rate is 28 percent—the national average for families—then the tax-equivalent yield of the California muni will be 7.1 percent [5.1 ÷ (1 − .28)]. In other words, the muni gives you as much after taxes as a Treasury paying 7.1 percent. But the Treasury actually pays 5.7 percent, so the muni is a better deal. If your tax rate was 39.6 percent—the top bracket at the time—then the yield to compare with the Treasury is a lofty 8.4 percent.

In these cases, munis are an easy choice, but they aren't always. The rates of munis and Treasuries don't move in tandem. Also, while you can buy T-bonds directly through the Treasury, munis are bought through brokers, who often charge stiff commissions. And you are not certain to get the best price, since muni issues are small and illiquid and their prices not very "transparent"—or widely reported. In addition, remember state taxes. Most states exempt interest on their own bonds, but not necessarily on the bonds of other states. Treasury interest is always exempt from state taxes. And, finally, Treasuries are never callable.

You can buy bonds individually or in mutual funds, closed-end funds, or unit-investment trusts. Remember that, since bond funds own ever-changing portfolios of dozens of debt issues, they never "mature." You can't be certain of getting your entire investment back—which is one of the big advantages of bonds. Still, diversification is an intelligent investing tactic, and we particularly like bond UITs.

An easy way to diversify and dampen interest-rate risk is by "laddering," or buying bonds that mature in successive years. Here's how it works: Say you have $50,000 to invest. Instead of putting all your money into bonds that come due in five years, you put $10,000 into bonds that mature in one year, another $10,000 into bonds that mature in two years, and so on.

At the end of year 1, the shortest-maturity bonds will mature. Take the proceeds and put them in new five-year bonds, which will mature at the end of year 6. Then continue the process. Your portfolio always contains five bonds, maturing one year after another.

Consider the bond investor's nightmare: rising interest rates. As the shortest bonds in the portfolio mature, you are able to invest the proceeds in new five-year bonds that have higher rates and longer maturities. A neat trick.

Credit risk is not a problem with Treasuries, nor with highly rated munis. Still, we feel much better holding muni issues from different states and in different fields—a turnpike bond, school bond, G.O., water plant bond, and so on.

What do bonds return? It depends on their credit risk, maturity, and the general interest-rate environment. But since 1926, according to Ibbotson, long-term government bonds have returned an annual average of 5.2 percent, including both the interest payments (yields) and price increases. Yields, however, can vary wildly. In 1951, Treasuries paid 2.1 percent interest; in 1982, they paid 13.5 percent; and in 1998, they fell below 5 percent.

Unlike stocks, bonds guarantee their returns (as long as you hold them to maturity). You know what you're getting before you sign up. Still, don't forget that even though stock returns aren't guaranteed, over time, stocks have proven even less risky than bonds after inflation is taken into account.

CASH

What financial professionals call "cash" isn't the green stuff. It is actually a term for a very brief loan. An interest-bearing checking account, for example, is actually a loan from you to your bank. You can get your principal back any time you want. A certificate of deposit, or CD, is also a loan, usually to a bank, with a longer maturity—from thirty days on up. And a Treasury bill is a loan of up to one year from an investor to the federal government.

Another widespread form of cash is the money-market fund—simply a mutual fund which, instead of holding stocks in its portfolio, holds short-term bonds and other kinds of loans, such as commercial paper, which is debt issued by large corporations directly to investors. Tax-exempt money-market funds are structured the same way, but their portfolios are filled with muni bonds that are just about to mature.

The yields of money-market funds change daily, as some securities (a word that encompasses all financial instruments) mature and are replaced by others. But unlike bonds, the prices of money-market funds never change: They always trade at $1 per share. Only the interest they pay varies. Since 1926, the yield on T-bills (the rate that tends to determine the rate of other ultra-short debt) has averaged 3.8 percent—just a little ahead of inflation, at 3.1 percent.

Cash is not really an investment. It's a resting place for money you might need in a hurry or plan eventually to put to use in stocks or bonds. Except in extraordinary circumstances—such as in 1980, when T-bills were paying 11 percent interest—you should carry as little cash as possible.

From 1987 to 1997, the value of a portfolio completely composed of T-bills, continually rolled over and reinvested, rose from $1,000 to $1,700, but a $1,000 bond portfolio rose to $2,920, and a large-cap stock portfolio to $4,590. T-bills are often called "safe," but the truth is they can cost you plenty in lost opportunities for large returns.

ALLOCATING ASSETS

Now that you know the building blocks—stocks, bonds, and cash—it's time to draw the blueprints for constructing a portfolio. This process is the first step in establishing a firm investment discipline. Your asset allocation does not have to be set in stone, but its flexibility has to be charted from the start. Unless you take your blueprint seriously, you won't be able to resist the urge to change allocations as the markets bounce up and down. If that happens, your whole investment edifice will weaken and even crumble. So get the numbers straight and stick to them.

The classic asset allocation, wrote Marshall Loeb in his book, *Lifetime Investment Strategies,* is 55 percent stocks, 35 percent bonds, and 10 percent cash. That's interesting, but not too helpful. The average male may wear a size 40 suit, but a man goes to a store for one that fits him, not the average male.

Your own broad asset allocation should depend on two factors:

1. *Your tolerance for risk.* Some investors just can't sleep at night, worrying about the fate of their shares. That's an expensive affliction, but it can be even more expensive if you buy lots of stocks and then dump them. "Know thyself" is a good rule for investors, and if you are an incurable hydrophobe, you shouldn't dive into the pool.

2. *Your own needs.* These are more complicated, but they come down mainly to time horizon—how long you can hold on to your stocks and bonds before you need to liquidate them (that is, turn them into cash). That horizon is usually a function of age.

If you are twenty-five years old and want to build a nest egg for your retirement at age sixty-five, then every dime you invest should go into stocks, except for a cash reserve against emergencies. There is no need to worry even about a ten-year bear market. You can survive it—indeed, benefit from it, as you continue to buy more shares for your account at lower prices. And remember the research that shows that over periods of twenty years or more, stocks have been no more risky—in fact, even less risky—than bonds and T-bills.

But many people cannot remain heavily invested in stocks as they get older. If you plan to leave your job at sixty-five, you will need cash to pay expenses in retirement. As you near the time when you need to start withdrawing money, you should own fewer stocks and more bonds and cash. The reason is simple: When you get close to retirement, short-term fluctuations can have a big impact on your life.

Suppose, for example, that you have built a nest egg of $1 million in stocks and that you are planning to turn all of that money into a laddered portfolio of Treasury bonds when you retire, so you can live on the interest checks of roughly $50,000 a year. For simplicity's sake, assume your entire portfolio consisted of 12,500 shares of Motorola stock, which was trading at $80 a share in the summer of 1997. Your plan is to retire in October 1998. But as the date approaches, Motorola goes into a sickening slide. By September, the stock is trading at $40. Your portfolio is now worth only $500,000, and if you convert to Treasuries, as planned, your consumption will be 50 percent lower for the rest of your life because of your bad luck. The solution is to begin shifting assets earlier, for a smoother transition to the time when you need the cash.

For 36ers, the standard asset allocations—the sort that Loeb and other financial advisors have advocated for years—must be adjusted. Anyone, even in retirement, who passes up the chance to gain from the one-time-only rise in stock prices that we see occurring, would be making an enormous mistake. *All* investors should have a substantial chunk of their money in stocks over the next ten years.

Here is a sample allocation, which operates on these assumptions: retirement at sixty-five, moderate risk aversion, nest-egg development the only goal, all other expenses paid from earnings at work.

Up to age 30: 95 percent stocks, 5 percent cash

Ages 31 to 40: 90 percent stocks, 5 percent bonds, 5 percent cash

Ages 41 to 50: 80 percent stocks, 10 percent bonds, 10 percent cash

Ages 51 to 60: 70 percent stocks, 20 percent bonds, 10 percent cash

Ages 61 to 65: 60 percent stocks, 30 percent bonds, 10 percent cash

After that, allocations depend on how much income you need to supplement Social Security (if it's still around) and other pension benefits. Bonds and cash provide two or three times as much current income as stock dividends.

ALLOCATIONS WITHIN ALLOCATIONS

Dividing your portfolio into stocks, bonds, and cash isn't enough. Under the heading "stocks," there are subcategories, allocations within allocations. The objective here is diversification. If, for example, your stock holdings comprised only micro-cap companies, the smallest of the small, you would be placing far too large a bet on a single sector that comprises only 5 percent of the U.S. stock market. But owning only the large-caps of the S&P 500 is a similar error.

One way to spread your money—at least among U.S. stocks—is to put all of it into a Wilshire 5000 index, such as Vanguard Total Stock Market Fund. That's acceptable to us, but it's not ideal. The Dow 36,000 Theory plays favorites. It leans toward solid growth stocks— companies with a long history, a stable franchise or broad moat, and earnings and dividends that are growing faster than the economy as a whole. Most of the stocks that meet these qualifications fit into the large-cap growth category. But again, it would be a mistake to put all your cash into a fund like T. Rowe Price Dividend Growth or Fidelity Fifty, which specialize in such companies.

In addition, all portfolios need some exposure to foreign stocks. Since foreign shares do not move in tandem with U.S. shares, they can moderate the lows (and the highs) in your portfolio. For example, a study by Sanford C. Bernstein & Co. found that between 1970 and 1995, foreign stocks outperformed U.S. stocks significantly in twelve years; U.S. stocks did much better in twelve years; and the two categories were about the same in only two years. Sometimes, the differences were extreme—in 8 of the 26 years, one category outscored the other by at least twenty percentage points. A dose of foreign stocks, research shows, provides returns that are about the same as an all-domestic portfolio but with as little as half the risk. Certainly, you *can* ride out the lows in the U.S. market, but will you have the discipline? A portfolio with lower risk is a portfolio that won't spook you into selling in tough times.

But our enthusiasm for foreign companies, as a whole, does not match our enthusiasm for U.S. firms. The risk premium, which is falling to zero in the United States, will persist for foreign stocks as their governments and corporate managements struggle to make the changes that have reassured investors here. As a result, we would substantially "underweight" foreign stocks in suggested portfolios.

In 1999, Morgan Stanley Dean Witter calculated that the United States, with 5 percent of the world's population and 20 percent of its

GDP, has a stock market that represents 51 percent of the world's market capitalization (the value investors assign to companies). Western Europe, with 6 percent of population and also 20 percent of GDP, has 25 percent of the world's market cap. Asia, 47 percent of population, 30 percent of GDP, and 15 percent of market cap. The rest of the world—Africa, Latin America, the Middle East, Russia, and Central Europe—has 35 percent of population, 30 percent of GDP, and less than 10 percent of market cap.

But U.S. stocks merit a higher proportion in your portfolio than 51 percent since this country is where risk premiums are declining most swiftly and surely. Our recommended geographic allocation looks like this:

U.S. STOCKS: 80 percent

EUROPE: 10 percent

JAPAN: 5 percent

EMERGING MARKETS (rest of Asia, Latin America, Central Europe, etc.): 5 percent

Be flexible, but keep a 20 percent foreign weighting as a goal. You could simply buy a foreign-stock fund and trust the manager to make the geographic allocations. But beware: Such managers are market timers; they are continually trying to guess which markets will be up and which down, and when. In 1997 and 1998, for instance, the best performers shoveled all their assets into Europe. But that meant they missed the 19 percent run-up in Asian stocks in the first quarter of 1999. The easiest way to avoid this problem is to own separate mutual funds, even index funds, for each region. For instance, you could buy Vanguard International Equity Index European Fund, which divides its holdings across the continent by the weighting each country has in the Morgan Stanley European stock index. The fund, by the way, "has produced outstanding long-term returns versus its . . . peer group," according to Value Line. A big reason is an expense ratio of just 0.3 percent, compared with 1.9 percent for the average European fund. For Japan, of course, you don't need an index fund—simply a fund like T. Rowe Price Japan. Vanguard also has an emerging-markets index fund, but again, you can pick a managed fund from a firm like Merrill Lynch, Fidelity, or Templeton and get the exposure you need. Buying the individual stocks of emerging-markets countries is not a sport we recommend.

Within the U.S.-stock category, you need diversification as well, with allocations to small-caps, income-generating stocks such as REITs, utilities, and high-dividend shares, plus value stocks with particularly low P/Es. Our suggested weightings for U.S. and foreign stocks in a typical 36er portfolio:

LARGE-CAP GROWTH: 50 percent

LARGE-CAP VALUE: 10 percent

SMALL-CAP (both growth and value): 10 percent

INCOME: 10 percent

FOREIGN: 20 percent

As with foreign stocks, the easiest way to own small-caps and REITs is through mutual funds. Turn back to Chapter 11 for some recommendations.

But remember that these allocations are flexible. If you believe you have an expertise in technology stocks or even Internet stocks, put them in a separate category. If you think you don't need income stocks, forget them. But remember that the single largest chunk of your equity assets should be dedicated to large-cap growth—companies that should boom under the Dow 36,000 Theory.

DON'T JUST ALLOCATE, RE-ALLOCATE

Having a plan to allocate assets is a necessity before you buy a stock or fund. But once you have made your purchases, remember to *re-allocate*. Every year, check to be sure the categories have not gotten too far out of kilter because one has boomed while another has busted.

Let's imagine a simple portfolio composed of individual stocks and bonds (or mutual funds) in different asset categories, with dividends and capital gains reinvested back into the same assets. In early 1994, it was set up with $100,000 and looked like this:

Large-cap stocks	$40,000 (40 percent)
Small-cap stocks	$10,000 (10 percent)
Tech stocks	$10,000 (10 percent)
International stocks	$10,000 (10 percent)
Emerging-market stocks	$10,000 (10 percent)

Treasury bonds	$20,000 (20 percent)
Total:	**$100,000** (100 percent)

During the next five years, some categories grew faster than others, and one (emerging markets) actually fell. Using statistics from Lipper, Inc., we calculated a new allocation in early 1999:

Large-cap stocks	$117,880 (56 percent)
Small-cap stocks	$14,735 (7 percent)
Tech stocks	$29,470 (14 percent)
International stocks	$14,735 (7 percent)
Emerging-market stocks	$6,315 (3 percent)
Treasury bonds	$27,365 (13 percent)
Total:	**$210,500** (100 percent)

The portfolio gained a delicious 111 percent, but the categories are now far out of whack. The top three groups (domestic stocks) represent 77 percent of the portfolio, up from 60 percent; foreign stocks, 10 percent, down from 20 percent; and bonds, 13 percent, down from 20 percent.

It is time to rebalance. Take large-caps: If you want to maintain an allocation of 40 percent, then large-cap assets should be worth about $84,000, not $117,880. So you should sell about $34,000 worth of large-caps and distribute the proceeds among small-caps, which now should be tanked up to $21,000 from about $15,000, and foreign stocks. Also sell tech stocks and put the proceeds into bonds.

The premise of this kind of rebalancing is that you want to keep your assets in roughly the same proportion as five years ago. You're certainly free to change the percentages, but only for the right reasons— that you're closer to retirement, for example, and need more bonds. But don't change proportions because you believe you can time the market, convinced, for instance, that small-caps will be dogs for decades.

Also, rebalancing is a way to buy low. When a category falls as a percentage of your portfolio, it is a sign that shares in that asset class are cheap.

The only disadvantage of re-allocating is that capital gains will generate a tax bill. The only way to avoid this is to keep as much of your portfolio as possible in a tax-deferred account. You can reduce the bill if you own stocks, in addition to mutual funds, in your portfolio. If, for example, you have ten large-caps, even with the group as a whole tripling, one or two of the stocks may have fallen in price. By selling those you can offset gains from other sales. A way to avoid extreme re-balancing—and evade the tax man—is to invest dividend payments and mutual-fund distributions in your worst-performing categories, rather than re-investing them in the stocks and funds they came from. But, in general, taxes are a small price to pay for the benefits of main-taining a portfolio with sensible asset allocation. Don't go nuts, how-ever. You don't need to reallocate every year or sell assets in a category that has risen from 10 percent of your account to 11 percent.

WHEN STOCKS AND BONDS RETURN THE SAME

Under the Dow 36,000 Theory, the prices of stocks will rise until they reach the perfectly reasonable price, or PRP. When that ascension is complete, stocks will be putting the same amount of cash in your pockets over the long run as bonds. Does this mean that it doesn't mat-ter whether you invest in stocks or bonds? Not exactly.

One asset may suit you better than the other. If your horizon is short-term, you'll still want to own bonds rather than stocks. If you be-lieve that you can find stocks that will outperform the market, then choose them over bonds. But for the market as a whole, you will have to expect lower returns from stocks that you purchase after the PRP is attained. Another consideration—as with the choice between Trea-suries and munis—is taxes. In taxable accounts, stocks should remain a better buy than bonds for many investors. In the highest brackets, Treasury bonds generate income that is taxable at rates close to 40 per-cent while capital gains taxes (only triggered by a sale) are half that.

The choice will be personal, but the main change is that bonds will become a better alternative for long-term investors than they are today. After the PRP is achieved by the stock market, a young investor could hold an all-bond portfolio in a tax-deferred portfolio and not be mak-ing a ridiculous decision.

When we developed our theory, the Dow was trading roughly at 9,000, and we concluded that P/E ratios, then about 25, would rise to 100 and still be reasonable. So we justified the Dow immediately soar-ing, in a one-time levitation, to 36,000, based on earnings and divi-dends that prevailed at this level. But understand that earnings of corporations will continue to rise, and even if average P/Es remain in the range of 100 when the PRP is reached, the *prices* of stocks—and the level of the Dow—will rise too. Let's assume that the Dow goes to the current PRP of 36,000 this afternoon and that the P/E for the typical stock is 100. Over the next five years, if earnings rise by 5 percent annually, the Dow will grow by more than 25 percent—to nearly 46,000.

But what if the Dow takes longer to get to the PRP? Assume, for instance, that at the end of the year 2001, the Dow is at 25,000 and the average stock carries a P/E ratio of 50. In that case, if P/Es double to their reasonable level of 100, the PRP for the Dow at that instant will be 50,000—not 36,000.

The point is that the PRP is a moving target, and it may not be easy to know just when the cash flow from stocks and bonds will be equivalent. We intend to make an announcement of this event on our website (www.dow36000.com) when it happens, but if you miss it, don't worry. You can't go far wrong simply by following the rules for asset allocation we have laid out here, shifting slowly from stocks to bonds as you get older but still taking advantage of the huge rise in equity prices.

CHAPTER 15

The Wealth Explosion

I draw the conclusion that . . . the economic problem may be solved, or be within sight of a solution, within a hundred years. This means that the economic problem is not—if we look into the future—the permanent problem of the human race.
—John Maynard Keynes, *Essays in Persuasion* (1931)

IF THE DOW JONES industrial average soars to 36,000 tomorrow—or even a few years after—the world will change.

Wealth will explode. Or to put it more precisely, the true value of investments in profitable U.S. corporations will be recognized. It will be as though you owned a family heirloom, an emerald brooch, thinking it was worth $1,000, then suddenly found from an appraiser that it was worth $4,000. But this reassessment will be happening to tens of millions of families, and the sums are massive.

At the end of 1998, American households owned $11 trillion worth of stocks—as individual shares or through mutual funds or pension plans. That figure was $2 trillion just ten years earlier, and we believe it will become about $40 trillion as the Dow rises to its perfectly reasonable price. Since there are roughly 100 million households, the average family owns about $100,000 in stocks. When the PRP is achieved, those stockholdings will become about $400,000.

Household net worth—assets minus liabilities—came to about $36 trillion, or $360,000 per family, in 1998. If the value of stocks quadruples, then net worth will jump to $660,000—an increase of 83 percent.

Imagine the average American becoming nearly twice as rich overnight because of stocks. How would the country be different?

POLITICS: THE POWER OF THE INVESTOR CLASS

The first change we expect is political. Just as the stock market crash of 1929 changed the face of politics for the next five decades, the stock market boom of the 1980s and 1990s will change the face of politics well into the next millennium. The crash was the catalyst for the modern welfare state. The market boom could have the opposite effect. As more and more Americans gain a larger and larger stake in stocks, their views undoubtedly will shift on such matters as business regulation, taxes, antitrust policy, trade, and even foreign affairs.

The crash set off a chain reaction that led to Social Security, a more pervasive regulatory regime, and, eventually, food stamps, subsidized housing, federalized welfare, Medicare, and Medicaid. The boom could result in the reduction or dismantling of many of these same programs and a move back to smaller government. In the late 1990s, even Democrats like Senator Daniel Patrick Moynihan of New York were proposing to change the most sacrosanct of these programs, Social Security, to allow Americans to invest money that now goes to payroll taxes in stock accounts.

The increase in stock prices creates a powerful feedback loop. Higher prices attract more investors into the market, and those investors bid up the prices of stocks, attracting even more investors . . . At the same time, this new "investor class," as it is called, is starting to have an influence on politicians, who pass laws more favorable to investment, further reducing the risk premium, pushing up stock prices, and attracting even more investors.

The investor class—that is, the group of people who own stocks—now comprises roughly half of all U.S. adults, up from one-tenth in 1965 and one-fifth in 1990. No longer is stockholding the province of just the rich and the middle-aged. More than half of America's shareholders have less than $50,000 a year in family income, and nearly 40 percent of households headed by someone younger than thirty-five own stocks, up from 13 percent in 1983.

Rising stock prices are not the only reason for this broadening ownership. Other reasons are:

• **The shift away from traditional, defined-benefit pension plans** (by which companies oblige themselves to pay a set amount to retirees) to defined-contribution 401(k) plans, run by employees themselves, who invest for high returns that will benefit them directly when they retire. In 1995, according to the Employment Benefit Research Institute, 45 percent of Americans had a 401(k) or its nonprofit or public-sector equivalent. Participation has increased fivefold in fifteen years.

• **Growing fears that Social Security is in deep trouble.** Research by Roper Starch Worldwide found that in 1997 only 46 percent of Americans believed they could "count on" Social Security as a source of income in retirement—down from 88 percent in 1974. Meanwhile, 42 percent said they could count on self-directed retirement accounts, up from 6 percent in 1980. If you don't think Social Security will be there when you retire, then it makes sense to invest in stocks on your own.

• **The rise in mutual funds**, which have made stock investing easier, safer, and more democratic. The Investment Company Institute reports that 44 million U.S. households—more than four in ten families—own mutual funds. Median family income of fund shareholders is just $55,000.

Federal Reserve data showed that in 1998 the value of the average household's stocks exceeded the value of its real estate. And, when you subtract mortgages, the net equity in homes is less than half the value of stocks. That's a huge change. Just ten years earlier, net home equity was 77 percent *greater* than the value of stocks.

Real estate has long been the asset favored by politicians, who have showered it with tax breaks and subsidies. But, suddenly, stocks are more important to the financial well-being of Americans than anything else they own. That fact is what is producing a sea change in politics. Economist Lawrence Kudlow contends that "the new Investor Class decided in 1994 to vote congressional Democrats out and a new crop of Republicans in . . . Call it stock market politics."

While Kudlow may be drawing battle lines that are too stark, the economic sophistication of the investor class has undoubtedly begun to change the world. Kevin Kelly, author of the book, *New Rules for the New Economy*, describes similar forces: "This new global economic culture is characterized by decentralized ownership and equity, by pools of knowledge instead of pools of capital, by an emphasis on an open society, and, most important, by a widespread reliance on economic values as the basis for making decisions in all walks of life."

President Bill Clinton must have had the investor class in mind when he agreed in 1997 to cut the capital-gains rate from 28 percent to 20 percent and to create Roth IRAs, which exempt retirees from paying taxes on withdrawals from special retirement accounts. With nearly half of Americans owning stock, he could hardly have said that these were tax breaks only for the rich.

At first glance, the class seems to lean Republican. A 1999 survey by Rasmussen Research looked at the party affiliations of people who owned stock portfolios worth at least $5,000 and at the affiliations of those who owned no stocks. Of the stockholders, 38 percent identified themselves as Republicans and 33 percent as Democrats; of the non-stockholders, Democrats outnumbered Republicans, 41 to 27 percent. Perhaps this result is not so surprising. Rich people are more apt to own stocks, and rich people are more apt to be Republican. But look at respondents in the *same* income group: $40,0000 to $60,000, the mid-range for families with a husband, wife, and at least one child.

For the stockholders here, 37 percent were Republicans and 31 percent Democrats. For the non-stockholders, the results were practically reversed: 35 percent were Democrats, 28 percent Republicans.

But the rise of the investor class is unlikely to be simply a partisan phenomenon. We suspect that shareholders, however disorganized, will affect the policies of *both* parties. In the future, the investor class could flex its muscles by becoming an advocacy group for the interests of corporations—for example, by pushing for lower taxes or more free trade or by opposing attempts to regulate Internet commerce.

But be wary of glib conclusions. Increased wealth could have surprising effects on politics. For example, in the 1998 congressional elections, newly rich voters favored Democrats, perhaps because they gave Clinton credit for the country's prosperity and the market's ascendancy, according to William Schneider of the American Enterprise Institute. Also, with the additional security that wealth brings, they may have been voting for the Democrats' fiscal or environmental policies—since they can *afford* to be more compassionate. Despite the rise of the investor class, which has pushed Americans into higher brackets, there was no clamor in the late 1990s for cutting taxes. One effect of increased wealth may be less concern for how much the government takes from you since you have enough to pay the bills.

Still, as Kevin Kelly emphasizes, the investor class will undoubtedly take a more benign view of free-market, or what was once called "liberal," economics—that is, policies that allow private competition to thrive and that limit the intervention of the government in transactions between consumers and producers or stock buyers and stock sellers. The success of stocks in the 1980s and 1990s is one reason the liberal economic view has spread so widely, infecting even the ranks of Keynesians, who believed that it was government spending that determined the health of an economy. In a remarkable interview with Daniel Yergin, Lawrence Summers, secretary of the Treasury under Clinton and an establishment Harvard economist with strong ties to that older, activist tradition (he is the nephew of Nobel Prize winners Kenneth Arrow and Paul Samuelson), said that Americans "have seen how badly the public sector can mess things up." He added:

> With competition, things seem to go better. Innovation happens. The world is more focused on variety than quantity. . . . Things will happen in well-organized efforts without direction, controls, plans. That's the consensus among economists. That's the Hayek legacy. As for Milton Friedman, he was the devil figure in my youth. Only with time have I come to have large amounts of grudging respect. And with time, increasingly ungrudging respect.

Summers is referring to the late Friedrich von Hayek, Nobel Prize winner and leading figure of the Austrian, or liberal (or libertarian), school of economics. Milton Friedman, another Nobel Prize winner, now at the Hoover Institution at Stanford University, is considered the leading heir to Hayek's free-market philosophy.

And the investor class has not finished growing. In 1999, Clinton, partly in an attempt to divert attention from plans to privatize Social Security, proposed universal savings accounts (USAs) for 124 million Americans. Under the plan, the government would give money directly to lower-earners so that they could set up their own retirement accounts. For example, a family making $40,000 would qualify for an annual $600 tax credit and get another $700 from the government if it puts $700 of its own cash into a USA, which would be invested in stocks and bonds. The most important effect of this plan is the same as that of the proposal of Moynihan and others who want to substitute private stock accounts for payroll tax contributions: Virtually every American would join the investor class.

Certainly, a market collapse—caused by a shock that would sharply increase the risk premium temporarily—would be a setback to investor class influence. But in the new environment, politicians (even governors of the Federal Reserve Board) would be reluctant to take the kind of steps that would contribute to such a debacle and would be eager to ameliorate it. Both parties will ignore the investor class at their very deep peril.

CULTURE: THE GOOD LIFE

One of the greatest of American politicians, John Adams, our second president, wrote to his wife Abigail in 1780:

> I must study politics and war, that my sons may have liberty to study mathematics and philosophy. My sons ought to study mathematics and philosophy . . . in order to give their children a right to study painting, poetry, music, statuary and porcelain.

The modern social science of economics did not exist in Adams's time, so today we would paraphrase his sentiments this way: In the past, people were concerned with building political and economic systems that would establish the foundation for building great wealth. Now, we are benefiting from their work.

As Lord Keynes says in the quotation at the beginning of this chapter, the "economic problem" is on its way to solution very soon. But what is the point of wealth? To Adams, it was to enable the pursuit of "poetry . . . and porcelain"—in other words, art and culture or, as Aristotle put it, "the Good," which is "that at which all things aim." We can also use terms like "spirituality," "personal achievement," "aesthetics," or "the good life." And, as we said in the very first paragraph of Chapter 1, stocks help Americans lead the good life—which is one reason we decided to write this book, as a response to a financial establishment that was scaring so many people away from gaining access to that life. The wealth that stocks represent is a means to a beneficial end.

Wealth, scientific researchers are convinced, makes health. But it makes a lot more.

"We serve physical concerns and creature comforts first, psychic needs later," write Michael Cox and Richard Alm. They cite the work of the psychologist Abraham Maslow, who created a famous pyramid, a hierarchy of needs that starts with a physiological base (food, clothing, shelter), then moves upward to safety, social needs, self-esteem, self-actualization and transcendence. As people grow wealthier, they climb Maslow's pyramid of needs, trying to make life more rewarding for themselves and their families. Among other pursuits, self-actualization and transcendence have has meant more philanthropy, travel, education, participation in culture and spirituality. But to reach the pinnacle of the pyramid, you need to satisfy more basic needs, which went unmet for much of history. "A typical American at the turn of the century spent $76 out of every $100 for food, clothing and shelter. By the 1990s, it had fallen to $37 out of every $100," write Cox and Alm.

The boom in stocks will mean that percentage will fall further, so it is no surprise that the boom in stocks has meant a boom in culture. As Nick Gillespie wrote in Reason magazine:

> Everywhere we look, the cultural marketplace is open and ready for business. The number of places where you can buy books has more than doubled during the past 20 years . . . More than 25,000 video rental stores are scattered across the United States, effectively functioning as second-run theaters and art houses. . . . More than 110 symphony orchestras have been founded since 1980.

Also, of course, the Internet has provided windows on the great museums of the world, translations of Dante, a reader-compiled database of 180,000 movies. Call up "Shakespeare" on Yahoo! and get 473 websites.

Wealth makes charity as well. In 1997, Americans contributed $143 billion to nonprofit organizations, an increase of 7.5 percent over the previous year. Three-quarters of that money came from individuals. Philanthropy, like culture and education, will be one of the growth industries created by a rising stock market. After all, one of the few loopholes in the tax code involves donations of appreciated stock. For example, an investment of $10,000 in IBM shares in 1980 was worth $108,200 by 1999. Donate that stock to charity, and both the donor and the recipient escape capital gains taxes. In fact, we believe that in the next five years, many individuals and foundations will have so much stock wealth that their biggest problem will be finding worthy causes to which to give money.

And wealth makes education. In 1970, only half the population had graduated from high school; by 1995, the figure had reached four-fifths. In 1970, only one-tenth had graduated from college; twenty-five years later, the figure was one-quarter. Education is directly correlated with producing and consuming culture. The National Endowment for the Arts reports that a college graduate is twice as likely as a high school graduate to read literature and three times as likely to attend a jazz concert or visit an art museum. Yes, there's a lot of schlock out there, but more good stuff than ever—and more people with the leisure and education to tell the good from the bad.

We don't deny that the wealth that we expect from the stock-market boom can lead to decadence. Wealth can be seen as an end in itself or as a means of acquiring a bad life instead of a good one. But by alleviating the burden of meeting basic needs, wealth allows us more choices—foolish or wise.

BILLIONS OF RECIPES

Increased wealth will have another effect. It will accelerate technological change, which will lead to greater economic growth, which itself will produce more wealth—another positive feedback loop, or virtuous circle. Paul M. Romer, the Stanford University economist and champion of what is called "New Growth Theory," writes that "economic growth occurs whenever people take resources and rearrange them in ways that are more valuable." He uses the metaphor of cuisine: We have a finite number of ingredients that we can mix in a nearly infinite variety of combinations. "Economic growth springs from better recipes, not just from more cooking." How many recipes can there be?

The periodic table contains about a hundred different types of atoms, so the number of combinations made up of four different elements is 100 × 99 × 98 × 97 or about 94 million. A list of numbers like 1, 2, 3, 7 can represent proportions for using the four elements in a recipe. To keep things simple, assume that the numbers in the list must lie between 1 and 10 and no fractions are allowed, and that the smallest number must always be 1. Then there are about 3,500 different sets of proportions for each choice of four elements, and 3,500 × 94 million (or 330 billion) different recipes in total. If laboratories around the world evaluated 1,000 recipes each day, it would take nearly a million years to go through them all.

In exploring new recipes—new ways of doing things—we have only scratched the surface. Increased stock market wealth should accelerate the process, with new capital being invested in companies, new and old, that will continue to experiment. As technology improves, we can use computer models to try new recipes out—the trial-and-error dynamic will speed up.

New Growth Theory identifies three special features that make growth possible, says Romer: (1) we live in a physical world with far more possibilities than we can imagine or explore, (2) our ability to cooperate and trade allows us to share and advance knowledge as never before, and (3) markets "create incentives for people to exert effort, make discoveries and share information."

The economist Robert Fogel, a Nobel Prize winner from the University of Chicago, has coined the term "technophysio evolution" to describe the process that started roughly three hundred years ago as mortality rates dropped, population increased, and technological breakthroughs vastly increased our food supply and revolutionized "manufacturing, transportation, trade, communication, energy production, leisure-time services, and medical services." Fogel points to "the realization in the twentieth century of humankind's ancient desire to fly." From the flight of Wilbur and Orville Wright at Kitty Hawk to Neil Armstrong's walk on the moon, a scant sixty-six years transpired. By contrast, it took six thousand years to go from the invention of the plough to the steam engine.

Fogel argues that technophysio evolution has given human beings "so great a degree of control over their environment that they are set apart not only from all other species, but also from all previous generations of *Homo sapiens.* This new degree of control has enabled *Homo sapiens* to increase its average body size by over 50 percent, to increase its average longevity by more than 100 percent, and to improve greatly the robustness and capacity of vital organ systems."

In the midst of such change, why should we believe that gross domestic product in the United States will simply grow at the same rate as it grew in the past century? Why not more powerfully than the 2 to 2.5 percent real rates that we used in the assumptions that led us to Dow 36,000? With growth in the range of 4 percent, Dow 100,000 is in sight.

IN PURSUIT

We are happy, however, to settle for our more circumspect inputs. They produce outputs that we consider modest but that most Americans still cannot believe true.

It is only natural to resist new paradigms, new ways of looking at the world—at least until it is clear that the old model (in this case, the regime of P/E ceilings and dividend-yield floors) has clearly failed.

Financial data going back more than a hundred years show that stocks, if they are held for the long term, are no more risky than bonds and Treasury bills. Equally risky assets should produce equal returns—just as two identical condos in similar neighborhoods should produce equal rents.

But stocks have been giving their owners far more cash than bonds, mainly because investors continue to act as though stocks are more risky than they really are. Stocks, as we put it earlier, were thought to be like "plague bonds"—buy them and you risk catching a terrible disease—or like a house thought to be in an earthquake zone. But when research proves that you really can't catch the plague and that the earthquake zone is two hundred miles to the north, a reassessment is necessary.

That is what we have done in this book: a reassessment. With stocks no more risky than bonds, we asked, what should stocks return so that their flow of cash to investors will be the same as the flow of cash from bonds? The answer is shockingly low—which means that the price of stocks should be shockingly high. The Dow must rise to 36,000 to reach a reasonable earnings yield, under very cautious assumptions.

To right this imbalance, the market is now in the process of a rapid rise to Dow 36,000. There will be bumps along the way, but when stocks reach their perfectly reasonable price, returns will level off. In the meantime, fortunes will be made from the one-time-only ascent.

How to cash in? The second half of the book offered suggestions—either through mutual funds or individual stocks. We also reminded you that, as Benjamin Graham, put it, "the investor's . . . worst enemy is likely to be himself." Even with the assurance that the logical direction for stocks is up—and up sharply—the human element prevails. "The ruling passion," wrote Alexander Pope nearly three centuries ago, "conquers reason still." We hope this book offers a way to tame those passions, to build wealth, and then to devote your energies (and other passions!) to pursuing a better life.

Glossary

Asset: Something of value. The three main assets for investors are stocks, bonds, and cash, with "cash" referring to very short term debt instruments, including Treasury bills, *money-market* funds, and certificates of deposit.

Basis point: One one-hundredth of a percentage point.

Bond: An IOU, or debt security, that is issued by a corporation or government entity. It usually carries a coupon, or fixed rate of interest. When interest rates rise, the market price of a bond you own will typically fall. When rates fall, the price will rise.

Book value: The value of a corporation, based on the assets and liabilities recorded on its balance sheet. A popular valuation measure for a stock is its price-to-book ratio, or P/B, derived by dividing the market price per share by the book value per share. For example, the *Dow Jones industrial average* had a P/B ratio of 6.8 in May 1999, high by historic standards.

Capital appreciation: The increase in the market value of an asset. If you buy a stock at $50 and it rises the next year to $75, then its capital appreciation is $25.

Capital gain: An event, usually taxable, that occurs when you sell the stock at a profit.

Closed-end fund: A way to own a diversified portfolio of stocks and bonds with only a small investment. A closed-end fund is similar to a conventional *mutual fund,* except that the company that manages the portfolio issues a fixed number of shares. Investors trade the shares among themselves on a stock exchange, rather than buying and redeeming them from the company itself. As a result, closed-end funds can trade above or below their *net asset value,* or market price, of their shares.

Coupon rate: The stated interest rate on a bond, paid by a corporation or government entity throughout the bond's life. For example, a $10,000 Treasury bond with a coupon of 5 percent will pay interest of $500 per year. While the coupon

Words in *italics* appear elsewhere in the glossary.

stays the same until maturity (when the principal goes back to the creditor), its "yield" changes from day to day. The current yield is the coupon rate divided by the market price, which varies with supply and demand. For example, if interest rates rise, the market price could be $8,000 on the same $10,000 bond, in which case the yield would be 6.25 percent ($500/$8,000 = 0.0625).

Diversification: Investing in a variety of assets and sectors in order to reduce overall risk.

Dividend: A payment, usually in cash but occasionally in stock, from a corporation to its shareholders. Most dividends are paid quarterly, but not all (see Chapter 3).

Dividend yield: A percentage derived by dividing a stock's annual dividend payments by its market price. Typically, the figure is expressed as an indicated dividend since it assumes that the current quarterly dividend will continue throughout the year (as it usually does).

Dow: The Dow Jones industrial average, composed of thirty blue-chip stocks and invented by Charles Dow in 1896. The Dow is often used as a stand-in for the market as a whole. The lineup of companies changes every few years, according to the considered judgment of analysts at Dow Jones & Co., which also owns *The Wall Street Journal.* The average is price-weighted, which gives smaller companies more influence on its ups and downs, unlike the *Standard & Poor's 500 index,* which is weighted by market capitalization. The thirty Dow stocks in 1999 were Alcoa, AlliedSignal, American Express, AT&T, Boeing, Caterpillar, Chevron, Citigroup, Coca-Cola, Walt Disney Co., E.I. du Pont de Nemours & Co., Eastman Kodak, Exxon, General Electric, General Motors, Goodyear Tire, Hewlett-Packard, IBM, International Paper, Johnson & Johnson, McDonald's Corp., Merck & Co., Minnesota Mining & Manufacturing, J.P. Morgan & Co., Philip Morris Cos., Procter & Gamble, Sears Roebuck & Co., Union Carbide, United Technologies, and Wal-Mart Stores. Of the thirty names, twenty (or their corporate successors) remain from the Dow in 1984. One way to purchase the thirty Dow stocks in a single security is by buying a share of the Diamonds Trust Series, which trades on the American exchange under the symbol DIA.

Earnings: A corporation's officially reported profits after taxes. The figure does not account for cash outlays for new plant and equipment or dividends, but it does account for such non-cash items as depreciation (gradually writing off the value of old capital investments). "Earnings per share," or EPS, are simply the profits (quarterly or annual) attributed to each share of stock: divide total earnings by total shares outstanding.

Earnings yield: A percentage derived by dividing a stock's earnings per share by its market price. An earnings yield is a stock's E/P, the inverse of its *P/E.*

Expense ratio: A mutual fund's costs, as expressed as a percentage of its share price, that are passed on to its investors.

401(k) Plan: An employer-sponsored retirement plan that allows employees to make tax-deferred investments (often matched by the employer) in stocks, bonds, and money-market funds. The title refers to a section of the federal law that enacted the program. A 403(b) Plan serves the same purpose for employees of universities, public schools, and non-profit organizations, and a 457 Plan is for employees of state and local governments.

Free-cash flow: The cash that a company generates that is not necessary for operations or investment in capital equipment.

Gross domestic product: Or GDP. The value of all goods and services produced by a country, including by corporations in that country that are owned by foreigners. GDP growth is the standard measure of economic vitality and is usually expressed in real (that is, inflation-adjusted) terms.

Intrinsic value: The fundamental, underlying, or "true" value of a corporation, as contrasted with its *book value* or value in the stock market. Intrinsic value is the discounted *present value* of all the cash that can be taken out of a business during its remaining life. Warren Buffett, who popularized the term, notes that it is "an estimate, rather than a precise figure. . . . Two people looking at the same set of facts . . . will almost inevitably come up with at least slightly different intrinsic value figures." (The quotation is from his 1993 letter to the shareholders of Berkshire-Hathaway, Inc., which he chairs.) The *perfectly reasonable price,* or PRP, is a measure of intrinsic value.

Long-run: Or long-term. A phrase with no precise meaning that is nonetheless used frequently in investment parlance. To us, a long-term investment is one that is intended to be held a minimum of five years and, better, ten or more.

Load: The fee or commission charged by some mutual funds when an investor buys (front-end) or sells (back-end) shares. A no-load fund has no such charges.

Market capitalization. Or "cap." The total value of all the shares of stock in a company, according to investors. To calculate market cap, simply multiply the price per share by the number of shares outstanding. In mid-1999, the stock with the largest cap was Microsoft, at $463 billion. While there is no strict definition, small-cap stocks are usually considered those with market caps under $1 billion; mid-cap, from $1 billion to $5 billion (sometimes $10 billion); and large-caps, above that.

Money-market fund: A *mutual fund* that invests strictly in very short-term debt instruments, typically maturing in days or months. The price of a money-market fund stays the same ($1 per share) while its yield varies from day to day.

Municipal bond: A bond issued by a state or local government agency. Interest on munis is exempt from federal tax, and many states exempt their own munis (and sometimes those of other states) from state tax.

Mutual fund: An investment company whose purpose is to hold a portfolio of stocks, bonds, or cash instruments like Treasury bills. The company sells shares to the investors, who can redeem them at any time at *net asset value*. A mutual fund gives small investors a way to own hundreds of stocks with only a small outlay of cash.

Net asset value: The value per share of a mutual fund or closed-end fund, calculated daily. To find the NAV, first add up the market value of the fund's assets (stocks, bonds, etc.) and divide that figure by the number of shares outstanding.

Nominal: Strictly by the numbers, unadjusted. If the real rate of GDP growth is 3 percent and inflation is 2 percent, then nominal growth is 5 percent.

Perfectly reasonable price: Or PRP. Our term for the price of a stock—or the level of a stock index—that takes into account the true level of riskiness of stocks and their likely earnings. Since stocks are no more risky than bonds over the long term, the PRP is the price where the cash flow from a stock is equivalent to the cash flow from a bond.

Perpetuity: A bond that never matures, but pays interest forever. The British government has in the past issued perpetuities called consols.

Present value: The value today of future cash flows from an asset. To calculate present value, you need to "discount" that flow of cash by making an assumption about interest rates in the future and sometimes add a risk premium. Say you win a lottery that will pay you $10,000 a year for twenty years. Present value is what an investor should pay you right now for the privilege of collecting those checks.

Price-to-earnings ratio: Or P/E. The share price of a stock on a given day divided by its annual earnings per share—in other words, the number of dollars it takes to buy one dollar of a company's earnings. There is no convention for the period over which those earnings are calculated. Usually, the P/E reported in newspapers is based on earnings during the most recent 12-month period. Often, however, the earnings are estimates for the year ahead.

Profits: An imprecise term that indicates the amount left over when expenses are subtracted from revenues. It is frequently used interchangeably with *earnings.*

Real: Adjusted for inflation, using the Consumer price index or GDP deflator.

Return: The *dividends,* interest, and *capital appreciation* (price increase) produced by an investment, expressed as a percentage of its cost. For example, if a stock begins a year at a price of $100 and ends the year at $118 while paying a dividend during the year of $2, then its return is approximately 20 percent (20/100 = .20). We say approximately, because in making precise return calculations, dividends are assumed to be reinvested in new shares of stock each quarter, so the returns end up slightly higher.

Risk: In general terms, the possibility of loss. In finance, risk usually is defined as volatility, the extremes of the ups and downs of returns. No single measurement captures risk adequately, but the most common are *standard deviation,* which compares a stock's movements to its own average, and beta, which compares the stock's movements to the market. Wal-Mart, for example, has a beta of 1.0, which means it has been just as volatile as the market as a whole, while Tiffany & Co. has a beta of 1.35, which means that, when the market has risen (or fallen) 10 percent, Tiffany has risen (or fallen) 13.5 percent. These risk measurements are historical. They cannot predict future volatility.

Risk premium: The additional *return* investors demand for putting their money into a riskier asset. The risk premium for stocks over Treasury bonds has averaged about 7 percent over the past century. The decline of the risk premium to between 2 percent and 3 percent in recent years has been the main reason for the rise in stock prices.

S&P 500: The popular Standard & Poor's 500 index, comprising, with a few exceptions, the largest 500 stocks, by *market cap,* on the three major U.S. exchanges: New York, American, and Nasdaq. The capitalization of the S&P stocks represented about three-quarters of the capitalization of all 7,000-plus stocks on those three markets in 1999. The S&P is the benchmark, or standard, against which most general-equity mutual fund managers measure their performance. It is a cap-weighted index, with the largest companies having the most effect on its movements.

Security: A *stock* or *bond.* Stocks represent the claims of owners on a corporation's assets; bonds represent the claims of debtors.

Standard deviation: A measure of risk—specifically, of how much a stock's annual returns vary from its average (mean) return. The higher the number, the more volatile the stock. For example, the average return of large-cap stocks over the past seventy years has been 11 percent and the standard deviation has been 20 percent, according to calculations by Ibbotson Associates of Chicago. This means that in two thirds of the years, returns fall between a range of the average return plus or minus 20 percent: that is, between −9 percent and + XO 31 percent.

Stock: Shares in a corporation. Another word is *equity.*

Tobin's Q: The ratio of the market value of a stock to the estimated replacement value of its assets. James Tobin, a Nobel Prize–winning economist, introduced the concept in an academic paper in 1969. Adherents of the Q ratio believe that a "safe" ratio is 1. The Q ratio is similar to the price-to-*book value* ratio, and its recent elevation has alarmed traditional analysts.

Treasury bond: A bond issued by the U.S. Treasury. Interest is exempt from state, but not federal, taxes. Technically, a bond is a debt instrument which, when issued, has a maturity of seven years or more. A note matures in one to seven years, while Treasury bills are issued in maturities of three, six and twelve months.

Unit investment trust: Or UIT. A portfolio of stocks or bonds, similar to a *mutual fund,* except that the assets in the portfolio are set when the UIT is issued and are held for a fixed term, rather than actively traded by a manager. At maturity, the UIT is dissolved, and investors receive the proceeds or roll them into a new one. Like closed-end funds, UITs are sold in a fixed number of units, rather than an ever-expanding number of shares. The units can be redeemed at any time, just like shares in a mutual fund.

Zero-coupon bond: A debt security that does not make regular interest payments. Instead, investors buy the bond at a discount and receive the full face value at maturity. For example, in May 1999 a Treasury zero maturing in November 2021 at $10,000 could be bought in the open market for $2,500.

Notes

CHAPTER 1. INTRODUCTION

3. Never before have so many people: Stock ownership is rising. Peter D. Hart Research Associates, "A National Survey Among Stock Investors" (conducted for the Nasdaq Stock Market), February 1997.

3. Today, half of America's adults are shareholders: When household real estate and equity holdings are compared, the net value of real estate is used (net value of real estate = value of home − value of mortgage). *Flow of Funds Accounts of the United States.* Washington: Board of Governors, 12 March 1999, p. 102. www.federalreserve.gov (last accessed May 26, 1999, last updated May 1, 1999).

4. Many small investors: Alan Greenspan's speech, "The Challenge of Central Banking in a Democratic Society," was delivered as the Francis Boyer Lecture of the American Enterprise Institute for Public Policy Research. Washington, 5 December 1996, p. 6. www.aei.org (last accessed May 26, 1999, last updated January 15, 1998).

5. Why were prices rising: Charles MacKay, *Extraordinary Popular Delusions and the Madness of Crowds.* Boston: L.C. Page & Co., 1932. MacKay's book was first published in 1841 under the title *Memoirs of Extraordinary Popular Delusions.*

5. As John Burr Williams, a brilliant young economist: "In short, a stock is worth only *what you can get out of it."* John Burr Williams, *The Theory of Investment Value.* Burlington, Vt.: Fraser Publishing Company, 1997, p. 57. Burr's groundbreaking book on valuation was originally published in 1938 by Harvard University Press.

8. On March 30, 1998, we unveiled our theory: James K. Glassman and Kevin Hassett, "Are Stocks Overvalued? Not a Chance," *Wall Street Journal,* 30 March 1998, p. A18.

8. At the same time, our views have led some professionals: ". . . the fair-market P/E multiple of the market could reach 100." Byron R. Wien, "U.S. Strategy: Levitating Above Dow Jones 9000." Morgan Stanley Dean Witter Letter to Clients, 21 April 1998, pp. 3–5.

9. It's smart to be skeptical when someone (like us) claims: ". . . when recognizing that something was, in fact, different paid off significantly." Ibid.

9. Still, a more common response: Glassman and Hassett, second *Wall Street Journal* article. James K. Glassman and Kevin Hassett, "Stock Prices Are Still Far Too Low," *Wall Street Journal,* 17 March 1999, p. A26.

9. Still, a more common response: "This stupid article does not make any sense." Beth Piskora, "Dow 10,000? No Problem!" *New York Post,* 18 March 1999, p. 37.

9. He's right. It doesn't make sense: "We're at an unusual point in history . . . Historically, after a period of success on the stock market . . ." Alan Schoenfeld, "Finance Guru Advises Stocking U.S. Against Risk," *Yale Herald,* 19 January 1999, pp. 6.

9. He's right. It doesn't make sense: In 1996, Robert Shiller told the Board of Governors of the Federal Reserve System that stocks were headed for a fall. A manuscript by Shiller and Campbell resulted from their Federal Reserve Board testimony. John Campbell and Robert Shiller, "Valuation Ratios and the Long-Run Stock Market Outlook," *Journal of Portfolio Management,* vol. 24 (Winter 1998), pp. 11–26.

10. But on Wall Street, the iron-clad rules: Barron's transcript from a discussion among nine strategists and money managers in which Oscar S. Schaefer said, "If you look at stock valuations on a historical basis . . ." Kathryn M. Welling, "Tulipmania," *Barron's,* 18 January 1999, pp. 25–35.

11. Mainly through the research and proselytizing of investment banker Michael Milken: Connie Bruck writes in her book about Milken, *The Predator's Ball* (New York: Penguin Books, 1988): "Milken encountered the Hickman study when he was at Berkeley. W. Braddock Hickman, after studying data on corporate bond performance from 1900 to 1943, had found that a low-grade bond portfolio, if very large, well diversified and held over a long period of time, was a higher-yielding investment than a high-grade portfolio. Although the low-grade portfolio suffered more defaults than the high-grade, the high yields that were realized overall more than compensated for the losses. Hickman's findings were updated by T. R. Atkinson in a study covering 1944–65. It was empirical fact: the reward outweighed the risk." pp. 27–28.

14. In 1962, Thomas Kuhn, a professor of linguistics: "Sometimes a normal problem, one that ought to be solvable by known rules and procedures . . ." Thomas Kuhn, *The Structure of Scientific Revolutions,* 3rd ed. Chicago: University of Chicago Press, 1996, p. 5.

15. "I'm kind of floored," said David Castellani: Interview with the authors, October 1998.

15. That education teaches that stocks: "[The] emergence of new theories is generally preceded by a period of pronounced professional insecurity . . ." Kuhn, p. 67.

15. In the years ahead, a new paradigm: "picking up the other end of the stick" (quote from Herbert Butterfield) cited in Kuhn, p. 85.

16. One reason that stock ownership is soaring: Peter D. Hart, "A National Survey."

16. Another reason is that with low-cost mutual funds: *Mutual Fund Factbook, 39th Edition.* Washington, D.C.: Investment Company Institute, 1999, p. 45. www.ici.org (last accessed May 26, 1999, last updated May 21, 1999).

17. The press and the financial analysts: "The market is not overvalued, in our view, if two conditions are met . . ." *Outstanding Investor Digest.* New York: Outstanding Investor Digest, Inc., vol. 13, nos. 3 and 4 (24 September 1998).

17. Stocks have historically paid shareholders a large premium: Martin Wolf, "The Equity Puzzle," *Financial Times,* 16 December 1998, p. 15.

CHAPTER 2. THE HISTORY OF STOCKS

20. "Berlin was ebullient about the market's prospects": Martin Fridson, *A Very Good Year: Extraordinary Moments in Stock Market History.* New York: Wiley, 1998, pp. 84–86. In this exceptional book, Fridson—a managing director at Merrill Lynch & Co. and that rare bird, a financial professional who can also write well—examines ten critical years in stock market history, from 1908 to 1995. We owe him a great debt for the Chaplin-Berlin anecdote upon which we have embellished.

21. On December 5, 1996, we both attended the annual dinner: Between December 6, 1996, and May 21, 1999, the Dow Jones Industrial Average returned 77.3 percent, including price appreciation and reinvested dividends.

21. On December 5, 1996, we both attended the annual dinner: The key passage from the Greenspan speech: "Clearly, sustained low inflation implies less uncertainty about the future, and lower risk premiums imply higher prices of stocks and other earning assets. We can see that in the inverse relationship exhibited by price/earnings ratios and the rate of inflation in the past. But how do we know when irrational exuberance has unduly escalated asset values, which then become subject to unexpected and prolonged contractions as they have in Japan over the past decade? And how do we factor that assessment into monetary policy? We as central bankers need not be concerned if a collapsing financial asset bubble does not threaten to impair the real economy, its production, jobs, and price stability. Indeed, the sharp stock market break of 1987 had few negative consequences for the economy. But we should not underestimate or become complacent about the complexity of the interactions of asset markets and the economy. Thus, evaluating shifts in balance sheets generally, and in asset prices particularly, must be an integral part of the development of monetary policy."

22. Greenspan is a smart economist and a brilliant Fed chairman: The passage from *Fortune:* "Alan Greenspan of Townsend-Greenspan, Inc., financial advisers, thinks the market will soar, and that's just the trouble. 'A sharp secondary liquidation of goods and securities was avoided in 1958,' he argues, 'by an artificial liquidity in our financial system. This excessive liquidity could conceivably power an explosive speculative boom.' Before World War I, he explains, the periodic

'over-exuberance' of the financial community was held in check by the automatic forces of the market. Stock prices could not get too far out of line with real values because the supply of credit for the market was automatically constricted by a limited money supply. The ensuing corrections, however sharp, were short lived. . . . Because the penalties for over-expansion and excessive credit do not materialize, says Greenspan, investors get over-confident. . . . So Greenspan is worried lest stock prices take off in a steep rise. Once stock prices reach the point at which it is hard to value them by any logical methodology, he warns, stocks will be bought as they were in the late 1920's—not for investment, but to be unloaded at a still higher price. The ensuing break could be disastrous. Panic psychology, Greenspan believes, cannot be summarily altered or reversed by easy-money policies or any built-in stabilizer." Gilbert Burck, "A New Kind of Stock Market," *Fortune,* March 1959, pp. 120–121, 199, 201.

22. Lesson 1: Stocks Have Been Steady: Ibbotson Associates, *Stocks, Bonds, Bills and Inflation: 1998 Yearbook: Market Results for 1926–1997.* Chicago: Ibbotson Associates, 1998. The excellent and accessible Ibbotson data were invaluable in the preparation of this chapter.

22. Lesson 1: Stocks Have Been Steady: Historical averages are drawn from Jeremy Siegel's important book, *Stocks for the Long Run,* unless they are specifically attributed to Ibbotson or Shiller data. Jeremy Siegel, *Stocks for the Long Run,* 2nd ed. New York: McGraw-Hill, 1998. Ibbotson Associates, *Stocks, Bonds, Bills and Inflation: 1998 Yearbook: Market Results for 1926–1997.*

26. Turn again to Jeremy Siegel: While Professor Siegel's work is the easiest to understand, it was not the first or most definitive evidence of declines in riskiness for stocks in the long run. The pathbreaking papers were those of James Poterba and Lawrence Summers in 1988, "Mean Reversion in Stock Returns: Evidence and Implications," *Journal of Financial Economics,* vol. 22, pp. 27–60, and Eugene Fama and Kenneth French, "Permanent and Temporary Components of Stock Prices," *Journal of Political Economy,* vol. 96, pp. 246–273. Siegel gathered data from various sources including the quoted G. William Schwert. Siegel, p. 5.

27. Siegel's research also shows risk declining over time: Siegel produces copious data, then concludes: "Although it might appear to be riskier to hold stocks than bonds, the opposite is true: the safest long-term investment for the preservation of purchasing power has clearly been stocks, not bonds." Siegel, p. 26.

28. In the television program *Early Edition:* Information about the television program can be found at the CBS web page: www.cbs.com (last accessed May 26, 1999, last updated May 20, 1999).

28. Lesson 3: Traditional Valuation Methods: Dividend data and stock data back to 1800's are drawn from data on Robert Shiller's web page: www.econ.yale.edu/~shiller/chapt26.html (last accessed May 26, 1999, last updated April 28, 1988).

31. The second popular measure is the P/E: shareholders appear to "peer through the corporate veil." Alan Auerbach and Kevin Hassett, "Corporate Sav-

ings and Shareholders Consumption." In D. Bernheim and J. Shoven, eds., *National Saving and Economic Performance.* Chicago: University of Chicago Press, 1991.

33. The third measure of market valuation: James Tobin, "A General Equilibrium Approach to Monetary Theory," *Journal of Money, Credit, and Banking,* vol. 1, no. 15 (February 1969).

35. Perhaps the greatest investment mania of all time: Garber argues that the run-up in prices may have been sensible. Peter Garber, "Tulipmania," *Journal of Political Economy,* vol. 97, no. 3 (1989).

CHAPTER 3. DIVIDEND AND CONQUER

46. This commonsense conclusion—that it doesn't really matter: Merton Miller and Francis Modigliani, "Dividend Policy, Growth, and the Valuation of Shares," *Journal of Business,* vol. 34, no. 4 (October 1961).

48. Remember that many companies pay no dividends: *Berkshire Hathaway, Inc., Annual Report, 1992.*

48. When we turn to figuring out the true underlying value: "Earnings are only a means to an end." Williams, *Theory of Investment Value,* p. 57.

52. But look what happened: Calculations for the three stocks were made by the authors using data from Bloomberg Business News and contemporary accounts.

CHAPTER 4. A CONSERVATIVE LOOK OF HOW HIGH THE STOCK MARKET CAN GO

57. The answer lies in the confusion many people: Suzanne Woolley, "It's Not So Bad, Honest . . . But Gurus Say the Highs For the Year Are Behind Us," *Business Week,* 14 September 1998, pp. 40–42.

58. Certainly, viewed from a conventional perspective: Mark Hulbert, "Joseph and the Amazing Technicolor Market," *New York Times,* 21 March 1999, p. 8, Business section.

59. For example, a study by Peter D. Hart Research Associates in 1997: Peter D. Hart, "A National Survey."

62. Under the assumptions: Throughout the book, we calculate the PRP using software we have developed. We plan to make the software generally available in some form in the near future. Check our website, www.Dow36000.com, for more details.

65. A bond is an IOU, a piece of paper: The Disney bonds and Coke bonds both mature in July 2093, while the IBM bonds mature in December 2096. The Disney and IBM bonds are "callable," which means that the companies can retire them before maturity, much as you can repay your mortgage or refinance it at a lower rate before its term is up. In the past, the British government issued bonds that *never* matured, simply paying interest year after year.

69. To start, assume that dividends will grow: If the cash payment grows faster than the discount rate, then the present value of the stream of payments becomes infinite, since the rate of increase of the cash payment is greater than the rate at which future cash declines in present value. One of the most interesting aspects of the recent history of stocks is that the growth rates of earnings and dividends have been higher than the interest rate for many years. One economist friend of ours looked at these data and asked, "The real question is: why aren't stocks worth infinity?"

70. In its forecast at the beginning of 1999: Congressional Budget Office, *Economic and Budget Outlook: Fiscal Years 2000–2009.* Washington: Government Printing Office, January 1999.

71. To accomplish this, we constructed: Technically, one needs to control for dilution from share issues when analyzing aggregate dividends as a measure of the cash flow from owning stocks. In Chapter 5, we show that this correction has little effect on these numbers. *Flow of Funds,* p. 102.

CHAPTER 5. A MORE REASONABLE LOOK AT HOW HIGH THE MARKET CAN GO

75. But, first, listen to Warren Buffett: "The business is wonderful." Response to question at 1998 shareholders' meeting of Berkshire Hathaway. Quoted in *Outstanding Investor Digest,* p. 36. Selected excerpts from Berkshire meetings can be found at the *Digest's* website at www.oid.com (last accessed May 26, 1999, last update unknown).

80. Again, it is not difficult to find firms: "Buffett comes up with a number he calls 'intrinsic value.' *Berkshire Hathaway, Inc., Annual Report, 1996.* The Berkshire site is www.berkshirehathaway.com (last accessed May 26, 1999, last updated May 5, 1999).

80. Making adjustments to earnings in order to derive free-cash flow: Copeland, et al., actually suggest that the "financial flows" approach also add interest payments to the measure of free cash flow. When you calculate the present value of this measure, you need to subtract the value of the firm's debt to get the current value of equity. We adopt the useful simplication of ignoring interest payments on the plus side and debt on the minus side. This assumption is acceptable because the present value of interest payments is a good measure of the market value of debt. Thomas Copeland, Tim Koller, and Jack Murrin, *Valuation: Measuring and Managing the Value of Companies.* New York: Wiley, 1994.

80. Making adjustments to earnings in order to derive free-cash flow: Multiple articles discussing James Ohlson's view can be found in *Contemporary Accounting Research,* vol. 11, no. 2 (Spring 1995).

81. The surprise is that this measure: "the depreciation charge is not inappropriate . . ." *Outstanding Investor Digest,* p. 38.

82. A share repurchase: Here is another simple example to help describe the impact on your wealth of a share repurchase. Suppose a firm has $100 in cash and 10 shares. If it pays each shareholder a conventional $1 dividend, then the firm gives shareholders $10 total, so it will have only $90 left. At that point, each share is worth $9 ($90 ÷ 10 shares), and each shareholder still has $10—$1 in cash and a share worth $9. If the firm repurchases one of the shares, then the fellow who sells his share has $10. The firm has only $90 left, and the nine remaining shares are worth $10 each. Absent taxes, shareholders should be indifferent between the two actions.

84. We like this method for measuring free-cash flow: *Flow of Funds.*

CHAPTER 6. UNRISKY BUSINESS

95. Again, on average, bondholders would probably end up: "Turmoil 1998: Effects on Financial Products." Boston: Dalbar, Inc., 13 January 1999. The Dalbar study found most investors took the high volatility of 1998 in stride, but lower-income investors were more frightened than others.

95. Earlier, we presented evidence that stocks are no riskier: Siegel, pp. 25–28.

100. To account for the high risk premium: John H. Cochrane, "Where Is the Market Going? Uncertain Facts and Novel Theories." NBER Working Paper No. W6207, Cambridge, Mass.: National Bureau of Economic Research, February 1998. www.nber.org (last accessed May 26, 1999, last update unknown).

102. Over the past few decades, investors have entered: In his book, *One Up on Wall Street* (New York: Penguin Books, 1989), Peter Lynch, the former manager of the Fidelity Magellan fund, discussed the October 19, 1987, crash that drove the Dow to a single-day loss of 23 percent: "I've always believed that investors should ignore the ups and downs of the market. Fortunately, the vast majority of them paid little heed to the distractions cited above. If this is any example, less than three percent of the million account-holders in Fidelity Magellan switched out of the fund and into a money-market fund during the desperations of the week. When you sell in desperation, you always sell cheap," p. 12.

CHAPTER 7. THE JUNGLE STOCKS LIVE IN

108. Observing that the market was frequently efficient: The quotation from Buffett is reprinted in *The Essays of Warren Buffett: Lessons for Corporate America,* a well-chosen compilation, drawn mainly from Berkshire Hathaway annual reports, by Lawrence A. Cunningham, professor of law at Yeshiva University in New York. The paperback is self-published by Cunningham but available through Amazon.com (www.amazon.com).

112. Thus, prices move from day to day: Malkiel, Burton, *A Random Walk Down Wall Street.* New York: Norton, 1991, p. 25.

113. A good example is the Dogs of the Dow: Michael O'Higgins, *Beating the Dow: A High-Return, Low-Risk Method for Investing in the Dow Jones Industrial Stocks with as Little as $5000.* New York: HarperCollins, 1991.

113. When James O'Shaughnessy, a Connecticut money manager: James O'Shaughnessy, *How to Retire Rich: Time-Tested Strategies to Beat the Market and Retire in Style.* New York: Broadway Books, 1998, p. 246.

114. The Dogs of the Dow story used to work: Michael O'Higgins, *Beating the Dow with Bonds: A High-Return, Low-Risk Strategy for Outperforming the Pros Even When Stocks Go South.* New York: HarperBusiness, 1999.

114. Wayne Nelson, a Merrill Lynch & Co. senior vice president: Interview with the authors January 8, 1998.

116. Irving Fisher, who is widely regarded: Biographical information on Fisher comes in part from Robert Allen Loring's *Irving Fisher: A Biography.* Cambridge, Mass.: Blackwell Publishers, 1993.

117. Now, fast-forward the tape several generations: Campbell and Shiller, p. 11.

118. Shiller and Campbell concluded their presentation with this admonition: Ibid, p. 19.

119. What matters is not whether market conditions: Leah Nathans Spiro, "Dream Team," *Business Week,* 29 August 1994, p. 50.

124. In his book, Malkiel tackled: Malkiel, p. 392.

CHAPTER 8. TODAY, WHEN STOCKS WERE STILL CHEAP

133. Answer: It's true that small changes: Robert Barro and Xavier Sala-i-Martin, *Economic Growth.* New York: McGraw-Hill, 1995.

136. In an article titled "Anomalies: The Equity Premium Puzzle": Jeremy Siegel and Richard Thaler, *Journal of Economic Perspectives,* vol. 11, no. 1 (Winter 1997), pp. 191–200.

138. As for the fears that governments will throttle earnings: Lawrence Kudlow, a former official of the Office of Management and Budget in the Reagan administration, is now chief economist for American Skandia, an insurance and investment management firm in Shelton, Connecticut. Kudlow discusses the "investor class" intelligently and often. See, for example, Lawrence Kudlow, "The Investor Class: U.S. Shareholders Are a Potent New Political and Economic Force," *Market,* vol. 3, No. 3 (July/August 1998), p. 6.

139. Something is out of whack: *Berkshire Hathaway Inc., Annual Report, 1998.*

CHAPTER 9. HOW TO PROFIT FROM THE DOW 36,000 THEORY

148. ADP provides payroll accounting and tax-filing services to firms: "Over half the major corporations in America and 80 percent of small businesses . . . still process their payrolls in-house." "Automatic Data by the Numbers," *Babson-United Investment Report, 1999.* Babson-United, Inc.: Wellesley Hills, Mass., 19 October 1998.

CHAPTER 10. HOW TO BUILD A WINNING RELATIONSHIP
WITH YOUR STOCKS

151. For example, the state of West Virginia recently passed a law: Richard Thaler, *The Winner's Curse: Paradoxes and Anomalies of Economic Life.* Princeton: Princeton University Press, 1992, pp. 93–94

152. In *The Intelligent Investor,* first published: Benjamin Graham, *The Intelligent Investor: A Book of Practical Counsel.* New York: Harper & Row, 1973, p. xv.

152. Don't take our word for it: "*Quantitative Analysis of Investor Behavior Study: 1997 Update,*" Boston: Dalbar, Inc., 22 May 1998.

153. This process may sound strange: "The investor may as well resign himself in advance to the probability . . ." Graham, p. 15.

155. In fact, as Buffett puts it: *Berkshire Hathaway Inc., Annual Report, 1993.*

155. Unfortunately, much of the commentary in the press: "After nearly fifty years in this business . . ." John Bogle, *Common Sense on Mutual Funds: New Imperatives for the Intelligent Investor.* New York: Wiley, 1999, p. 20. Bogle's book is an excellent primer on mutual funds.

155. In a series of books, David Dreman: See, for example, David Dreman, *Contrarian Investment Strategies: The Next Best Generation: Beat the Market by Going Against the Crowd.* New York: Simon & Schuster, 1998.

155. "Overall," wrote William A. Sherden: William A. Sherden, *The Fortune Sellers: The Big Business of Buying and Selling Predictions.* New York: Wiley, 1998.

156. Andrew Metrick of Harvard looked at the performance: Andrew Metrick, "Performance Evaluation with Transactions Data: The Stock Selection of Investment Newsletters," National Bureau of Economic Research Working Paper No. W6648 Cambridge, Mass.: National Bureau of Economic Research, July 1998.

156. Even if you happen to stumble: Philip A. Fisher, *Common Stocks and Uncommon Profits,* New York: Wiley, 1996, p. 82. Fisher's book, originally published half a century ago, remains a classic. His discussion of when to sell stocks has never been surpassed.

156. Another reason not to try to time the market: Terrance Odean and Brad M. Barber, "Trading Is Hazardous to Your Wealth: The Common Stock Investment Performance of Individual Investors," forthcoming, *Journal of Finance.*

157. If you learn one practical lesson from this book: "If you aren't willing to own a stock for ten years," writes Buffett, "don't even think about owning it for ten minutes." Buffett, *Berkshire Hathaway Inc., Annual Report, 1996.*

CHAPTER 11. MAKING SENSE OF MUTUAL FUNDS

164. For a buyer of individual stocks: "If you are intellectually honest with yourself . . ." James K. Glassman, "Diversification Works Best in Small Doses," *Washington Post,* 14 May 1995, p. H-1.

164. Warren Buffett is fond of quoting Mae West: And Peter Lynch likes to call spreading your money across too many stocks "diworseifiction." He adds, "A foolish diversity is the hobgoblin of small investors." Peter Lynch, *One Up on Wall Street.* New York: Penguin Books, 1989, p. 242.

165. At the start of 1999, a total of $3 trillion: *Mutual Fund FactBook: A Basic Guide to the Trends and Statistics Observed and Recorded in the Mutual Fund Industry.* Washington: Investment Company Institute, 1999.

171. With small-cap funds, the discrepancy was even broader: "The results of our analysis." James K. Glassman, "Funds' Lofty Fees Add Insult to Injury," *Washington Post,* 13 September 1998, p. H-1.

175. In 1978, writing the third annual report for Vanguard: Bogle, p. 109.

176. But the S&P 500, as we said: For details on the index, see www.spglobal.com.

177. Why buy the market: *Berkshire Hathaway Inc., Annual Report, 1993.*

179. But if you buy mutual funds: James K. Glassman, "Beware the Tax Bite When Picking Mutual Funds," *Washington Post,* 26 March 1995, p. H-1.

183. Low turnover. Even if you hold your mutual fund: "It is only occasionally that there is any reason for selling at all." Fisher, p. 83.

187. Another growth fund: "If you've got good visibility of earnings, there aren't many stocks that are too expensive." Russell Hawkins, interview with the authors, November 1998.

188. If you are looking for a single value fund: The Whitridge quote is from the *Value Line Mutual Fund Survey.* New York: Value Line Publishing, 5 January 1999, p. 642.

CHAPTER 12. GETTING STARTED IN STOCKS

198. The simple fact is that mutual funds: "the art or science of managing revenues and resources . . ." Ambrose Bierce, *The Cynic's Word Book,* New York: Doubleday, Page & Co., 1906.

199. Such behavior explains the findings: "Quantitative Analysis of Investor Behavior Study." Boston: Dalbar, Inc., 1999.

199. Suppose you put all of your money: Rudolph Barbara, "Buy Stocks? No Way!" *Time,* 26 September 1988, p. 54.

211. But DPP's are even better: Charles Carlson, *No Load Stocks: How to Buy Your First Share and Every Share Directly from the Company.* New York: McGraw-Hill, 1997.

CHAPTER 13. WHICH STOCKS SHOULD YOU BUY?

216. His name is Elliott L. Schlang, and we'll bet: Schlang's institutional newsletter is also called the LJR Great Lakes Review. His office address is 1111 Chester Ave., Suite 820, Cleveland, Ohio 44114.

219. Schlang's second criterion is that a firm: Graham, p. 277.

223. One of Peter Lynch's top finds: "Taco Bell, I was impressed with the burritos on a trip to California . . ." Lynch, p. 19.

224. In 1999, once again: General Electric finished: GE information on this and subsequent pages, www.ge.com and Thomas F. O'Boyle, *At Any Cost: Jack Welch, General Electric, and the Pursuit of Profit.* New York: Knopf, 1998.

225. While GE is a respected company: with the second-largest capitalization: "A stock is worth the present value . . ." Burr, p. 397.

225. From Thomas Edison to Jack Welch: "speed, stretch, and boundaryless," *General Electric Company Annual Report, 1993,* p. 5.

229. So, like Microsoft, Tootsie Roll is building up its cash: Tootsie Roll Industries, Inc., SEC Form 10-K, SEC File No. 001-01361, filed 30 March 1999. See www.sec.gov/Archives/edgar/ for similar data on publicly traded companies.

230. Don't laugh: The Buffett statement comes from *Warren Buffett Talks Business,* broadcast by the University of North Carolina Center for Public Television in Chapel Hill, North Carolina, in 1995. The quotation is found in a fine little book, Janet Lowe, ed., *Warren Buffett Speaks.* New York: Wiley, 1997, p. 143.

CHAPTER 14. STOCKS, BONDS, OR CASH?

249. The classic asset allocation: Marshall Loeb, *Marshall Loeb's Lifetime Investment Strategies.* New York: Time Warner, 1996.

252. Be flexible, but keep a 20 percent foreign weighting as a goal: Vanguard International Equity Index European Fund "has produced outstanding long-term returns . . ." *Value Line Mutual Fund Survey,* 2 March 1999, p. 1432.

CHAPTER 15. THE WEALTH EXPLOSION

257. I draw the conclusion that . . . the economic problem: The Keynes quotation is cited by Myron H. Ross in his excellent, but little-noticed book, *A Gale of Creative Destruction: The Coming Economic Boom, 1992–2020.* New York: Praeger, 1989. At a time of pessimism, Ross argued presciently, "The United States is on the brink of a radical economic and social transformation," p. 1.

259. Growing fears that Social Security is in deep trouble: "Americans Aren't Counting on Social Security," Roper Starch Worldwide Hot Facts, August 1998, www.roper.inter.net/hotfacts (last accessed May 25, 1999, last updated September 8, 1998).

259. The rise in mutual funds: 44.4 million U.S. households—more than four in ten families—own funds. *Mutual Fund FactBook,* p. 45.

259. Federal Reserve Data showed that in 1998: *Flow of Funds.*

259. Real estate has long been the asset favored by politicians: Kudlow, p. 6.

259. While Kudlow may be drawing battle lines: Kevin Kelly, *New Rules for the*

New Economy: 10 Radical Strategies for a Connected World. New York: Viking, 1998, p. 156.

260. But be wary of glib conclusions: William Scheneider, "To the 'New Rich,' Bill's OK," *National Journal,* 14 November 1998. A version of this paper can be found at www.aei.org (last accessed May 26, 1999, last updated May 20, 1999).

261. Still, as Kevin Kelly emphasizes: Daniel Yergin and Joseph Stanislaw, *The Commanding Heights: The Battle Between Government and the Marketplace That Is Remaking the Modern World.* New York: Simon & Schuster, 1998, pp. 150–151.

262. One of the greatest of American politicians: John Adams, letter to Abigail Adams, 12 May 1780.

262. As Lord Keynes says in the quotation: The Aristotle quote is from *Nichomachean Ethics.*

263. "We serve physical concerns and creature comforts first, psychic needs later": Richard Alm and Michael Cox, *Myths of Rich and Poor.* New York: Basic Books, 1998, p. 266. "A typical American . . ." p. 271.

263. The boom in stocks will mean that percentage will fall further: Nick Gillespie, "All Culture, All the Time," *Reason,* April 1999. An excellent discussion of culture can be found at www.reason.com (last accessed May 25, 1999, last updated April 25, 1999).

264. Increased wealth will have another effect: David R. Henderson, ed., "Economic Growth," *Fortune Encyclopedia of Economics.* New York: Warner Books, 1993, pp. 183–190.

265. The economist Robert Fogel: Robert Fogel, "Catching Up with the Economy," *American Economic Review,* March 1999, p. 2. Fogel is a Nobel Prize winner in economics.

267. How to cash in?: Graham, p. xv.

267. How to cash in?: Alexander Pope, *Moral Essays, Epistle II, To Mrs. M. Blount,* 1735.

Index

A

Adams, John, 262
Adams Express, 174
adolescence *vs.* adulthood, 61–63, 64, 65, 77–80, 85
ADP, Inc., 147–49
Advanced Micro Devices, 231
Advanta Corp., 212
aggressive-growth funds, 167, 189–91
AIM Developing Markets fund, 195
Alcoa, 83, 232
Alger, David, 190
Allen, Paul, 226
Allied Capital Corp., 223
Allied Signal, 96, 232
Alm, Richard, 262
Alternative Living Services, Inc.
Amazon.com, 36, 42, 92, 189, 201, 214, 235
American Brands, 7, 51, 52, 53–54
American Can Co., 51
American Enterprise Institute, 21
American Express, 129, 232
American Heritage Fund, 167
America Online, 44, 168, 187, 189, 236, 237–38
Ameritrade, 209
Amex Diamonds, 182
Amgen, 192
AMR Corp., 188
Apache Corp., 197–98
arbitrage, 112, 114, 116, 119
Arrow, Kenneth, 261
Artisan International, 193–94
Asian funds, 194
asset allocation
    allocations within, 250–53
    defined, 108, 239
    diversification in, 251–53
    re-allocating assets, 253–55
    role of bonds, 241–48, 254
    role of cash, 248

role of stocks, 240–41
    sample, 250
    tax issues, 254–55
    and time horizon, 249–50
assets, 28–29, 269. *See also* asset allocation; bonds; cash; stocks
AT&T, 94, 114, 163, 188, 236
Automatic Data Processing, Inc., 147–49
automobile companies, 129
Aware, Inc., 237

B

Babson Value fund, 188–89, 189
Banc One Corp., 185
bank CDs, 67
Barber, Brad M, 156–57
Barro, Robert, 133
Barron's, 233
basis points, defined, 269
Berkshire Hathaway, 129, 183, 189. *See also* Buffett, Warren
Berlin, Irving, 20–21
Bethlehem Steel, 51
Biogen, 79–80, 84, 192
Blodgett, Henry, 236
Boeing Co., 31, 159
Bogle, John C., 155, 175, 176
Boich, John, 194
bonds. *See also* Treasury bonds
    in asset allocation, 241–48, 254
    vs. bank CDs, 67
    callable, 244
    convergence trading, 119
    corporate, 93, 241, 242–43, 245
    defined, 241, 269
    inflation-protection, 244–45
    and interest rates, 132–33, 242, 243–44, 247
    junk, 11, 243
    laddering of purchases, 247
    municipal, 246–47, 272

bonds (*cont'd*)
  in mutual funds, 247
  return on, 242, 247–48
  and risk, 92–93, 97, 99, 242–43
  vs. stocks, 7–8, 27–28, 35, 50, 54, 65–70, 95
  tax issues, 87–88, 157, 246
  zero-coupon, 244, 274
book value, defined, 269
Bosack, Leonard, 77
Brandywine Fund, 197
Bristol Myers Squibb, 185
Broadfoot, James, 191
brokers
  advantages of using, 159–60
  discount, 208–9
  fees for buying and selling stocks in mutual
    funds, 169
  fees for closed-end funds, 174
  full-service, 206–8
  online trading, 209–10
  questions to ask, 207–8
  setting up accounts, 205
  types of, 205–10
Brusca, Bob, 9
bubbles, investment, 35–36
Buffett, Warren, 17, 48, 75, 80, 81, 129, 139,
    155, 157, 164, 177, 214, 217
Bunker, Michael, 194
Butterfield, Herbert, 15
buy-and-hold portfolios, 173–74

C
callable bonds, 244
Campbell, John, 117–18
Campbell Soup Co., 63–64, 211
capital appreciation, 167, 269
capital gains, 88, 178–81, 260, 269
capital investments, 81, 82
capitalization, 167. *See also* large-cap stocks; small-
    cap stocks
Capital Research and Management Company, 159
car companies, 129
Carlson, Charles, 178, 211
Carter-Wallace, 181
cash, 248
cash flow
  deriving estimates, 5–6, 80–85
  and earnings, 74–76, 80–82, 85, 130–32
  and Iron Law, 41–44
  relationship to dividends, 47–48, 130, 131
  viewing yield, 84–85
cash return, calculating, 65–70, 96, 144–46
Castellani, David, 15
Castro, Oscar, 194
CDA/Wiesenberger, Inc., 170
CGCM Small-Cap Equity fund, 191
Chaplin, Charlie, 20–21

charity, 263–64
Charlson, Josh, 181
Chase Manhattan Corp., 189, 212
Cheung, Alexander, 237
Chrysler, 51, 52–53
Cintas Corp., 220
Cisco Systems, 77–78, 127, 191, 236
Citigroup, 232
classical model, 129
Cleco Corp., 30
Clipper Fund, 164, 165–66, 183
closed-end funds, 174–75, 181, 269
Coca-Cola, 39, 86, 114–15, 129, 180, 181, 183,
    187, 213, 217, 221
Cochrane, John, 100
Cohen & Steers Realty Shares, 191
Colgate-Palmolive, 212
Compagnie Financiere Richemont, 193
companies, good. *See also* General Electric Co.;
    Microsoft
  Biogen, 79–80
  Campbell Soup Co., 63–64
  Cisco Systems, 77–78
  criteria for choosing, 147, 230–33
  Fannie Mae, 64–65
  Microsoft, 78–79
  Tootsie Roll Industries, Inc., 215–16, 217, 222,
    228–30
  Wells Fargo & Company, 60–63
Compaq Computer, 168, 212
computer models, 118–21
Contrafund, 186–87
convergence trading, 119
Copeland, Tom, 80
corporate bonds, 93, 97, 241, 242–43,
    245
Cottt Corp., 221
coupon rates, defined, 269–70
Cox, Michael, 262
credit risk, 93, 242, 243, 247
currency fluctuations, 193
CVS Corp., 185

D
Dalbar survey, 152–53, 159, 199
Danoff, Will, 187
Datek, 204, 209, 210
day-trading, 210, 213
debt, low, as Schlang requirement, 221–22
defined-benefit pension plans, 258–59
defined portfolios, 173–74
Dell Computer, 42, 168, 187, 189, 191
DeVry, Inc., 220, 221–22
Diamond Series Trust, 178
direct investment, 210–12
direct purchase plans, 210–12
discount brokerage firms, 208–10

Index

Disney Co., 188, 212
diversification
  and asset allocation, 251–53
  defined, 270
  and mutual funds, 163
  too much, 164–65, 172
dividend reinvestment plans (DRIPs), 210–11
dividends
  defined, 270
  vs. earnings, 48, 85–86
  and free-cash flow calculations, 82–83
  General Electric Co., 7, 46, 47–48, 224–25
  growth of, 6–8, 12, 49, 50, 51–54
  impact of declining growth, 137–38
  importance of, 6–8
  and Iron Law, 41–44
  lowering, 47–48
  and mutual fund stock holdings, 181
  relationship to cash flow, 47–48, 130, 131
  relationship to earnings, 85–87
  tax issues, 85, 88, 179
  vs. Treasury bond interest rates, 29, 68–70
  whether companies pay, 44–48
dividend yields
  vs. bond interest rates, 29, 68–70
  defined, 270
  vs. P/E ratios as stock valuation measure, 31–32
  relationship to stock price, 29–31, 71–72
  as traditional measure of stock valuation, 29–31
DLJ Direct, 209
Dogs of the Dow, 113–15, 173
DoubleClick, Inc., 237
Dow 36,000 Theory
  archetypal stock, 215–16
  as basis for stock-picking, 198–99
  General Electric Co. illustration, 224–26
  Microsoft illustration, 226–28
  overview, 3–8, 143
  and perfectly reasonable price, 121, 122, 144, 255–56
  and Schlang's stock-picking strategy, 216–17
  suggested mutual funds, 184–95
  three elements, 132–33
  Tootsie Roll Industries as illustration, 228–30
Dow Jones industrial average
  in 1980s and 1990s, 3, 4, 38, 158
  composition of, 51–54
  defined, 270
  and Dogs of the Dow, 113–15, 173
  and index portfolios, 178
  vs. mutual funds, 168–69
Dreman, David, 155, 183
Dreyfus funds, 187, 193
du Pont (E.I.) de Nemours, 189
Dutch tulip-bulb mania, 10, 35–36
Dutton, Bill, 190

E

Early Edition, 28
earnings
  and cash flow, 74–76, 80–82, 85, 130–32
  defined, 270
  impact of decline, 137–38
  importance of growth, 219–20, 231–32
  and Internet stocks, 44
  relationship to dividends, 48, 74, 85–87
  and Schlang requirements, 217–20
earnings-to-price ratio, 87
earnings yield, 32, 270
Ebay, Inc., 235
education, investor, 15, 39, 101–2
emerging-markets funds, 193, 194–95, 252
Emerson, Ralph Waldo, 165
energy stocks, 197–98
Enterprise Growth fund, 183
EntreMed, 44, 213
equities. *See* stocks
equity funds. *See* mutual funds
equity-income funds, 167
E-Trade, 209
Excite@Home, 214
expense ratios, 169, 170, 171, 182, 271
Exxon, 41, 51, 52, 54, 159, 192, 211

F

Fannie Mae, 64–65, 165, 166, 212
Federated Capital Appreciation, 170
Fidelity funds, 171–72, 180, 181, 182, 185, 186–87, 191, 192, 197, 223, 251
Financial Research Corp., 170–71
Fisher, Irving, 116–17, 132
Fisher, Philip A., 156, 183
Ford Motor Co., 47, 81–82, 144–45
foreign stocks and funds, 167–68, 192–95, 251, 252
Fortune Brands, 7–8
Foulkes, Richard, 194
401(k) plans, 103, 181, 271
Franklin Growth, 180
Franklin Templeton, 184
Freddie Mac, 165, 166
free-cash flow, 80–85, 271
free trade, 104
Fridson, Martin, 20
Friedman, Milton, 261
Friedman, Rob, 193
Friess, Foster, 196–97
Fuji Photo Film, 194
Fuller, Lawrence, 188
full-service brokerage firms, 206–8

G

Gabelli, Mario, 184
gambling, stock trading as, 240

Index

GAM Pacific Basic fund, 194
Gardner, Tom and David, 14, 214
Gates, Bill, 226
GDP. *See* gross domestic product
Genentech, 192
General American Investors Co., 174
General Electric Co., 46, 47–48, 159, 163, 181,
    185, 201, 212, 234
    dividends of, 7, 46, 47–48, 224–25
    as illustration of Dow 36,000 Theory, 224–26
Gillespie, Nick, 262
Gillette, 127, 129–30, 183, 218
Gipson, James, 164
Glimcher Realty Trust, 98
global funds, 168, 187, 192, 193
Goldman Sachs International Equity fund, 194
government bonds. *See* municipal bonds; Treasury
    bonds
Graham, Benjamin, 152, 153–54, 193, 219, 224
Great Depression, 102–3
Greenspan, Alan
    as Fed chairman, 21–22, 104
    "irrational exuberance" remark, 4, 21–22, 118
gross domestic product, 133, 271
growth-and-income funds, 167, 184–86
growth funds, 167, 184, 186–89
growth stocks, 41, 186
Guinness Flight Wired Index Fund, 188

H
Hanes, 223
Harley-Davidson, 234
Harrah's Entertainment, 181
Hart (Peter D.) Research Associates, 59
Hawkins, Russell, 187
Hayes, Helen Young, 193
Hazard, Caroline, 117
health sector funds, 192
hedge funds, 118–20, 193
Hewlett-Packard, 231, 232
high-yield bonds, 243
Holowesko, John, 193
Home Depot, Inc., 211, 212
Hulbert, Mark, 58

I
Ibbotson Associates, 26–27, 190
IBM, 30, 42–43, 212, 232, 242
Idex funds, 180, 193
income stocks, 41, 42
index funds, 175–78, 180
individual retirement accounts (IRAs), 181
inflation
    allowing for, 70–72, 128
    and bonds, 70, 132, 243, 244–45
    and stock prices, 70–72, 128
Intel, 187, 191

interest rates, bond, 132–33, 242, 243–44, 247
international funds, 168, 169, 193–94
Internet
    as business information resource, 233–34
    stock trading on, 210
Internet mutual funds, 237
Internet stocks, 36, 44, 49–50, 189–90, 210,
    235–38
Internet UITs, 237
intrinsic value, 48, 80, 271
Intuit, Inc., 202–3
Invesco Asian Growth, 179
Investment Co. of America, 170
investors
    behavior of, 14–15, 110, 152–54
    and education, 15, 39, 101–2
    political power of, 258
    risk aversion of, 100
    short-term *vs.* long term, 22–24, 115, 126–28,
        199–201, 240
Investor's Business Daily, 233
Iron Law, 41–46
"irrational exuberance" remark, 4, 21–22, 118
Ivy U.S. Emerging Growth, 190–91

J
Janus funds, 183, 187–88, 193
Johnson & Johnson, 81, 83, 166, 187, 198–99,
    222, 223
JP Morgan & Co., 232
junk bonds, 11, 243

K
Kaufmann Fund, 169
Kaul, Rajiv, 192
Kelly, Kevin, 261
Kemper-Dreman High Return fund, 183
Keynes, John Maynard, 164, 262
Koller, Tim, 80
Krulwich, Robert, 134–35
Kudlow, Lawrence, 138, 259
Kuhn, Thomas, 14

L
Landauer, Inc., 221, 222
large-cap stocks
    in asset allocation, 253, 254
    in mutual funds, 184, 186
    vs. small-cap stocks, 190
Legg Mason, Inc., 168, 189, 206
Lerner, Sandra, 77
Lexington Corporate Leaders fund, 162, 180,
    184, 188, 232
life cycles, corporate, 61–63, 64, 65, 77–80, 85
limit orders, 210
Lipper Analytical Services, 191
load, 160, 169–70, 271

Longleaf Partners Realty, 191
long-run, defined, 271
Long-Term Capital Management, L.P., 118–20
Lucent Technologies, 212, 236
Lynch, Peter, 164–65, 189, 197, 223

M
MacKay, Charles, 5
Mairs & Power Growth fund, 181
Malkiel, 124–25
manias, investment, 10, 35–36
Marcus, David, 193
market capitalization, defined, 271
market efficiency, 114
market timing, 154–57
Marsico, Tom, 183, 184, 187
Maslow, Abraham, 262
Matthews Pacific Tiger fund, 194
Maytag Corp., 223
MCI WorldCom, 191, 202
Merck & Co., 33, 50, 130–31, 192
Meriwether, John, 119
Merrick, Andrew, 156
Merrill Lynch, 173, 179, 188, 194, 197–98, 206, 236
Merton, Robert, 119
Merton-Modigliani theorem, 46
Mexico Fund, 194
Microsoft, 31, 41, 84, 130, 159, 176, 187, 188, 191
    and dividends, 44–45
    as illustration of Dow 36,000 Theory, 226–28
    as Internet company, 236
    and perfectly reasonable price, 78–79, 89
Milken, Michael, 11, 103
Miller, Merton, 46
Miller, William, 168, 189
Minimed, Inc., 202
Minnesota Mining and Manufacturing (3M), 232
Mobius, Mark, 184
Modigliani, Franco, 46
money managers, 15
money-market funds, 248, 271
Montgomery International Growth fund, 194
Monument Internet fund, 237
Moretti, Arthur, 197–98
Morgan, Burton D., 181
Morgan Funshares, 181
Morgan (J.P.) & Co., 201
Morgan Stanley Dean Witter, 251
Morgan Stanley stock indexes, 194, 252
Motley Fool, 14, 235
Moynihan, Daniel Patrick, 258, 262
Mullins, David, 119
Munder Net Net fund, 237
municipal bonds, 246–47, 272
Murrin, Jack, 80

Mutual Discovery fund, 193
mutual funds
    aggressive-growth, 189–91
    for bonds, 247
    vs. buying stocks individually, 196–98, 203, 204
    closed-end, 174–75, 181
    concentrated, 183
    cost of buying, 203
    covering redemptions, 166–67
    defined, 272
    emerging-markets, 193, 194–95, 252
    expense ratios, 169, 170, 171, 182
    fees charged by, 160, 169, 170–71
    foreign-stock funds, 192–95
    growth, 184, 186–89
    growth-and-income, 184–86
    increase in ownership, 16, 259
    Internet, 237
    investor behavior, 152–54
    loads, 160, 169–70, 271
    low-turnover, 180–81, 183
    management of, 168–73, 180, 182–84
    and market timing, 171–72
    overview, 165
    performance of, 168–73
    reasons for owning, 163–65
    small-cap, 171, 189–91
    tax issues, 178–81, 205
    types of, 167–68

N
Nasdaq 100 index, 191
national security, 104–5
natural resources, 192
Navistar, 51
Nelson, Wayne, 114
net asset value, defined, 272
net debt, 82, 83–84
Net Stock Direct, 211
net worth, 257
New England Business Service, Inc., 190
Nike, 166
no-load mutual funds, 160
nominal, 70, 132–33, 272
Nucor, 188
Nuveen, 173, 192

O
Oakmark Small-Cap Fund, 179
Odean, Terrance, 156–257
O'Higgins, Michael, 113
Ohlson, Jim, 80
Olstein, Robert, 168
online trading, 209–10
O'Shaughnessy, James, 113
Owens-Illinois, 51

Index

P

PaineWebber, 208
Palmieri, Jerry, 181
paradigm shift, 14–16
PepsiCo, 129, 159, 166
P/E ratios
    100 as outer limit, 146, 233
    defined, 272
    Ford illustration, 145–46
    and growth funds, 186, 187–88
    of Internet stocks, 235
    market distribution of, 88–89
    as stock price valuation indicator, 4, 5, 8, 10,
        11, 31–33, 58
    volatility of, 32
perfectly reasonable price (PRP), 6, 58, 59–60
    ADP, 149
    Biogen, 79–80
    calculating precisely, 145
    Campbell Soup Co., 63–64
    Cisco Systems, 78
    defined, 95, 127, 272
    and Dow 36,000 Theory, 121, 122, 144,
        255–56
    Fannie Mae, 64–65
    Ford Motor Co., 144–45
    Microsoft, 78–79, 89
    skewness in, 88–89
    tax issues, 87–88
    Wells Fargo & Co., 62–63
perpetuities, 66–67, 272
Pfizer, 39, 187, 188
Philip Morris, 51, 165, 166, 181, 232
politics, 259–61
present value, 43, 272
Priceline, 44, 235, 237
price-to-book ratio, 12
price-to-earnings ratios. See P/E ratios
Procter & Gamble, 98, 163
profits, 137–38, 220–21, 230–31, 272
PRP. See perfectly reasonable price (PRP)

Q

Q ratio. See Tobin's Q
quantitative analysts, 119

R

random walk, 111–16, 124
Rasmussen Research, 260
Reagan, Ronald, 103–4
real, defined, 272
real estate, and asset allocation, 259
real estate investment trusts (REITs), 98, 131,
    191–92
RealNetworks, Inc., 237
regional funds, 193, 194
REITs, 98, 131, 191

repurchases, share, 82
retirement plans, 16, 103, 258–59
return
    calculating, 65–70, 96, 144–47
    defined, 5, 272–73
    and mutual fund expenses, 169–71, 182
    and risk, 25–27
    on Treasury bonds, 242, 247–48
risk. See also credit risk
    and bonds, 92–93, 97, 99, 242–43
    as decision factor, 40–41
    defined, 273
    and diversification, 164–65
    overview, 91–94, 123–24
    and stocks, 4, 16, 24–28, 38–39, 59, 91,
        95–98
    stocks vs. bonds, 27–28, 91, 94–96
    and volatility of investment returns, 25–26, 27,
        95
risk aversion, 94, 100–101
risk premium
    defined, 94, 99, 273
    impact on stock price, 122–23
    rising and falling, 39, 97–98, 99–100, 102–5,
        116, 134–37
Roth IRAs, 260
RPM, Inc., 218–19
Ruane, Bill, 183
Russell 2000 Index, 25, 190, 191

S

S & P 500 Index. See Standard & Poor's 500
    Index
Safeco Equity fund, 182
Sala-i-Martin, Xavier, 133
Samuelson, Paul, 261
Sarofim, Christopher, 187
Schaefer, Oscar S., 10
Schlang, Elliott L., 216–17
Schneider, William, 260
Schoelzel, Scott, 168, 187
Scholes, Myron, 119
Schwab 1000 Fund, 177
Schwab (Charles) brokerage, 208–9, 213
Schwert, G. William, 26
Scudder Latin America fund, 194
Seagram, 181
Sears, Roebuck & Co., 163, 212, 232
sector funds, 191–92
securities, defined, 273. See also bonds; stocks
Securities & Exchange Commission, 170, 202
Sequoia fund, 183
Seriologicals Corp., 191
shareholders. See investors
share repurchases, 82–83
Sherden, William A., 155
Shiller, Robert, 9, 26, 29, 68, 71, 99, 117–18

Siegel, Jeremy, 24, 26, 95, 115, 136
Singapore Fund, 194
Singapore Press Holdings, 193
Skyline Special Equities, 190
SLM Holding Corp., 189
small-cap stocks
  in asset allocation, 253, 254
  defined, 167
  vs. large-cap stocks, 190
  in mutual funds, 171, 189–91
Smith Barney, 208
Social Security, 259
Spartan Market Index Fund, 176
SPDRs, 178
Spears, John, 184
Spectra Fund, 190
standard deviation, defined, 273
Standard & Poor's 500 Index, 5, 25, 51, 89,
  163
  in 1980s and 1990s, 38, 118, 152, 153, 158
  defined, 273
  and Dogs of the Dow, 113–15, 173
  and index funds, 175–76, 182
  makeup of, 173, 176
  vs. mutual funds, 168–69, 173
Standard & Poor's Depositary Receipts, 178
Stansky, Bob, 181
Steers, Robert, 191
stockbrokers. *See* brokers
stockholders. *See* investors
stock market
  big drops and crashes, 15, 20–21, 29, 116–17,
    135, 158
  historical lessons, 22–37
  predictions about, 20–22
  short-term investing, 115, 126–28, 240
  studying, 108–21
  timing, 154–57, 171–72
StockPower website, 212
stocks. *See also* companies, good; investors
  in 1980s and 1990s, 3, 4, 5, 38, 56, 58
  allowing for inflation, 70–72, 128
  in asset allocation, 240–41
  vs. bonds, 7–8, 27–28, 35, 50, 54, 65–70, 95
  buying individually *vs.* buying mutual funds,
    196–98, 203, 204
  buying through brokers *vs.* buying directly,
    159–60
  calculating expected return, 65–70, 96, 144–47
  choosing, 147, 230–35
  cost of buying, 204–5
  defined, 273
  direct investment, 210–12
  diversification, 164–65, 213–14, 253
  foreign, 167–68, 251, 252
  fun and games accounts, 158
  historical view, 9–12

holding long-term, 22–24, 126, 127–28,
  199–201, 240
how to think about value, 39–41
investment catechism, 161
need for price rise, 72–73
ownership by company management, 222–23
paradigm shift, 14–16
and P/E ratios, 4, 5, 8, 10, 11, 31–33, 58
pleasures of owning, 201–3
as random walk, 111–16, 124
reasons to buy individually, 196–205
reversion to mean, 115–16, 123
riskiness of, 4, 16, 24–28, 38–39, 59, 91,
  95–98
supply and demand, 109–10
tax issues, 87–88, 179, 204–5
trading, defined, 156–57, 240
as undervalued, 4, 13–14, 17–18, 139–40
valuation of, 5, 10–13, 29–34
value per household, 159
ways to buy, 205–12
stock splits, 7
Stromberg, William
Strong Dow 30 Value fund, 178
Suez Lyonnaise des Eaux, 193
Summers, Lawrence, 261
Suretrade, 209

T
T. Rowe Price funds, 184, 185, 189, 192, 194,
  198, 251
tax issues
  in asset allocation, 254–55
  and bonds, 87–88, 157, 246
  capital gains, 88, 260
  deferral of taxes, 181
  and dividends, 85, 88, 179
  and index funds, 178, 180
  and mutual funds, 178–81, 205
  and perfectly reasonable price, 87–88
  and stocks, 87–88, 204–5
Templeton funds, 193, 195
ten-dollar bill story, 124
Terrana, Beth, 185
Thaler, Richard H., 136
Third Avenue Value, 184
TIAA/CREF Growth & Income fund, 186
Tidewater, Inc., 197–98
Time Warner, Inc., 185, 236
timing the market, 154–57, 171–72
Tobin's Q, 33–34, 273–74
Tootsie Roll Industries, Inc., 215–16, 217, 222,
  228–30
Torray, Bob, 184
trading, stock, 156–57, 240. *See also* day-trading
Transamerica Premier Aggressive Growth fund,
  189, 198

Treasury bills, 27–28, 35, 248
Treasury bonds
  in asset allocation, 241–48, 254
  defined, 50, 241, 274
  and inflation, 70, 132, 243, 244–45
  interest rates, 132–33, 243–44, 247
  interest rates *vs.* stock dividends, 29, 68–70
  vs. municipal bonds, 246–47
  overview, 65–66
  return on, 242, 247–48
  and risk, 92–93, 99
  vs. stocks, 7–8, 27–28, 35, 50, 54, 65–70,
    95
  tax issues, 87–88
Tri-Continental closed-end fund, 174
Trieck, Philip, 189
tulip-bulb mania, 10, 35–36
TWA, 243
Tweedy Browne funds, 184, 193

U
UITs. *See* unit investment trusts (UITs)
unemployment, 20–21
United Technologies, 232
unit investment trusts (UITs), 173–74, 178, 192,
    237, 274
universal savings accounts, 261
USA Today, 233

V
valuation, stock
  defined, 10
  historical, 10–12
  traditional measures, 5, 12–13, 29–34
value stocks *vs.* growth stocks, 186
Vanguard funds, 175, 176, 177, 180, 184, 192,
    194, 203, 251, 252
VeriSign, Inc., 237

Vinik, Jeff, 171–72, 181, 197
Vivendi, 194
volatility, 25–26, 27, 32, 95, 105
Volcker, Paul, 104
von Hayek, Friedrich, 261
Vornado Realty Trust, 131

W
Walgreen, 212
Wall Street Journal, 8–9, 108, 233
Wal-Mart, 188, 212
Warner-Lambert, 187
Washington Post Co., 183
Waterhouse WebBroker, 210
wealth, 105, 262–64
Weiner, Jason, 187
Weitz, Wallace, 171
Welch, Jack, 225
Wells Fargo & Company, 60–63
Whitman, Marty, 184
Whitridge, Nick, 188
Wien, Byron, 8–9, 11–12
Williams, John Burr, 5, 48, 225
William Wrigley Jr., Co., 212
Wilshire stock indexes, 156, 176, 177, 251
Wired magazine, 188
Wolf, Martin, 17
Woolworth, 51
WWW Internet fund, 237

Y
Yacktman, Ron, 184
Yahoo!, 188, 235
Yergin, Daniel, 261
Yockey, Mark, 193–94

Z
zero-coupon bonds, 244, 274

ABOUT THE AUTHORS

James K. Glassman, former financial columnist for *Reader's Digest* and *The Washington Post* and host of the PBS show *TechnoPolitics* and the CNN show *Capital Gang Sunday,* is a resident fellow at the American Enterprise Institute. He is also host of www.TechCentralStation.com, a website that covers technology, finance, and public policy.

Kevin A. Hassett is a resident scholar at the American Enterprise Institute who formerly served as a senior economist at the Federal Reserve Board. He received his Ph.D. in economics from the University of Pennsylvania. He is the coauthor, with R. Glenn Hubbard, of *The Magic Mountain: Defining and Using a Budget Surplus.*